Top 100 Golf Courses

of the British Isles

Top 100
Golf Courses
of the British Isles

Keith Baxter

Top 100
Golf Courses

of the British Isles

Keith Baxter

1st Edition June 2005

Copyright © Top 100 Golf Courses Limited and others by arrangement.

Graphic design by Nick Oliver.
Course descriptions by Keith Baxter and Andy Newmarch.
Photography by Top 100 Golf Courses, except where stated.

ISBN 0-9549172-1-9

Published by Top 100 Golf Courses Limited.
PO Box 160, Cambridge, CB3 0HT
www.top100golfcourses.co.uk
admin@top100golfcourses.co.uk
Designed, printed and bound in the British Isles

Uncaptioned photographs
Front cover – Carne. End paper front – Liphook 7th hole (Rachelle Baxter). Page 2 – Lindrick.
Page 3 – Hillside. Back cover – Royal St David's. End paper back – Downfield.

CONTENTS

ACKNOWLEDGEMENTS

We are most grateful to each and every person who has visited the Top 100 website (www.top100golfcourses.co.uk), especially those who have taken the time to post course reviews and to send through stunning photographs. This book would not have been possible without their input.

Thanks also must go the many golf club officials, too numerous to mention by name. We are touched by their kind words, support and for allowing us to print some of their photographs.

Lee Westwood requires no introduction but we must raise our glass to Lee and to Sarah Harris from International Sports Management for his foreword.

We also recognise that Golf Magazine, Golf Digest, Golf World, Golf Monthly and the Peugeot Guide and their various teams of panellists have given a great deal of consideration over the years to golf course ranking and rating. Long may they continue to do so.

Special thanks go to:
Jenny Needham for fantastic editing, patience and that wicked sense of humour.
Andy Newmarch for relentless energy and organisational skills.
Nick Oliver for creative design, ideas and genuine enthusiasm.
Rachelle Baxter for photographic work and for having Nick as her partner.
Jim Hannigan and the Aztech web team for making the Top 100 website a reality.
Lee Abbey for photography and dulcet wit.
John Skeet and Wayzgoose Print for printing and publishing advice.
David Richards for being a great sounding board.
Dr. Eurof Walters for statistical help and guidance.
And last but not least, thank you Sally for unconditional love and total support.

DEDICATIONS

To Sally for giving me courage and belief.
To Daniel and Rachelle for buying me that first golf lesson.
To Tesco for giving me the opportunity.

"Thus ends the course, and I know it so well that I find it very hard to criticise or appraise at its just worth."

Bernard Darwin on Aberdovey

Wentworth - one of Lee Westwood's favourites.

FOREWORD
by
LEE WESTWOOD

European Ryder Cup team member 1997, 1999, 2001 (2002) and 2004

The excitement of playing a golf course for the first time is a very special feeling indeed and I have been lucky enough to play many of the finest courses in the world. But there is no doubt in my mind that the ultimate collection of golf courses lies scattered across the tiny landmass that is geographically known as the British Isles. Each course is unique, from the diverse land used to the architect's influence. These Isles are blessed with rich, natural golfing terrain, from rippled seaside links to sandy heathland, from majestic parkland to rugged moorland. We are lucky enough to have it all.

Each year, thousands of golfers from all over the world make the pilgrimage to play our great courses, and I'm sure they return home much happier as a result of their experience.

Naturally, ranking golf courses is a subjective business and we all have our favourites, but I'm sure everyone will agree that we have a colourful golfing heritage. As for my personal favourites... well, I like so many different courses – and new ones appear regularly on my list – that it is almost unwise to list any, but amongst my favourites are Royal Birkdale, Turnberry, Wentworth, St Andrews and Lindrick.

I still get a thrill each time I tee it up on the 1st, at some of our lesser-known courses as well as our championship venues, but my golfing heart lies at Worksop, a hidden gem if ever there was one.

Lee Westwood

Introduction

It was more than a decade ago that I was, for the first time, charmed by a truly great course – Walton Heath – and since then I have remained totally captivated. Golf courses leave an indelible impression on me, so I never take for granted our good fortune in having the greatest collection of courses in the world.

There is nothing new about rating and ranking our greatest golf courses – Golf Monthly, Golf World, Golf Magazine, Golf Digest and the Peugeot Guide all produce their own ratings. Some of these publications have been ranking our courses for more than 20 years, using all types of criteria: design, visual appeal, quality, condition of the courses, etc. They use teams of experts from all walks of golfing life to produce their own lists. Judging panels include golf course architects/designers, amateur and professional champions, commentators, photographers and executive members of all types of golfing institutes.

But after studying ranking lists, it became apparent that there was an opportunity to present this information in an entirely new way. We have taken the ranking lists of the publications mentioned above and applied a series of rules and weightings, favouring the world rankings and the most recent lists. Ranking golf courses is entirely subjective and always open to criticism. Nevertheless, we persevered, and we have created the most comprehensive ranked list of the greatest golf courses of the British Isles. The Top 100 website (www.top100golfcourses.co.uk) features every course that has ever appeared on a Top 100 list (over 250 in total) and this book includes the first 100 ranked courses with independent course descriptions for each one.

We have also included in this book summarised course reviews that have been posted on the Top 100 website by thousands of visitors – all passionate golfers. We are all unique, as is each course and each hole. Everyone has their own opinion and we've noticed that the collective opinion of the ordinary golfer is often quite different to the opinion of esteemed Top 100 judging panels. For example, many ordinary golfers prefer North Berwick and Prestwick to Muirfield and Troon, but Muirfield and Troon are always the higher flyers in the traditional rankings. We felt it was essential to give everyone the opportunity to express what he or she thinks about our greatest courses, so we developed our unique rating system which, is built in to the course review process on the Top 100 website:

ALBATROSS - Excellent
EAGLE - Very Good
BIRDIE - Good
PAR - Average
BOGEY - Poor
DOUBLE BOGEY - Very Poor

We decided to make the rating system simple and set no specific rules for rating a golf course except, naturally, that the reviewer should have played it. Important factors, such as course location, condition (or presentation), difficulty and historical importance are all left for the reviewer to judge. See page 212 for the Top 100 list based purely on reviews posted by visitors to the Top 100 website (www.top100golfcourses.co.uk).

The Top 100 website began in May 2004, and since then, hundreds of thousands of golfers have taken the time to visit the site. Thousands of well-written, informed and honest course reviews are posted online and hundreds of stunning course photographs have been sent in. We've edited and summarised the course reviews for this book and we have tried to balance the comments to ensure fairness. However, as a principle, we have let honesty and passion come through. Additionally, and uniquely, many of the photographs used to illustrate this book were sent in by visitors to the Top 100 website.

We thought we were on safe ground when, after great deliberation, we decided on the title "Top 100 Golf Courses of the British Isles". After all, the name "British Isles" is geographical rather than political. It simply comprises all the main and offshore islands of the United Kingdom and Ireland, as well as the Isle of Man and the Channel Islands. But following a conversation with Pat Ruddy – the Irish architect and owner of the European Club – it became clear that we might well have overlooked something fundamental. Although pleased to have a great many British friends, Pat was quick to point out that his native island has long since ceased describing itself as a "British Isle". A thousand apologies in advance should we have offended anybody.

The Top 100 website and this book have been put together by a remarkably small team of ordinary club golfers with mixed handicaps. We are totally independent and not associated with any of the golf publications mentioned in this book. What we are is passionate about golf and addicted to playing great golf courses.

If you have any views or comments, we will be delighted to hear from you. Please use the Contact Us section on the Top 100 website - www.top100golfcourses.co.uk - and don't forget, you too can have your say about the courses you've played.

And so, without further ado, we present you with the finest courses in the land.

Keith Baxter - Editor

ST ANDREWS LINKS
St Andrews, Fife, KY16 9SF, Scotland
Telephone: +44 (0)1334 466666

Average Reviewers' Score:

Website: www.standrews.org.uk
Architect: Unknown
Visitors: Book well in advance - by ballot

Reviewers' Comments

Whole experience is fantastic... Rush of adrenaline compensates for faults in the golf course... Was very nervous about teeing off in front of the clubhouse... Has an aura about it... Humbling experience... One of the most disappointing golf experiences of my life... Course grows on you... Play it more than once to start to understand the beauty... I'm fed up hearing that you have to play it several times – most of us only get one chance... Play with someone who knows the course... Can get away with some dreadful shots and be punished for good shots... Distances hard to judge... Apart from bunkering, many holes are featureless... Weak round the turn... Greens are an experience; don't think your putting stroke has left you if you three putt regularly... You'll have more 90 footers here than anywhere... Coming up the 18th through the Valley of Sin, looking at the old town is one of the finest feelings... Overall a must-play but you may feel underwhelmed by the actual golfing experience... Whether you come away liking it or not, when you are old and the arthritis kicks in, you will be very glad you can tell your grandchildren that you played it... Best golf course in the world, bar none.

St Andrews (Old)

The Old course is a very special links, designed by Mother Nature. Surely there is little left to write about St Andrews; the spiritual home of golf, the world's most famous links course, the mother of golf and so on. It is probable that golf was played here way back in the 12th century; it is certain that this is the oldest course in the world.

In 1553, the Archbishop of St Andrews administered confirmation, at last allowing the community to play golf over the 22-hole links. The St Andrews Club was founded in 1754 and ten years later the course was reduced to 18 holes. The Royal and Ancient Golf Club – the world's oldest surviving "Royal" golf club – was formed in 1834, following the bestowal of royal patronage by William IV. In 1867, Women's golf began at St Andrews with the foundation of the world's first ladies' golf club.

"There are those who do not like the golf at St Andrews," wrote Bernard Darwin in his 1910 book, *The Golf Courses of the British Isles*, "and they will no doubt deny any charm to the links themselves, but there must surely be none who will deny a charm to the place as a whole. It may be immoral, but it is delightful to see a whole town given up to golf; to see the butcher and the baker and the candlestick maker shouldering his clubs as soon as his day's work is done and making a dash for the links."

The course itself usually isn't an instant hit, it's a course you have to get to know and love. Dr Alister MacKenzie wrote in his book, *The Spirit of St Andrews*: "A good golf course is like good music or anything else: it is not necessarily a course which appeals the first time one plays over it; but one which grows on a player the more frequently he visits it."

Every true golfer should play this course at least once. It sends shivers down the spine when the starter announces your name, setting those first tee nerves jangling. Oozing familiarity with names like the Swilcan Burn and its famous bridge – thought to have been built by the Romans – and the Valley of Sin. There are many memorable holes and the 17th, the Road hole – is the most famous hole in the world.

The greens are the most extraordinary and interesting putting surfaces in the world. There is little definition between the fairways, fringes and greens; what's more, the fairways are probably faster and certainly more undulating than the average golf club's greens. Their size is absolutely staggering – they are gigantic, occupying more than an acre in some cases. When you are on the green, forget about having the pin tended – take a pair of binoculars instead.

So, get yourself in the ballot and keep your fingers crossed. You will definitely remember the Old course experience for the rest of your life.

THE HONOURABLE COMPANY OF EDINBURGH GOLFERS
Duncur Road, Gullane, East Lothian, EH31 2EG
Scotland
Telephone: +44 (0)1620 842123

Average Reviewers' Score:

Website: none
Architect: Old Tom Morris, Harry Colt and Tom Simpson
Visitors: Tue/Thu - Contact Secretary in advance

Reviewers' Comments

Muirfield is a gentleman's club that also happens to have a golf course attached, albeit a brilliant one... Clubhouse is a throw back in time to a bygone age... Welcome was friendlier than expected... Lunch is an old schoolboy affair... You half expect the dinner ladies to come around with the jugs of water... Too formal for me... No idea as to why this course is regularly voted the best in the British Isles... It's not as good as it's cracked up to be... Can't understand fawning comments from so many others who play it... Good track but barely makes my top five in Scotland... Doesn't have that WOW factor... Doesn't have the scenery but it's a great golf course that is challenging but fair... Undeniably a great course and very tough... Could quite happily play golf here for the rest of my life... It's not the hardest, that's Carnoustie, it may not be the prettiest, (Royal County Down?), but we generally all agree it's the best... Layout gives relief against the elements... Holes are devious and aimed squarely at the big boys... Strong collection of par threes but there are few memorable holes... Has remained my favourite since first playing it over 10 years ago.

Muirfield

Muirfield is the course of "The Honourable Company of Edinburgh Golfers" (HCEG), the world's oldest golf club, formed in 1744. In those days, the members played over Leith Links, originally a five-hole course. In March 1744, the first official rules of golf were drawn up by the "Gentlemen Golfers of Leith" in readiness for a tournament which was due to be played over Leith Links the following month. These original 13 rules became the basis for the game of golf and shortly afterwards, the HCEG was formed.

Almost 150 years later, in 1891, the course at Muirfield opened for play. Old Tom Morris designed it, originally as a 16-holer. A further two holes were added a few months later. In 1928, Harry Colt and Tom Simpson were brought in to make alterations to the layout. Many golf historians believe that the course became truly great as a consequence of the changes made by Colt and Simpson. The design layout is a masterpiece and highly unusual for links courses of this era. Most courses were laid out simply, nine out and nine back. Muirfield is different; it was the first to be designed with two concentric rings of nine holes. The outward nine holes run clockwise around the edge and the inward nine run anti-clockwise, sitting inside the outward nine. The layout ensures that the wind hits you from all directions, but it is as difficult to play downwind as it is upwind.

Host to fifteen Opens, most recently in 2002, Muirfield is considered by many of the top professionals to be one of the fairest Open Championship golf courses. Bernard Darwin loved it, and in his 1910 book, *The Golf Courses of the British Isles*, he wrote: "There is a fine view of the sea and a delightful sea wood, with the trees all bent and twisted by the wind; then, too, it is a solitary and peaceful spot, and a great haunt of the curlews, whom one may see hovering over a championship crowd and crying eerily amid a religious silence."

This is an eccentric but traditional golf links of the highest calibre. The fairways have that lovely spongy seaside turf, there's some unbelievable bunkering (many of which are small and deep) and there's that thick, thick rough to contend with. The greens are relatively small too, which makes you think carefully about your approach shots and once you are safely on the putting surface, you'll need to interpret them well because the borrows are subtle and tricky to read.

In recent years it has become easier to get a tee time at Muirfield, especially if you are a gentleman. They do allow visitors on Tuesday and Thursday and ladies are allowed to play if accompanied by a man. Many people think that Muirfield is the best golf course in the British Isles, but is it the best golf club?

ROYAL COUNTY DOWN GOLF CLUB
Newcastle, County Down, BT33 0AN, Northern Ireland
Telephone: 028 4372 3314

Average Reviewers' Score:
●●●●●●

Website: www.royalcountydown.org
Architect: Old Tom Morris, Harry Vardon
Visitors: Contact in advance - not Sat or Wed

Reviewers' Comments

By some distance the best course I have ever played… Loved it… This is the best course in the UK & Ireland… What makes Northern Ireland's finest so special? – A sense of drama, as much as anything… The Mountains of Mourne provide the backdrop… Almost every hole is at once thrilling and terrifying… It's no place for a novice… A slight criticism, it is that there are a few blind shots… Some holes require a blind tee shot to carry fully 200 yards to reach the fairway… There are no marker posts here, only small, whitewashed stones, invariably surrounded by the roughest rough imaginable… High quality greens… The greens are as good as greens can be – lightning fast, true and devilishly contoured… The huge bunkers are deliberately unkempt around the edges – they appear bearded… It's a great layout and was in fantastic condition… Old Tom Morris's design is genius itself, from the ticklish short 7th to the unique – I use the word advisedly – dogleg 15th… Great front nine… There is one poor hole, the 17th. That apart, County Down is the ultimate links experience… It's worth almost any green fee… A day here is an experience you'll never forget… Well worth its high rating… I'll be back.

Royal County Down

There is always lively discussion about which golf course is better than another, but none is more passionate than the debate over the relative merits of Royal County Down and Royal Portrush. If you haven't played either of them yet, we recommend a golf trip to Northern Ireland.

Royal County Down is at Newcastle, a little holiday town nestling at the feet of the majestic Mountains of Mourne. It's an exhilarating location for a classic links golf course where the Bay of Dundrum sweeps out into the Irish Sea and where the mighty peak of Slieve Donard (3,000 ft.) casts its shadow over the town.

Old Tom Morris was paid the modest sum of four guineas to design the course and it opened for play in 1889. Harry Vardon modified it in 1908, the same year King Edward VII bestowed royal patronage on the club. Royal County Down maintains tradition; the "Hat Man" still mixes the pairings for the Saturday matches (foursomes in the winter and four-balls in the summer) as he did around 100 years earlier.

Old Tom was presented with an idyllic piece of ground on which to design a golf course. The sand dunes are rugged but beautifully clad in purple heather and yellow gorse, the fairways are naturally undulating, shaped by the hands of time. The greens are small and full of wicked borrows, or to put it in Bernard Darwin's words, "they lie, moreover, in a good many instances, in those pleasing little hollows which are the most adroit flatterers in the whole world of golf."

Measuring more than 7,000 yards from the back tees, Royal County Down is a brute. It's an absolute mystery to us that this fantastic course, with one of the finest outward nine holes in golf, has never hosted an Open. Factor in the ever-changing wind and you have as stern a test as any Open Championship venue.

The 3rd, a huge par four, has a wonderful elevated tee and one of the fastest greens on the course. The 4th and 9th holes are both featured in the book, *The 500 World's Greatest Golf Holes*. The 4th must be one of the most scenic long par threes in golf: "Innumerable gorse bushes, ten bunkers, three mountain peaks, and one spire equal the most magnificent view in British golf". The 9th, a long par four, is perhaps one of the world's most photographed holes, the line from the elevated tee is directly at the Slieve Donard peak and the sweeping fairway lies eighty feet below - magnifique.

Sure, the course has a level of eccentricity; there are a number of blind drives and some of the bunkers are fringed with coarse grass, which gathers the ball with alarming regularity, but this simply adds to the charm. If a measure of a great golf course is the number of holes that you can remember, then Royal County Down is one of the greatest courses of them all.

ROYAL BIRKDALE GOLF CLUB
Waterloo Road, Birkdale, Southport, Merseyside
PR8 2LX, England
Telephone: +44 (0) 1704 567920

Average Reviewers' Score:

Website: www.royalbirkdale.com
Architect: George Low, FW Hawtree and JH Taylor
Visitors: Contact in advance - Not Sat

Reviewers' Comments

If Muirfield didn't exist, this would be my number one… Best links course played so far… The course has everything, and matches the best… Royal Birkdale is the most complete of the Open venues… Can there be two better courses in such a small area as Birkdale & Hillside? A seriously tough course, especially when the wind blows – playing to handicap nigh on impossible… Birkdale is a supreme test of golf… Keep out of that rough… It's a fair course with relatively flat fairways but the dunes give each of the holes tremendous form and definition… The opening hole is one of the toughest I've ever played… played the 1st on more than ten occasions and never even bettered bogey… If you don't know a member, it's expensive to play here… Well worth a visit to Southport… Every true links lover should play this course at least once and I guarantee that you'll want to play it again and again and in doing so, you'll love it more and more… Excellent all-round condition… The art deco clubhouse is the perfect place to reflect on the round.

Royal Birkdale

The Birkdale (as it was originally called) was a nine-hole golf course located at Shaw Hills and it opened for play in October 1889. In 1894, the committee decided to extend the course to 18 holes and move it to its current home at Birkdale Hills. Designed by George Low, the course was ready in 1897. In the 1930s, the course was remodelled and upgraded to championship standard by F.W. Hawtree and J.H. Taylor. In his book, *Golf Between Two Wars*, Bernard Darwin writes: "J.H. Taylor was the architect and he has unquestionably made of Birkdale a 'big' course on which it is good fun to see the big men stretch themselves... no bad player is going to win over Birkdale, and yet it is no slogger's paradise, for in the English Championship the final was fought between Arnold Bentley and W. Sutton, who are neither of them particularly long drivers."

The club was simply known as Birkdale until 1951 when King George VI bestowed the royal charter on the club. Royal Birkdale has hosted all the important events – the Ryder Cup, Walker Cup, Curtis Cup, Ladies British Open Championship. The British Open Championship has been hosted at Birkdale no fewer than eight times (most recently in 1998).

It truly is a famous links and widely recognised for its fairness. If you hit the fairways, rarely will the ball be thrown off course. The fairways are laid out in the flat-bottomed valleys between the towering dunes. These dunes, in turn, provide superb viewing platforms for spectators. Invariably in immaculate condition, Royal Birkdale is a very tough cookie to master. The greens were re-built prior to the 1998 Open and despite their youth, are extremely difficult to read.

Birkdale has a superfluity of great golf holes. The 12th, a 183-yard par three is a classic hole and as natural as you can get. From a raised tee, the ball must carry across a hollow, whilst avoiding four deep pot bunkers before coming to rest on a narrow, raised green that nestles at the feet of tussocky sand dunes. The par five 15th is Birkdale's longest hole and one of the most heavily bunkered on the course; knock it straight down the middle off the tee and then using a long iron or a fairway wood, avoid the bunkers spread-eagled across the fairway; chip it on and bingo, an easy five! The monstrous 18th has seen drama over the years, a heavily bunkered par four measuring 476 yards. Only our best two shots in the bag will see us putting for a birdie.

Royal Birkdale can be a torrid experience when the wind is up, with white horses kicking and rearing their heads in the Irish Sea, crashing like kamikazes onto the beach. In these conditions, many of the carries from tees to fairways into the prevailing wind can be too much for the average golfer. But whatever the weather, Royal Birkdale is a provocative place to play golf.

ROYAL PORTRUSH GOLF CLUB
Dunluce Road, County Antrim, BT56 8JQ
Northern Ireland
Telephone: +44 (0)28 7082 2311

Average Reviewers' Score:

Website: www.royalportrushgolfclub.com
Architect: Harry Colt
Visitors: Contact in advance - restrictions Wed & Fri pm, Sat & Sun am

Reviewers' Comments

Portrush has a lack of blind shots, unlike County Down… Both are classics, and I'm undecided… They are both extremely difficult, but I personally prefer Portrush because it is a lot fairer… In my opinion this is the third best course behind Royal County Down and Muirfield… No doubt a classic links but have recently come away a little disappointed… First three holes did not really give me the inspired feel that I hoped for… A tough opener with out of bounds on one side, bushes on the other… My favourite hole is the 4th – a humdinger – aim for the gap in the fence off the tee… Certainly some really fine holes – 5th, 8th, 14th and 15th are my choices – and the views by the coast are exceptional… The 5th "White Rocks" and the stunning par three "Calamity" will remain lodged in my memory for ages… Let down by the weak 17th and 18th holes – pity, otherwise it would be my No.1… Expected to get the WOW factor here but it just did not show up… Not the most attractive course in the world but it is certainly a tough and fair challenge (and the condition is superb)… A great course and should not to be missed… A classic.

Royal Portrush (Dunluce) th

"Portrush stands on a rocky promontory that juts out into the Atlantic, and, if I may allude to such trivialities," wrote Bernard Darwin in, *The Golf Courses of the British Isles*, "the scenery of the coast is wonderfully striking. On the east are the White Rocks, tall limestone cliffs that lead to Dunluce Castle and the headlands of the Giant's Causeway. On the west are the hills of Inishowen, beyond which lie Portsalon and Buncrana and the links of Donegal."

Since its foundation in 1888, Royal Portrush has undergone a transformation in more ways than one. It was originally a 9-hole course, known as the County Club. The following year it was extended to 18 holes. In 1892, its name changed to the Royal County Club, with the Duke of York as patron. In 1895, the Prince of Wales came along and the name finally changed to Royal Portrush. Why? Who knows? However, the biggest transformation came along when Harry Colt redesigned the course prior to the Second World War. Colt felt that Portrush was his finest achievement, even though Muirfield was one of his earlier projects.

The Dunluce links is named after the ruined Dunluce castle that overlooks the course. It was the venue for the first professional golf tournament in Ireland, won by Sandy Herd in 1895. The Open Championship has been held outside of Scotland and England only once; that occasion was here in 1951, when Max Faulkner triumphed. Faulkner was the last British Open champion, until Tony Jacklin lifted the claret jug in 1969 at Royal Lytham & St Annes.

Surely Royal Portrush has the most dramatic entrance to any golf course. As you wind your way towards the course along the coastal road, the crumpled, undulating links land suddenly appears in front of you, flags fluttering in the breeze. This is a seaside links paradise, located in an evocative setting on the north Antrim coastline, blessed with magnificent ocean views. On a clear day (from the 3rd tee) you can see the Paps of Jura and the island of Islay. The fairways nestle in natural valleys between towering sand dunes. The small greens blend perfectly into the landscape, one of Colt's masterstrokes. The greens are generally protected by natural grassy hummocks rather than sand bunkers, further adding to the understatement.

The most spectacular parts of the course are down by the shore. The 5th hole (called "White Rocks") is an absolute stunner. It's a short, downhill par four with a left to right dogleg. The elevated tee provides a platform to soak up the vista. The green is perched on the very edge of the course, some 50 feet above the seashore. The 14th, called "Calamity", is a 210-yard par three; a deep chasm to the right of the green makes it a nervous tee shot.

Royal Portrush is a seriously tough cookie and requires solid driving to hold together a decent score. A trip to the Giant's Causeway may provide some respite after a gruelling round, followed by a nip of whiskey at nearby Bushmills, the world's oldest distillery.

1

THE WESTIN TURNBERRY RESORT
Turnberry, Ayrshire, KA26 9LT, Scotland
Telephone: +44 (0) 1655 334032

Average Reviewers' Score:

Website: www.turnberry.co.uk
Architect: Philip Mackenzie Ross
Visitors: Contact Golf Reservations Office

Reviewers' Comments

There is not a more spectacular golf course in Scotland, dare I say, Britain... The magnificent course speaks for itself... A true testament to the game of golf... A fantastic facility to visit... Experience was daunting but the staff were most welcoming... The staff offered no personal touch... A brilliant Scottish golf experience... People who run it make you feel larger than life... Holes 4 to 12, hugging the coastline between the dunes and then past the lighthouse, are just fabulous... Standing on the back tee at number 9 with the waves crashing is something every lover of links golf should experience... Holes are well designed and testing... Remember that old Pro-celebrity golf TV series from the 70s? Aye, this brings it all back... Wonderfully atmospheric... Having played Troon, Carnoustie and Royal Liverpool, Turnberry would be the one I rush back to... Over the closing holes, who are you going to play, Watson or Nicklaus from 1977?... My number two course ever (only behind the sublime Woodhall Spa, Hotchkin) and I urge you, forget the cost, go play it... Truly a 5-star facility with exceptional staff and a golf course that is second to none... My biggest regret was not having my camera for the sunset over Ailsa.

Turnberry (Ailsa) 6th

The Ailsa course at Turnberry is probably the most scenic Open Championship course, often referred to as Scotland's Pebble Beach. Located right next to the Irish Sea, with craggy rocks and superb views across to the Isles of Mull and Arran, it's an unusual links course, because there are no dunes protecting the holes that run close to the sea (4th to the 11th). This makes for an interesting challenge when there's a freshening wind.

Golf at Turnberry began in 1903; five holes were laid down for a private course on land owned by the Marquess of Ailsa. The course was then extended and developed further, thanks to the Marquess and the Glasgow and South Western Railway Company.

Turnberry twice came close to extinction; it was requisitioned during both World Wars and used as an airbase. During the Second World War, a number of holes were flattened and turned into expansive concrete runways. It was the tenacity of the then owners that saved the course. Philip Mackenzie Ross was given the task of returning the flattened land back to its former glory. It was a huge task, but in 1951, after two years of intensive work, the links reopened.

Mackenzie Ross did a great job; the highest compliment being paid when, in 1977, the Ailsa course hosted its first of three Opens. The 1977 Open was a classic, notorious for the famous battle between Jack Nicklaus and Tom Watson. Watson hit an amazing 65 in the last two rounds to beat Nicklaus by one shot. To commemorate this incredible head-to-head tussle, the 18th hole has been renamed the "Duel in the Sun".

In the 1986 Open, Greg Norman had an amazing second round in windy conditions. He went out in 32, despite two bogies, and had a putt on the 18th for a back nine score of 29. Unfortunately, he three-putted, but his round of 63 is still considered to be one of the very best in Open Championship history. He went on to win by five clear shots.

The resort at Turnberry is run as a commercial operation so there is no problem in securing a midweek tee time. The Ailsa is an absolute "must-play" course; it has a wealth of excellent holes. There are no huge dunes but the holes, which are sometimes subtle and often dramatic, make up for the lack of dune definition.

Essentially it's an out and back layout with the prevailing wind usually at your back for the outward nine. The stretch of holes from the 4th to the 11th is thrilling and the scenery breathtaking. The tee shot on the par four 9th fills you with trepidation as you drive over the rugged shoreline to a blind fairway. This signature hole, called "Bruce's Castle", takes you past the famous lighthouse and Robert the Bruce's ruined castle.

The Ailsa is an appealing course and possibly contains the finest stretch of coastal holes in the British Isles.

BALLYBUNION GOLF CLUB
Sandhill Road, Ballybunion, County Kerry, Ireland
Telephone: +353 (0) 68 27146

Average Reviewers' Score:

Website: www.ballybuniongolfclub.ie
Architect: Philip Mackenzie Ross, Jo McKenna, Lionel Hewson, Tom Simpson & Molly Gourlay
Visitors: Contact in advance - not at weekends

Reviewers' Comments

Simply magnificent. A course of great variety, challenge and truly memorable scenery, it has to be on everybody's must play list… One place I never tire of playing… Sometimes, because of expectation based on wonderful reviews, a film disappoints. This was my feeling about Ballybunion… Played seven rounds in southwest Ireland and found it to be the most interesting and strategic layout of the bunch… Great variety and you will have great respect for this course once you have played it… Too many holes best described as 'ordinary'… Prepare to be challenged on every approach to greens that are difficult to hit… Some complain about the opening holes and then you talk about them. 1st hole is a nice test for an opening hole, 2nd a great par four where you have to get your tee shot down the left to get on to the elevated green in two, 3rd a par three from an elevated tee is as challenging a par three as any I have played… It has it all and the finishing four holes must rank amongst the best finishes anywhere… Finishing hole is disappointing… Somehow I expected more… Links golf at its best… And don't forget they have a second excellent links – the Cashen.

Ballybunion (Old)

The town of Ballybunion was named after the Bunion family, who owned the local 15th century castle. For many people, the name conjures up a vivid image of a wild links golf course on the edge of the Atlantic with fairways set amongst the gigantic duneland. Herbert Warren Wind, the distinguished American golf author, described Ballybunion as "nothing less than the finest seaside course I have ever seen".

As you drive from the historic town of Ballybunion, along the winding road to the golf course, your eyes feast upon the most spectacular links land imaginable. It will come as no surprise that this course, located on Sandhill Road, has the largest, most formidable sand dunes in the British Isles.

Originally founded in 1893 as a 12-hole course, the 1897 Irish Golfer's Guide names the designer as Jo McKenna. The club struggled financially at this time and then folded in 1898. The course was re-established in 1906 as a 9-holer, designed by the prominent Irish golf journalist Lionel Hewson; the Old course was extended to 18-holes in 1926. The Old course remained relatively anonymous until it hosted the Irish Championship in 1937; prior to the tournament, Tom Simpson and Molly Gourlay were called in to make suitable alterations to the layout. Little has changed since.

The Old course is a thrilling challenge, a supreme test of golf. If you are a very good golfer and there's a gentle breeze blowing, you might score well. If there's an onshore gale blowing, you are best to forget scoring well and simply try to enjoy this exhilarating golf course. Bill Clinton played here in 1998, apparently taking more "mulligans" than you can shake a golf club at!

There are so many excellent holes on the Old course that it is fickle to single out one, so we'll select three. The 2nd is a long 445-yard par four, the line for the tee shot a narrow gap between two towering sand dunes. A strong accurate drive will leave a long approach shot to a raised plateau green. The 7th is another tough par four, measuring 432 yards, with its tee perched on the cliff-edge overlooking the seashore. It's an absolute cracker. If there is such a thing as a signature hole then it would have to be the 11th, yet another supremely challenging par four of 453 yards.

Tom Watson fell in love with this place and he goes out of his way to extol the course's virtues. After several visits, Watson agreed to write an article for the course guide/planner. He writes: "After playing Ballybunion for the first time, a man would think that the game of golf originated here. There is a wild look to the place, the long grass covering the dunes that pitch and roll throughout the course making it very intimidating ... in short, it is a course on which many golf architects should live and play before they build golf courses. I consider it a true test of golf.".

CARNOUSTIE GOLF LINKS
Links Parade, Carnoustie, Angus, DD7 7JE, Scotland
Telephone: +44 (0) 1241 853789

Average Reviewers' Score:

Website: www.carnoustiegolflinks.co.uk
Architect: Old Tom Morris, James Braid
Visitors: Contact in advance - not Sat/Sun am

Reviewers' Comments

Tough as nails but fun to play... A brute, the rough can be impossible... Definitely the hardest course I've played, and we played on a calm dry day... Don't go expecting to shoot your handicap and you will have a fantastic day out... Loved it because of the Open history and the challenge... Intimidating, frustrating, unfair, incredible... No opportunity to relax at any stage... Welcome was excellent, the greens true and the course awesome... I thought the terrain very bland and featureless – if it wasn't for the burn, it would be pretty boring... So many memorable holes... I can probably remember more of my shots on this course than any other I've played... With the exception of a few holes, I found the course a bit dull... Play this course – tee up on the 17th and scratch your head and wonder how one drive can confuse you so much... You come up against so many different situations and require so many different types of shot that every one seems different... An overrated track in my mind... The finest course I have played... I got a par on the last, so nice to beat Jean Van de Velde.

Carnoustie (Championship)

Carnoustie is a big natural seaside links and it's one of the most difficult courses in the British Isles.

The first record of golf being played across this links land dates back to 1650; a 10-hole course was laid out in 1842. Fifteen years later, in 1857, an 18-hole course was fashioned by Old Tom Morris. James Braid extended the course in 1926 and it has hardly changed since.

Much has been written about Carnoustie over the years. The finishing holes are especially brutal and many consider that it has one of the greatest back nines in championship golf. Others will recall John Van de Velde's barefoot paddle in the Barry Burn at the 18th hole. Bernard Darwin perhaps had Van de Velde in his mind when, in 1910, he wrote in his book *The Golf Courses of the British Isles*: "he had got burns badly on his nerves… there really is some justification for the nervous golfer who has water on the brain after a round at Carnoustie." You have to cross the snaking burn no less than five times whilst playing the closing two holes. We mustn't forget to mention the wee Jockie's Burn either – he's the young son of Barry, and he comes in to catch your approach shot to the 3rd green.

In addition to burns, Carnoustie has some of the most formidable bunkers to contend with. There's a plethora of them and some are alarmingly cavernous. The par five 6th, called "Long", measures 520 yards from the white tees and is regarded as one of the world's best holes. "Hogan's Alley", with two fearsome looking bunkers in the middle of the fairway and a third bunker to the right hand side, ensures that the tee shot is daunting.

The 15th, 16th and 17th are considered the world over to be three of golf's very best closing holes. "Lucky Slap", the 15th, is a 460-yard par four, where the fairway slopes from left to right into the path of two waiting bunkers and the approach shot must avoid a cluster of three bunkers sited to the right of the green. "Hardest par three in golf; downwind it is difficult, into an easterly wind it is practically impossible", according to the yardage guide. We won't argue because the 16th, called "Barry Burn" measures 245 yards from the white tees; for the ladies, it's an easy par four measuring 212 yards. The 17th is a complete conundrum, called "Island" because the Barry Burn snakes in front of the tee and then loops back, cutting across the fairway. Into the prevailing wind, it is tough to know what to do on this brutal 400-yard-plus par four.

Carnoustie isn't the prettiest golf course - rarely do you catch glimpses of the sea - but it is a delightfully rough monster, even from the forward tees. Bring your "A" game here and pray for the weather to be kind.

ROYAL ST GEORGE'S GOLF CLUB
Sandwich, Kent, CT13 9PB, England
Telephone: +44 (0) 1304 613090

Average Reviewers' Score:

Website: www.royalstgeorges.com
Architect: William Laidlaw Purves, Frank Pennink
Visitors: Contact in advance - not at the weekend - fourballs on Tue

Reviewers' Comments

Royal St George's is a fantastic experience... Somewhat unspectacular from the tee unlike its near neighbour Royal Cinque Ports... The course condition left nothing to be desired... Condition was spectacular...You will definitely get some unlucky bounces during your round. Apart from that you will find it hard to fault... It's a tough, tough course but one that must be played... We experienced neighbouring Deal as the tougher course but this is probably due mainly to the narrower fairways and tougher rough... Sandwich is worth a trip, especially if you can combine with Prince's or Deal... A friendly welcome and a great overall experience... Walk down the hall to the bar and you will be surrounded by wonderful golfing memories. Getting your pint of bitter in a silver tanker will top off what will no doubt be a very good days golf... The green keeping staff get maximum marks for the immaculate results... Fairway width and rough were manageable which contributed positively to a great experience... A must.

Royal St George's

In 1885, doctor William Laidlaw Purves spotted from the vantage point of St Clement's church a spectacular piece of undulating land with expansive sand dunes. Being a Scot and a keen scratch golfer, he decided that there was only one thing to do with this links land; create a golf course. In 1887, the course opened for play and was named "St George's" after the English patron saint.

After only seven years of play, in 1894, Sandwich hosted its first of 13 Open Championships. This was the first Open to be played outside Scotland. Royal patronage was granted in 1902 and the Prince of Wales (later King Edward VIII) became club captain.

It's not a traditional out and back layout. In a similar style to Muirfield, each nine is broadly circular, a loose figure of eight. There is nothing artificial, just a natural look and feel to the course that blends beautifully into the surroundings. Wild flowers, dune grasses and the sweet song of the lark, commanding views over Pegwell Bay and the white cliffs of Dover ensure an amazing experience.

All the holes are very different and memorable, a true sign of a great golf course. There are also some unique features; thatched roof shelters, the red cross of St George on the flags, and that bunker on the 4th hole cut into a huge dune, the UK's tallest and deepest bunker. If you can carry that famous bunker on this 470-yard par four, then you can enjoy the peace of the fairway beyond, called the "Elysian Fields". The 15th is considered architecturally to be one of the most impressive holes in golf because the fairway bunkers are virtually symmetrical.

Some hazards are not clearly visible from the tees, but in the past things were much worse. In the mid 1970s, blind shots were considered passé, so Frank Pennink was brought in to ring the changes. Three new holes were built and tee changes were made to two other holes. Many, except for the real traditionalists, believe that these changes have further improved the layout.

Here we have one of the most difficult tests of golf, requiring courage, confidence and solid ball striking. Severely undulating fairways make good scoring very tough indeed. Often the tee shot will come to rest on an up slope or a down slope, then one needs to hit a long iron or fairway wood into the green from an uneven lie.

Ian Fleming, the author of the James Bond books, was a member here. The golf scenes from the film Goldfinger were filmed at Stoke Park, but Fleming called the course "Royal St Marks" in the film, no doubt inspired by his home club. Like Muirfield, Royal St George's is a private men's club and there are no female members. Women can play the course as a member's guest, but there are no ladies' tees.

Sandwich is a classic links course, summed up nicely by Bernard Darwin: "My idea of heaven as is to be attained on an earthly links". Darwin went on to become president of the club between 1952 and 1961.

PORTMARNOCK GOLF CLUB
Portmarnock, County Dublin, Ireland
Telephone: +353 (0) 184 62968

Average Reviewers' Score:

Website: www.portmarnockgolfclub.ie
Architect: William Pickeman
Visitors: Contact in advance - not Sat, Sun & Public Hols

Reviewers' Comments

It's rather flat - no towering dunes - but it's brilliant nonetheless - you get a feeling of quiet isolation... The moment you step on the first tee you know that you're about to play a very special course and you won't be disappointed... Your game needs to be in order because it's a tough cookie... The ultimate test – you'll love it here... Natural course that cannot fail to impress any links lover... No weak holes and many are stunning... If the wind is blowing it will test every part of your game... From the off you're under pressure to play to handicap but what a pleasure it is... Distance, accuracy and control are a must and if you leave any of these in the locker room you're in for a tough day... Forget reaching most of the par fours in regulation... After playing the 3rd stand and look back from the 4th tee and admire the hole you've just played - brilliant... Favourite holes are the 14th (tough approach to the green) and the par three 15th along the coastal boundary (aim 30 yards left and watch nature do its thing)... Final two holes are tough... Highly recommended... I love this course, top quality in every aspect.

Portmarnock (Old)

Portmarnock is situated on its own sandy peninsula, approximately two miles long and covering some 500 acres. In 1893, William Pickeman, a Scottish insurance broker, and his friend George Ross, rowed across the sea from Sutton to the peninsular and immediately realised that this was prime golfing terrain. In those days, the peninsular could only be reached by boat.

The land belonged to the famous distiller, John Jameson, and from around 1850, the links was used as the Jameson's private golf course. Nine "proper" holes opened for play in October 1894 and, two years later, the course was extended to eighteen holes. Pickeman was the driving force behind the original course and went on to design others in Ireland.

There is nothing man-made – it's a natural links, and considered to be a very fair golf course. With water on three sides, the course is at the mercy of the wind. Laid out broadly in two loops of nine holes, you are invariably playing in different directions, and measuring over 7,300 yards from the back tees, it is a formidable test of golf. You will need your very best putting game because the greens at Portmarnock are lightning fast and true.

There are superb views to the south of the Ireland's Eye (a small island), home to important seabird colonies, and the Hill of Howth (once famous for its electric trams). On a clear day looking northwest, the Mountains of Mourne are visible.

Portmarnock has hosted a number of important events including, on 12 occasions, the Irish Open and the Canada Cup. The closing five holes are especially brutal. Bernard Darwin once commented: "I know of no greater finish in the world than that of the last five holes at Portmarnock". The first of the closing five holes, the 14th is featured in the book The 500 World's Greatest Golf Holes – "One of the most beloved par 4s in golf. The narrow, elevated green demands a precise second shot if par is to be made, or in Joe Carr's case, a precise first shot." Apparently Carr, an amateur, made a hole-in-one on this 385-yard par four. How on earth did he miss those greenside bunkers?

The par three 15th – measuring 188 yards – plays along the seashore. Any hint of a left to right shaped tee shot will almost certainly end up on the beach, whilst the green is protected at the front by three fearsome bunkers. Ian Woosnam almost came a cropper on this hole in the second round of the 1988 Irish Open. His opening tee shot ended up in the sea, but playing three off the tee, he somehow managed to find the edge of the green and then he holed a 40-footer for a bogey. Clearly inspired by this miraculous save, Woosnam went on to win the title.

ROYAL LYTHAM & ST ANNES GOLF CLUB
Links Gate, St Annes on Sea, Lancashire, FY8 3LQ
England
Telephone: +44 (0) 1253 724206

Average Reviewers' Score:

Website: www.royallytham.org
Architect: Harry Colt, Herbert Fowler, Tom Simpson & C.K.Cotton
Visitors: Mon & Thu - Contact in advance

Reviewers' Comments

One of the finest courses anywhere... Sense of history makes Lytham a worthy Open venue and an unforgettable experience for the average club golfer... Historic atmosphere is quite humbling... Practice facilities are excellent... Not a course for the high handicapper – it's tough with a capital T... A challenging layout, especially when the wind is up... Tough course but a bit lacklustre... Immaculately conditioned and the greens were as good as any I've ever experienced... Not the most idyllic setting but always in immaculate condition... It would be nice to see the sea rather than suburbia... Try to keep out of the traps – they'll ruin the card... Bunkers are truly magnetic... The back nine, as everyone knows, is brutal... Felt as though I played good solid golf and I dropped twelve shots coming home and there was only a 15-20 mph wind... What a warm and friendly Lancashire welcome, those folk really know how to make you feel at home and the food was delicious... Will return one day... Really would like to come back and stay in the Dormy accommodation to gently soak up the atmosphere... Should be on everyone's must-play list... It was a pleasure to play this cracking links course.

Royal Lytham & St Annes 11th

Royal Lytham & St Annes is the most northerly of the English championship links courses, situated only 10 miles, as the seagull flies, from its illustrious neighbour, Royal Birkdale. This monster links opened for play in 1886, fashioned by George Lowe, the club's first professional. In the early part of the 20th century, three great architects joined forces to remodel the course – Harry Colt, Herbert Fowler and Tom Simpson. C.K. Cotton later modified the layout.

This is definitely a links course, but it is no longer beside the sea. It now lies about one mile inland but there is evidence that the sea is nearby because you can spot Blackpool Tower in the distance. The links is positioned – rather unusually – surrounded by red brick houses and flanked on the west by the railway line while the guardian Victorian clubhouse watches sternly over the course. The conditioning of the course is exceptional and not as rough and ready as many of its contemporaries. The ground is relatively even, except perhaps on a couple of holes, where the land is slightly wrinkled.

The course itself is extremely tough. Only Carnoustie (on the British Open circuit) is thought to be tougher. Bernard Darwin describes Lytham's challenges in his book, *The Golf Courses of the British Isles*: "The trouble, besides the rough grass and pot-bunkers, consists of sandhills, both natural and artificial. To build an artificial sandhill is not a light task, and it is characteristic of the whole-hearted enthusiasm of the golfers of St Anne's that they have raised several of these terrifying monuments of industry." At this stage we should remind ourselves that Darwin penned this in 1910 and, in those days, it was highly unusual to build anything other than bunkers, talking of which, the bunkers are many and annoyingly magnetic.

The 1st is unique because this is the only par three starting hole on the Open Championship circuit and it's a long one, measuring 206 yards from the back tees. Ian Woosnam hit a fine tee shot here in the 2001 Open and then sank the putt, thinking he'd made a birdie, only to find that he had 15 clubs in his bag. This cost Woosie £225,000 and possibly the Open Championship title; it also cost his caddy around £20,000 and his job.

The 17th hole, a 467-yard par four, belongs to the esteemed Bobby Jones. As an amateur, he won the 1926 Open Championship, beating Al Watrous by two shots. A plaque, located close to the spot from which he nailed his second shot onto the green from a rough, sandy lie during the final round, commemorates Jones's triumph. The mashie that Jones used for this remarkable shot is displayed in the clubhouse. The final hole is a relatively ordinary 414-yard par four and it's a simple case of straight hitting to avoid the 15 bunkers that are trying hard to swallow the ball. The resurgence of British golf occurred here in 1969, when Tony Jacklin's final drive avoided all the bunkers and he putted out to win the Open in a sea of emotion.

Nathan Tucker

SUNNINGDALE GOLF CLUB
Ridgemount Road, Sunningdale, Berkshire, SL5 9RR
England
Telephone: +44 (0) 1344 621681

Average Reviewers' Score:

Website: www.sunningdale-golfclub.co.uk
Architect: Willie Park, Harry Colt
Visitors: Contact in advance - Not Fri, Sat, Sun or public hols

Reviewers' Comments

Without doubt the best inland course in the country... One of the prettiest courses around - a heathland delight... Not the most difficult course in the Top 100... Play this one before all others on your list of courses to play. You won't be disappointed.... This classic layout is very tight off the tee with heather and pine trees bordering every fairway... You'll need to read the greens properly in order to score well... Greens sometimes come in for criticism in that they are less firm than classic heathland courses... At least you can fly the ball at the greens... To score well you'll need to shape the ball in both directions to negotiate the doglegs... Keep out of the heather - it can be a nightmare... Stop off on the way round at the glorious halfway hut but before you do, enjoy that drive on the elevated 10th tee, it's a cracker ... It's pricey, but worth every penny... One of the most exclusive clubs in the land but it's cheaper than Wentworth and in my book it's better... The clubhouse is simply gorgeous and the food is scrumptious too... A stunning golf club.

Sunningdale (Old)

The Old course at Sunningdale is one of the British Isles' most aesthetically pleasing inland courses. Arguably, it was the first truly great golf course to be built on the magical Surry/Berkshire sand-belt. The land was (and still is) leased from the freeholder, St John's College, Cambridge. It is a Willie Park masterpiece and opened for play in 1901, becoming known as the Old after the opening of the New Course in 1923.

Lined with pine, birch and oak trees, it is a magnificent place to play golf. The emblem of the club is the oak tree, no doubt modelled on the huge specimen tree standing majestically beside the 18th green. It's incredible to believe that originally the golf course was laid out on barren, open land. Harry Colt was a big influence at Sunningdale; he was Secretary and Captain in the club's early years and redesigned the Old course, giving it a more intimate and enclosed feel.

In 1926, during qualification for the British Open, amateur Bobby Jones played the Old Course perfectly, scoring 66, made up of all threes and fours (taking 33 putts). This type of scoring was unheard of in those days. Bernard Darwin brilliantly summed up Jones's round as "incredible and indecent". "Few joys in this world are unalloyed," wrote Darwin in *Golf Between Two Wars*, "and though Bobby was naturally and humanly pleased with that 66, he was a trifle worried because he had 'reached the peak' rather too soon before going to St. Anne's." Jones went on to Royal Lytham & St Annes and won the 1926 Open by two strokes, beating fellow American Al Watrous.

If you have already played the Old course, you will surely remember the elevated 10th tee, a fabulous driving hole and one of our all-time favourite holes. By the time you have putted out on the 10th, you will be ready for refreshments at the excellent halfway hut that sits welcomingly behind the green. What sheer delight! The 5th, a lovely par four, is beautifully described in *The 500 World's Greatest Golf Holes*: "From an elevated tee, the fifth is clearly defined. The fairway is bordered by heather, golden grass and dark green forest. There are two fairway bunkers in the right half of the fairway; a small pond and four sentinel bunkers protect the green. Success calls for two pure shots…" The 15th is also featured in the same book – it's a superb par three, measuring 226 yards.

Many people regard Sunningdale as the perfect golfing venue. The Old and New courses taken together are probably the finest pair of golf courses anywhere. On a sunny autumn day, walking on that perfect heathland turf, surely there is nowhere better to play golf with a few friends. "If we have not been too frequently 'up to our necks' in untrodden heather – nay, even if we have – we ought to have enjoyed ourselves immensely," as Darwin said in his 1910 book, *The Golf Courses of the British Isles*.

LOCH LOMOND GOLF CLUB
Rossdhu House, Luss by Alexandria, Dunbartonshire
G83 8NT, Scotland
Telephone: +44 (0) 1436 655555

Average Reviewers' Score:

Website: www.lochlomond.com
Architect: Tom Weiskopf and Jay Morrish
Visitors: Members' guests only

Reviewers' Comments

Could not fault this course… Would have any golfer drooling for a very long time… It's not that good… Delightful, satisfying, thankful, wonderful, amazing, dumbstruck, sensational – I could go on… Single most memorable round of golf in the UK… Played the course on five separate occasions and have yet to be disappointed… Very scenic but mediocre golf course… Location is stunning but there are only a couple of genuinely great holes... Each hole is varied and immensely challenging… Design of holes would look good anywhere… No attention to detail missed… Design is masterful… Wouldn't rank in my Top 25 parkland courses played previously… Becomes an instant entry into my personal Top 3 courses… Great shame that it's not open to "ordinary" people… Conditioning is quite fabulous - no doubt due to the fact that it's only open for six months of the year… If you like manicured parkland, then it's as good as it gets… More staff here than golfers, so expect to be looked after well… Genuine feeling of welcome… Sheer luxury and the Loch Lomond brand go together like eggs and bacon… Truly a taste of the dream lifestyle… As close to golfing heaven as I expect I'll ever get on this earth.

Loch Lomond

It doesn't matter whether you take the high road or the low road, a visit to the bonnie banks o' Loch Lomond is a romantic experience. A hop, skip and a jump from Glasgow, under the watchful guard of Ben Lomond, lies the largest expanse of fresh water in Great Britain. And midway along the western banks of the loch lies the most exclusive private members' golf club in the land.

Loch Lomond Golf Club is set in more than 600 acres of sheltered seclusion, sandwiched between the mountains and the historic lochside. The golf course contains two Sites of Special Scientific Interest – protecting rare plants and unusual woodland – and the site is designated as a National Scenic Area. Dozens of inhabited bat boxes nestle amongst the branches of some of the 46 different types of trees, there's even an inhabited owl box. It's a heaven for wildlife and conservationists, and apart from Valderrama, Loch Lomond is the only other European golf club to be awarded full Audubon status (Audubon's mission is to conserve and restore natural ecosystems).

The course, designed by the successful Jay Morrish and Tom Weiskopf partnership, opened for play in 1993 to a fanfare. Weiskopf regards Loch Lomond as his "lasting memorial to golf" and who could argue with him? It is already a classic course and the long-term home to the Scottish Open. According to Colin Montgomerie, "wherever Loch Lomond is ranked, it ought to be higher".

In such a beautiful area it would have been easy to allow the views to do the talking, but Morrish and Weiskopf have designed a spectacular course, which would stand proud without the stunning scenery. Each hole – except for the linked 2nd and 4th greens – is isolated from the next. None of the hazards are hidden from view – either from the tee or from approach shots – and there are no tricks up Loch Lomond's sleeve.

Measuring 7,100 yards from the back tees, this is a tough and long course for the average club golfer but it's sad that not everyone can share the experience. If you are lucky enough to get a game, don't expect to threaten Retief Goosen's course record of 62, but do expect to use every club in the bag.

For a course that is so young, there is so much architectural history. The Colquhoun Clan built Rossdhu House in 1773 and Mary Queen of Scots wrote her love letters in Rossdhu Castle – the remains of which overlook the 18th green. The whole experience is truly remarkable and if you are lucky enough to receive an invitation, do not pass it by.

LAHINCH GOLF CLUB
Lahinch, County Clare, Ireland
Telephone: +353 (0) 65 7081103

Average Reviewers' Score:

Website: www.lahinchgolf.com
Architect: Old Tom Morris, Dr Alister MacKenzie, John Burke, and Martin Hawtree
Visitors: Contact in advance

Reviewers' Comments

Few courses can be said to have *no* weak holes, but Lahinch is one of them... A course that has everything... I agree with Old Tom, Lahinch is a most natural golf course... Holes are laid out in the most flowing and natural manner... Following the changes made by Martin Hawtree, it is possibly the best course in Ireland and UK... Great condition, hugely challenging weather, friendly staff and a wonderful layout make this an absolute must... Enjoyed playing Lahinch more than any in southwest Ireland because of the layout (great variety and use of the terrain) and the scenery (great ocean and beach views)... Great variety of holes... No two holes are alike, no weak holes and each presenting a different challenge... Keeps you captivated from beginning to end... Some greens were in need of sunshine but the way the course winds its way through the dunes gives a feeling of great exhilaration... 6th is a killer straight into the Atlantic wind and there is a barrage of long par fours on the back nine that make getting to the 19th more of a physical challenge than you could ever imagine... Good and knowledgeable golfers will appreciate this magnificent test of golf. Worthy of a higher ranking... Links golf at its finest - whatever the weather.

Lahinch (Old) th

Lahinch is derived from the old Irish name Leithinsi, a half island. The village dates back to the 18th century and grew in popularity thanks to George I, who believed that eating periwinkles and sea-grass was healthy.

Golf here dates back to 1892 when three local Limerick golfers laid out an 18-hole course, assisted by officers of the Scottish "Black Watch" regiment who were stationed in Limerick. In 1894, Old Tom Morris was commissioned to make improvements to the layout and he made excellent use of the natural terrain, especially the giant sand dunes. Old Tom believed that Lahinch was the finest natural course that he had seen.

In the mid-1890s, the West Clare Railway made the town more accessible and consequently, people flocked to Lahinch to stay at the new Golf Links Hotel. The whole town lives and breathes golf. Bernard Darwin wrote the following in his book, *The Golf Courses of the British Isles*, published in 1910: "The greatest compliment I have heard paid to Lahinch came from a very fine amateur golfer, who told me that it might not be the best golf in the world, but was the golf he liked to play best. Lest this may be attributed to patriotic prejudice, I may add that he was an Englishman born and bred."

In 1927, Dr Alister MacKenzie redesigned the course, relocating a number of holes closer to the bay. The redesign work took one year to complete and featured undulating triple tiered greens. MacKenzie was pleased with his work and said: "It will make the finest and most popular course that I, or I believe anyone else, ever constructed".

Unfortunately, in 1935, the same time that MacKenzie was designing Augusta with Bobby Jones, the committee decided that his greens were too tough for the average golfer. John Burke was granted the remit to flatten them out. Happily, in 1999, Martin Hawtree reinstated MacKenzie's characteristics, completing the restoration.

This is an enchanting place to play golf. It's rugged, distinctive, unusually varied and immensely entertaining. It's a traditional out and back layout, situated next to the lovely beach of Liscannor Bay.

Each September, Lahinch hosts the South of Ireland Championship, an annual occurrence since 1895. The "South" is a matchplay competition, which attracts many spectators and some great amateur golfers, although it is unlikely that anybody will beat John Burke's record. The "King of Lahinch" was the South of Ireland champion 11 times between 1928 and 1946.

The 4th hole, a 428-yard par four has a blind drive to a hidden fairway and the approach to the green is obscured by a hill on the right. Views across the bay are uplifting. Another great hole is the 5th, a short par five, named Klondyke, one of the most celebrated in golf and an Old Tom speciality. The tee shot needs to find a narrow rippled fairway located in a valley between dunes. A blind second shot then has to negotiate Klondyke, a towering sand dune that straddles the fairway some 200 yards away from the green.

ROYAL LIVERPOOL GOLF CLUB
Meols Drive, Hoylake, Wirral, Merseyside, CH47 4AL
England
Telephone: +44 (0) 151 632 3101

Average Reviewers' Score:

Website: www.royal-liverpool-golf.com
Architect: George Morris, Harry Colt, and Donald Steel
Visitors: Not Thu am or weekends - contact in advance

Reviewers' Comments

If it's tradition you're looking for, look no further… Hoylake is a true links… Make no mistake, it's a true, honest and tough test of links golf… Bring your A game or you'll be in trouble… Not the most inspiring course in the land and many would say that it's flat and boring… As good a test of your inner game as any I have come across… Not keen on the internal OOB – which comes in to play right from the off… You will get bad bounces, be beaten senseless by the wind and have chips and putts to make you feel ill… Some genuinely stunning holes and the 10th and 11th stand out for me… Not to be tried if you like your greens soft and receptive… Maintained to impeccable standards and a truly memorable round of golf… To venture onto Royal Liverpool is a true privilege… Clubhouse is full of old wood and silverware and the course saw the beginnings of golf in England… Will look on with interest when the Open returns in 2006… I have no idea how they will cope with the crowds and tented villages… Undeniably a top quality course that has to be played but I personally prefer Birkdale and Hillside… Serious course for serious golfers.

Royal Liverpool

The Open Championship returns to Royal Liverpool in 2006. Hoylake, as it is called by those in the know, has a long and illustrious history of playing host to the Open, and has hosted ten, its first in 1897 and its most recent in 1967. Founded in 1869, Hoylake is the second oldest seaside links course in England — only Royal North Devon is the more senior.

George Morris, the brother of Old Tom, originally laid out a 9-hole course on the site of a racecourse and for the first seven years, golfers shared the land with members of the Liverpool Hunt Club. Three extra holes were soon added and in 1871, the course was extended to 18 holes. In 1872, the club received royal patronage from Prince Arthur, Duke of Connaught.

Bernard Darwin reported on the coming of the Haskell, which burst onto the scene at the Amateur Championship at Hoylake in 1902. The winner, Charles Hutchings, and the runner-up, Sidney Fry, used the rubber-core ball. Later that same year, Sandy Herd used a Haskell and won the Open at Royal Liverpool, sounding the death knell for the "gutty" ball.

Harry Colt made alterations to the 11th and 17th holes, named Alps and Royal. He also created a new 13th hole and changed the greens at the 8th and 12th holes. In his book, *Golf Between Two Wars*, Bernard Darwin describes Colt's changes and the alteration to the 16th, called the Dun: "I do not criticise the disappearance of the old cross-bunker at the Dun because that had been made inevitable by the modern ball and modern driving. It was sad to see it go if only because the soberest might fall into it after dinner — I have seen them do it — in finding their way home across the darkling links; but it had to go and the present Dun is a fine long hole. Trying not to be Blimpish and die-hard and to look at the course with eyes unblurred by sentiment, I solemnly and sincerely declare that Mr Colt made a great job of it".

Donald Steel was commissioned to make alterations to the course; these changes included a number of new greens, tees and bunkers. The work was completed in 2001 and the course now stretches out in excess of 7,000 yards.

The land is unusually flat, offering little in the way of definition — three sides of the course are bordered by houses and the Dee Estuary lies on the western side. When you get out onto the course, the undulations become more pronounced and, as you move away from the houses, the overall experience improves. The holes alongside the shore (9th, 10th, 11th and 12th) are the most visually appealing and very challenging.

Without doubt, Royal Liverpool is a tough links. Only a couple of holes are in the dunes — otherwise there is little protection from the ever-changing wind. There is nothing artificial about the course — it represents a traditional, genuine test of golf and will examine the very best players.

KINGSBARNS GOLF LINKS
Kingsbarns, St Andrews, Fife, KY16 8QD, Scotland
Telephone: +44 (0) 1334 460860

Average Reviewers' Score:

Website: www.kingsbarns.com
Architect: Kyle Phillips
Visitors: Course closed Dec-Mar – contact in advance

Reviewers' Comments

It surpassed my experience at Turnberry... Simply the best new course I have ever played... Played on five occasions and each time it gets better... Too expensive for what you get, double the cost of Dornoch... You'd never believe it was new... You can play like an absolute idiot (and I did) and still come away with a smile on your face... A big course in every sense of the word yet full of subtle nuances... Modern risk/reward design elements are at play on most holes... The sea is in view at all times...Has much variety with big hitting par fives, short par fours and glorious varied par threes... Dramatic views along the coastline... Bring your putting game or you will easily perish with three (or four!) putts on greens... Some think the last hole is weak. I think it's a wonderful end to a wonderful series of golf holes... If you make it an annual pilgrimage as I do, then it becomes one of the highlights of the golfing year... Have played most of the Top 100 links courses and I still rate this the best... Well worth the green fee and a tremendous addition to the St Andrews experience... A special course.

Kingsbarns

According to golf historian Bobby Burnet, golf at Kingsbarns dates back to 1793. A nine-hole golf course once played over part of the current layout. The "nine-holer" was commandeered by the military at the outbreak of the Second World War because they felt that the beach at Kingsbarns was an invasion risk. The golf course disappeared until American architect Kyle Phillips came along at the close of the 20th century.

Phillips studied various courses, including Royal Dornoch, to ensure that the end design would look natural. The earthmovers then rumbled in and shifted hundreds of thousands of tonnes of earth to create the moonscape that is now Kingsbarns.

The course opened in July 2000 and was welcomed by rapturous applause. The course appears so natural that you would think that it had been there for years, an outstanding achievement.

One of the many delights is that you can see the North Sea from virtually every part of the course. It has its own burn (the Cambo), which was uncovered during all that earth moving. The terrain is perfect for golf, rippling fairways, humps and hollows. What's more, the course is always maintained in immaculate condition. The green fee is not insignificant, however, the goody-bag that is handed out on the first tee is a really nice touch.

Situated just six miles from St Andrews, Kingsbarns is an important addition to the superb links courses in this area. It is feasible that this might be the last true links course to be built along Scotland's coastline and if so, it is just as well that this course is an absolute cracker and deserves to be bracketed alongside the greatest courses in the world.

Julie

ROYAL TROON GOLF CLUB
Craigend Road, Troon, Ayrshire, KA10 6EP, Scotland
Telephone: +44 (0) 1292 311555

Average Reviewers' Score:

Website: www.royaltroon.com
Architect: George Strath, Willie Fernie & James Braid
Visitors: May to Oct - Mon, Tue & Thu only

Reviewers' Comments

A fine and true test of links golf and well worth playing when visiting the Ayrshire coast... Not very scenic but a nice layout and not tricked up... My No.2 in Scotland behind Dornoch... Warm welcome from the staff... Caddies are something else with a wicked sense of humour... Don't come expecting to play to handicap, the back nine is as tough as old boots... We played on a day when it was impossible to stop the ball downwind, and very difficult to reach the later holes into the elements... Frankly a bit of a slog, and probably my least favourite of the Open courses... Opening holes and the equivalent number of closing ones are fairly featureless... Most interesting stretch is around the turn... Course really comes alive at the "Postage Stamp" and then the run of holes through to the 13th are especially memorable... It's worth playing for the "Postage Stamp" alone... All in all a great experience, but not quite living up to my expectations... For the price, the poorest value in UK.... They've a tricky little par three course and the Portland course too, so you can make a day of it here... A quality links course and an absolute must for traditional links lovers.

Royal Troon (Old) **17**th

Troon was founded in 1878 as a five-hole golf course following a meeting in the local pub by a group of golf enthusiasts. It was George Strath, Troon's pro, who was largely responsible for the original course design. Willie Fernie and James Braid later modified and extended the layout. In 1923, Troon hosted its first Open and finally moved out of the shadow of its famous neighbour, Prestwick. (By 1923, Prestwick had already hosted 23 Open Championships).

"The course at Troon is perhaps a little overshadowed by its more famous neighbour," wrote Bernard Darwin in his 1910 book, *The Golf Courses of the British Isles*, "but it is a very fine course nevertheless, especially since it has been lengthened of late years. It has, moreover, one of the finest short holes to be found anywhere."

In 1978, Troon's centenary year, royal patronage was bestowed. Royal Troon remains the first (and last) club in Great Britain to have been granted Royal status under the long reign of Queen Elizabeth II.

It's a traditional out and back links course and the opening few holes are relatively gentle, with a series of short par fours running along the Firth of Clyde. It's from these early holes that you get the chance to soak up the views. On a clear day, you can see the distant Ailsa Craig in the south, and to the west, the majestic mountains on the Isle of Arran.

The course measures 7,150 yards from the back tees but line is more important than distance from the tee. Bunkers are everywhere, the majority of which are not visible from the tees. There's plenty of deep rough and a smattering of gorse and broom to punish the wayward shot. Make your score on the outward nine holes; the inward holes are severe, often playing into the prevailing northwesterly wind. The stretch of holes from the 7th to the 13th provides an interesting and varied challenge.

The 6th is the longest par five in Open Championship golf and the 8th, the "Postage Stamp", is the shortest par three on the Open circuit (123 yards). The name stuck after Willie Park referred to the hole in an article for Golf Illustrated: "a pitching surface skimmed down to the size of a postage stamp". It was here, in the 1973 Open, at the age of 71, Gene Sarazen holed out in one. The following day, he holed his bunker shot for a two at the same hole. It was an amazing return for Sarazen, who had played in Troon's inaugural Open in 1923.

The 11th is a short par five for the members but a brutal 481-yard par four for the pros. Either way, this hole is considered to be Troon's toughest hole — out-of-bounds and the railway line runs along the right hand side. The 133rd Open Championship returned to Royal Troon in July 2004.

John Skeet

WOODHALL SPA GOLF CLUB
The Broadway, Woodhall Spa, Lincs, LN10 6PU
England
Telephone: +44 (0) 1526 352511

Average Reviewers' Score:

Website: www.woodhallspagolf.com
Architect: Harry Vardon, Harry Colt & Colonel S.V. Hotchkin
Visitors: Contact in advance - handicap certificate required

Reviewers' Comments

A wonderful example of how a golf course should be… I was expecting a lot the first time I played here and I wasn't disappointed… This is undoubtedly my favourite course and has to be the best inland course in the country… It not only lived up to expectations but exceeded them… Course is very fair - play straight and you can score well… Course has fair greens, decent size fairways and punishing rough and bunkers… Take your bucket and spade with you - the bunkers are something else. Some are so deep a de-compression chamber is recommended… This is a course that should only be played by 'decent' golfers otherwise you will have a very frustrating day… Condition was excellent, welcome was friendly and professional, and they serve a good pint of Bateman's! - What more can one ask for… It's good value for money… Often compared to Sunningdale as the 'Best Inland' course in the UK - the Hotchkin is better value for your money… A genuine golf course… I look forward to my regular pilgrimage to Woodhall… This is truly one of the best courses I've played… Visit this course at least once in your life.

Woodhall Spa (Hotchkin)   18th

The Hotchkin course at Woodhall Spa invariably fights with Loch Lomond and Sunningdale Old for the coveted position of "best inland course" in the British Isles. Originally, Harry Vardon laid out the course and it opened for play in 1905. Harry Colt, just before the Great War, made further modifications to the layout. But in the 1920s, the owner, Colonel S.V. Hotchkin, put the course through one last major redesign phase before the Hotchkin finally matured into its present layout. The English Golf Union purchased Woodhall Spa in 1995 for a reputed £8m and turned it into their headquarters.

An oasis in the heart of Lincolnshire, set amongst glorious pine, birch and broom, this heathland course is an absolute delight to play. The sandy subsoil allows all-year-round golf, the springy turf making walking a real pleasure. Keep your ball in play and do your best to avoid the heather, gorse and the bunkers. See if you can copy the feat of J.A. Wilson (8 h/cap) and his opponent L.D. Henshaw (12 h/cap). In 1982, Wilson holed in one at the 12th (a beautiful, long par three) but only managed a half because Henshaw also holed in one. Apparently they were hurrying their shots too because they had just been invited to play through. The four-ball standing behind the green were gobsmacked!

The Hotchkin is bunker heaven (or hell), notorious for its deep, cavernous sand traps. It is also helpful if you can hit the ball long and straight. Otherwise you will be presented with some very tough second shots. Woodhall Spa isn't a tournament course, but it is supremely challenging and plays host to a number of distinguished national and international amateur competitions. Many important matches have been decided on its famous 18th hole. This short 491-yard par five finishing hole typifies what is so special about Woodhall Spa. If we can strike the ball with solidity off the tee and avoid the hazards, then we give ourselves a chance of scoring well. We can see the flag clearly in the distance but the drive is tight. We must land left of the sentry oak, but not too far left, otherwise we will be bunkered. We must be dead straight in order to find the crisp, sandy fairway and if we achieve all these things, and if we are a stout hitter, we may be tempted to go for the green with our second shot. It is tempting - the route to the green is open and its meagre protection is a solitary bunker guarding its left flank. What can we say? "Go for it" perhaps?

It is definitely worth making the trip to play this gem and the green fee is tremendous value for money too (especially if you are a member of an English golf club). And remember - the Hotchkin is undoubtedly one of the premier inland courses in the whole of the British Isles. Can you afford not to play it?

John Moody

WATERVILLE GOLF LINKS
Waterville, County Kerry, Ireland
Telephone: +353 (0) 66 947 4102

Average Reviewers' Score:

Website: www.watervillehouse.com
Architect: Claude Harmon, Eddie Hackett, and Tom Fazio
Visitors: Contact in advance

Reviewers' Comments

Waterville is a tough links golf course that requires accurate driving… Tough…long…tight…enough said… It's exceptionally tough with some top class holes and it's also fair without tricks… A great location… Play here for the stunning location alone… I found the front nine to be quite undistinguished for links golf but the back nine is superb with the par five 18th skirting the Atlantic… Undeniably a great course but outclassed by Ballybunion, Lahinch and Old Head… The course was in great shape and the staff were very friendly… Enjoy the warm and friendly Irish welcome… Well worth a visit… You should add this course to your itinerary when golfing in southwest Ireland… Not to be missed.

Waterville

The town of Waterville is a famous angling centre, located on a strip of land that separates the Atlantic Ocean from one of the most beautiful lakes in Ireland, Lough Currane. The name Waterville, or An CoireÁn (Little Whirlpool), is the premier coastal tourist centre of South West Kerry. Every year, Charlie Chaplin came to Waterville with his family, and they have named the annual two-day AM-AM after him. The AM-AM has been held since 1984, a two-day golfing extravaganza involving teams from all over Ireland. It also involves a certain amount of merriment!

Golf at Waterville started around 1889 with a modest 9-hole course, laid out on the eastern section of the present course. In the 1950s, the club folded until Jack Mulcahy (an Irish American) bought the links in the late 1960s. Mulcahy commissioned Claude Harmon, his friend and the 1948 Masters champion and Eddie Hackett, Ireland's most prolific architect, to design a new course. In 1973, the "beautiful monster" course opened for play. Tom Fazio was recently commissioned to update the course.

Waterville plays on a promontory surrounded by the sea. It's a stunning, remote location with views to the northeast of the Macgillycuddy's Reeks mountain range and to the southwest across the beautiful Ballinskelligs Bay and the Atlantic Ocean. The fairways are gently undulating, the front nine plays across relatively flat ground whilst the back nine weaves its way through avenues of tall dunes. The view from the elevated 17th tee, an excellent par 3 called "Mulcahy's Peak" after the founder Jack Mulcahy, is simply breathtaking.

There are few courses that can boast such a fine collection of unique and great golf holes. Waterville has three outstanding par threes and three excellent par fives, the par fours are pretty good too. The 11th is a heavenly short par five with a rippling fairway protected on both flanks by towering dunes. The 366-yard par four 16th was once called "Round the Bend" because it follows the natural curvature of the Atlantic coastline. It was here that Liam Higgins, the local pro, had a hole-in-one on his way to setting a course record of 65. Fittingly, the hole is now called "Liam's Ace".

The remote location of the Waterville links has precluded it from hosting any big competitions, but many famous golfers find their way here and they all leave with the feeling that this is a very special place.

Payne Stewart was due to be Honorary Captain of Waterville in 2000. Tragically, in October 1999, he died when his private jet crashed in South Dakota. A bronze life-sized statue pays tribute to him and his affiliation with Waterville.

ROYAL DORNOCH GOLF CLUB
Golf Road, Dornoch, Sutherland, IV25 3LW, Scotland
Telephone: +44 (0) 1862 810219

Average Reviewers' Score:

Website: www.royaldornoch.com
Architect: Old Tom Morris and J.H. Taylor
Visitors: Contact in advance

Reviewers' Comments

There's something mystical about Royal Dornoch... I found myself stopping to take in the beauty of the view... My favourite course in Scotland... Do whatever you can to grace the fairways of Dornoch... After a gentle start the course opens out in front of you... It can't be rushed when you've waited this long... The course simply tests every aspect of your game, especially your short game... I had the good fortune to play this course on the longest day... Arrived at midnight and it seemed light enough to play... The greens were fast, firm and in superb condition... The rough was not very punishing... The bunkers were penal in many places... 4th, 5th, 6th, 9th 14th and the 17th were fantastic and really got the pulse racing... Superb linking of holes... Superb variety... I will be back to play this fabulous course again as soon as I can... Without wishing to name drop, I have played Valderrama and Pebble Beach but Dornoch leaves both firmly in its wake... Its design, atmosphere and scenery cannot be faulted... A first class pure golf experience... Just a real pleasure to play and one of my all-time favourites... Magic.

Royal Dornoch (Championship)

Royal Dornoch is spellbinding. It seems to mesmerise amateur and professional golfers from all over the world and many make the pilgrimage to this natural links at some point in their lives.

In 1630, according to the *Guinness Book of Golf Facts and Feats*, Sir Robert Gordon described the course in glowing terms. Dornoch… "doe surpass the fields of Montrose or St Andrews", he wrote. There are also written records showing that golf was played at Dornoch in 1616, long before its first nine-hole golf club was founded in 1877. This makes Dornoch the world's third oldest golf course (behind St Andrews and Leith). In 1886, Old Tom Morris "updated" the original nine holes and came back three years later to extend the course to 18 holes. J.H. Taylor later made changes to Old Tom's layout with guidance from the club's secretary, John Sutherland.

It's the timeless setting that makes Royal Dornoch such a pleasing place to play golf. It's wild, isolated and, at the same time, absolutely beautiful; there's the blaze of colour in early summer when the gorse is in flower. The pure white sandy beach divides the links from the Dornoch Firth and it all feels very humbling.

Ostensibly the course itself is pretty straightforward: it's an out-and-back layout. Many of the greens, though, are built on natural raised plateaux, making approach play especially challenging. It's the raised domed greens that became the trademark of Dornoch's most famous son, Donald Ross. Born in 1872, Ross became the club's head green-keeper and professional. He later emigrated to the States and became one of the greatest golf course architects of all time. Many of his designs, most notably Pinehurst No.2, bear the hallmark of Royal Dornoch's greens.

There are plenty of great holes to choose from at Royal Dornoch. The 4th is in the middle of a stretch of three excellent par fours. The line from the tee is the statue of the Duke of Sutherland. "Whinny Brae" is the par three 6th that signals the change from the low-lying holes to the more elevated ones. It requires an accurate tee shot across a swathe of gorse that wraps its way around the plateau green. The 14th, called "Foxy", is a long par four, measuring almost 460 yards, and it is one of the most simple and natural holes in golf featuring a classical Donald Ross domed green.

The town of Dornoch is steeped in history; there has been a human settlement in the area for over 4,000 years. The witch's stone stands in a local garden, commemorating Scotland's last "witch" burning. The stone says 1722, but Janet Horne, the alleged witch, was tried and condemned to death in 1727.

Most people know about Dornoch and many have this course on their "must-play" list. All we can say is that you shouldn't leave it too late - this course must be played sooner rather than later.

GANTON GOLF CLUB
Ganton, North Yorkshire, YO12 4PA, England
Telephone: +44 (0) 1994 710329

Average Reviewers' Score:

Website: www.gantongolfclub.com
Architect: Tom Chisholm, James Braid, Ted Ray, J.H. Taylor, Alister MacKenzie, Tom Simpson and C.K. Cotton
Visitors: Via prior arrangement – not at weekends

Reviewers' Comments

One of the friendliest and most welcoming clubs I have ever visited... They made my day when I last visited with truly personal service... Ganton is an honest course set in a delightful spot... The course itself is a complete dream; only the sea is missing from this perfect place... In a similar vein to Woodhall Spa, you need to plot your way round here and stay out of the gigantic bunkers... Stay out of the colossal bunkers and the rough and you've got a fighting chance to play to your handicap... Even if you do stay on the straight and narrow you'll need your finest putting game to score well... One of the most unusual and varied courses that I've played... It feels linksy, heathland and moorland... This is the genuine article and should be played at least once... If I lived in this neck of the woods I'd want to be a member here... Simply magnificent.

To classify Ganton as a heathland course is a misnomer – one could just as easily categorise it as an inland links, as it's situated in the rural Vale of Pickering, nine miles from the sea. This sandy, gently undulating site was once a North Sea inlet. Consequently it has all the characteristics of a links and a heathland course. Either way, it is a perfect place to play golf.

The Scarborough Golf Club (as it was originally called) opened for play in 1891, laid out by St Andrews' Tom Chisholm. The great Harry Vardon became the club's pro in 1896, the same year he won his first Open title at Muirfield. This immediately put Ganton on the map. In 1905, Ted Ray, along with James Braid and J.H. Taylor made alterations to the layout. Alister MacKenzie and C.K. Cotton made further changes over the next 50 years.

The bunkering is quite extraordinary, a real feature of the course, with over 100 cunningly placed bunkers, some of which are simply huge, both in breadth and in depth, whilst others are small. Only lucky (or very good golfers) will avoid the sand traps.

If you blend the Old course at Walton Heath with Woodhall Spa's Hotchkin course and then throw in a touch of Muirfield, you've got Ganton. Nearly 100 years ago, Bernard Darwin compared it to being "a little like Woking, a little like Worplesdon; and, generally speaking, it is the type of course that one would expect to find in Surrey rather than in Yorkshire." Occupying open, windswept heathland, it's a supreme thinking man's and woman's test of golf; the fast greens and firm fairways test the very best players. Various types of thick gorse, heather and broom highlight the course during the spring and summer months.

Three short par fours provide the opportunity of a game of risk and reward for the big hitters. There are only two par threes but the strength of the par fours more than compensates for this. The 4th hole – a 406-yard par four – requires a solid drive to a wide fairway before an undulating green sited on a raised plateau is unveiled. The approach shot must carry across a gully and avoid a canny bunker on the right-hand side of the green. From the raised tee 5th tee – a short 157-yard par three – you have a great view of the well-protected green. Only an arrow-straight tee shot will suffice. Stray to the left and you will be swallowed up by one of two bunkers, stray to the right and you'll be trapped by a huge curved bunker, which wraps itself around the entire right-hand side of the green.

Ganton is used to holding important competitions – it hosted the 1949 Ryder Cup (the USA won seven matches to five), the 2000 Curtis Cup and the 2003 Walker Cup. It's also a friendly club that opens its doors warmly to visitors. If you are a serious golfer and have never played here, we strongly recommend it.

THE EUROPEAN CLUB
Brittas Bay, County Wicklow, Ireland
Telephone: +353 (0) 404 47415

Average Reviewers' Score:

Website: www.theeuropeanclub.com
Architect: Pat Ruddy
Visitors: Book in advance

Reviewers' Comments

Simply enjoy a setting that feels as far from reality as any course I know... This course has a soul that is so often lost on today's courses... This course is up there amongst my all time favourites... Surely the European is the most friendly and welcoming club on the planet... We were met by Mr. Pat Ruddy himself, he was full of passion and enthusiasm and offered us the warmest welcome I have ever received from any golf club... The course itself is a beast... The keyword here is excitement... I love this course and you must play all 20 holes, they are all memorable in their own right... Lots of great golf holes ensuring that every single club in the bag is given an airing... The 7th is rightly the showpiece and what a golf hole. Rough grass, dunes and water all protect this stunning golf hole... Each and every time you stand on the tee it generates a thrill. Sheer delight... The course, for me, still needs time to develop... Mr. Ruddy, may I say you have made a great layout and I hope that nature allows this course to develop into a true great... In my eyes, a modern day classic.

The European Club is located in the garden of Ireland, between the coastal towns of Wicklow and Arklow, about 30 miles south of Dublin. It's Pat Ruddy's creation and he and his family have stayed there ever since. This is a unique experience, a 20-hole links set amongst rugged dunes. It opened for play in 1993 with only one thing missing – history.

Ruddy's continued involvement with the European Club will no doubt only improve matters; the course needs time to evolve and he will be there to help it on its way. We are especially pleased to see that a charming burn has replaced the out-of-place lake in front of the 18th green. It's an old adage to say that many of the holes look so natural that you'd think they'd been there forever, but it's true. Ruddy has done an equally good job here as that of Kyle Phillips at Kingsbarns.

This is an inspiring place for golf, huge dunes provide tremendous definition and the Irish Sea is very much a backcloth. It's a bit of a monster too; the 18-hole layout stretches to more than 7,000 yards, a challenging par 71. Two par threes (7a & 12a) make up the par 77 20-hole layout and they are definitely worth playing, making a refreshing break from tradition. There is no doubt that Ruddy has a sense of humour – the scorecard is full of witticisms, even the green on the par four 12th is humorous at over 125 yards long, with any three putt being an achievement.

This is an enjoyable and memorable course. Many of the holes are varied and capture one's attention and there are some great holes too. The 7th (stroke index 1) is a long 470-yard par four with a burn that runs along the entire length of the hole. Brittas Bay glistens behind the green. The 13th – four evil bunkers on the left-hand side and the Irish Sea on the right – amply protect this very long 596-yard par five. The 14th is an arresting par three, measuring 165 yards with a plateau green shielded by huge dunes.

This is an absolute must-play gem of a golf course and quite likely one of the last links courses to be built in Ireland. Golf Magazine ranked the European Club at number 98 in their World Top 100, an incredible achievement for a youngster.

ROYAL PORTHCAWL GOLF CLUB
Rest Bay, Porthcawl, Mid Glamorgan, CF36 3VW, Wales
Telephone: +44 (0) 1656 782251

Average Reviewers' Score:

Website: www.royalporthcawl.com
Architect: Charles Gibson, Harry Colt, Tom Simpson, CK Potter, Donald Steel
Visitors: Contact in advance – weekdays only

Reviewers' Comments

Royal Porthcawl is a thoroughly enjoyable experience... Tradition, tradition, tradition... It's worth playing simply for the sea views - quite stunning... Beautiful golf course - you can see the sea from every hole... This is real quality from start to finish - great setting with the waves crashing dramatically right from the start... This is a very fair course, which played relatively easily from the yellows, but from the whites it's a different proposition... I really couldn't fault the course... This course is so tough when the wind blows – a real test of golf... Holes towards the end of the round are long and tough with the 16th the hardest - long par four, tricky to get on in two and it would probably make its way on to a list of the hardest finishing holes... Unusual wooden clubhouse with a very traditional olde worlde golf club atmosphere... They could improve the service in the clubhouse, ordering bar food by telephone seems strange in the extreme... Golfing experience is simply stunning and it's a fantastic day out.

Royal Porthcawl

Royal Porthcawl is located off the beaten track, east of Swansea and west of Cardiff. Despite being the highest ranked course in Wales, it remains relatively unknown.

The club was founded in 1891 and Charles Gibson, Royal North Devon's professional, laid out a 9-hole course on Lock's Common. In 1895, an adjacent piece of land became available and Ramsey Hunter designed a proper 18-hole course. Porthcawl was granted its royal title in 1909 by King Edward VII. Over the years, the layout has been extensively modified: 1913 by Harry Colt, Tom Simpson in 1933, 1950 by C.K. Potter and finally, in 1986, by Donald Steel.

The first four holes and the last six holes represent classic links golf, but the holes in the middle rise up onto higher ground, offering fantastic views across the Bristol Channel. This middle section of the course, with plenty of gorse, has distinct heathland characteristics. Darwin completely disagrees with our sentiments. He wrote about "the very excellent links of Porthcawl. Links they may worthily be called, for the golf at Porthcawl is the genuine thing – the sea in sight all the time, and the most noble bunkers."

It's not a long track at a little over 6,600 yards from the back tees, but it's a very subtle course where position from the tee is more important than distance. Gary Wolstenholme will vouch for this. Wolstenholme played Tiger Woods in the 1995 Walker Cup and despite being constantly out-driven by Woods, Wolstenholme controlled and positioned the ball better and secured a famous victory at the last hole.

The Bristol Channel acts as a funnel for Atlantic gales and the course is fully exposed to the wind. It's not a traditional out and back layout, the holes loop back on one another, playing in various directions. With an absence of trees and dunes, the wind plays a powerful role, but whatever the wind, Royal Porthcawl is a convivial, relaxed place to play golf in beautiful surroundings.

WENTWORTH CLUB
Virginia Water, Surrey, GU25 4LS, England
Telephone: +44 (0) 1344 842201

Average Reviewers' Score:

Website: www.wentworthclub.com
Architect: Harry Colt
Visitors: Handicap certificate required - contact in advance - not at weekends

Reviewers' Comments

Nothing quite like playing a course that you can see the pros play on TV... It was great fun to play such a famous course; I didn't want the round to end... Not the cheapest green fee, but it's certainly one of the most memorable and engaging golfing experiences available around the London area... Too expensive for what you get... It's money well spent at any time of the year... From the first tee shot until the last putt drops the feeling is captivating... You'll recognise the holes as you step onto the tee... Good, but doesn't live up to its reputation... Wentworth lives up to its billing as one of the top 20 courses... A birdie on the 2nd, followed by watching Colin Montgomerie bogey the very same par three two weeks later, is quite satisfying... Keeping the ball in play is crucial... Greens are beautifully maintained but difficult to read, with cunning borrows intended to fool players of any calibre... Let down by its condition... Always in great condition... It's a tough test but manageable from the normal tees... The 17th is a very special hole... A course that makes a bad round feel very bearable.

Wentworth (West)

The West course at Wentworth is the most famous of the Surrey heath and heather courses. It is also the most televised course in Britain, hosting three professional tournaments every year (World Matchplay, PGA and the Seniors Masters). It was also the venue for the fiercely contested 1953 Ryder Cup, resulting in a single point American victory 6½ 5½.

It must have been an absolute delight for Harry Colt when he was asked to design the course, which opened for play in 1926. After all, he was already familiar with this landscape, having designed the East Course (founded two years earlier). It's a relative youngster in the scheme of things. Many of Surrey's famous sand-belt courses were established around the turn of the 19th century. Wentworth was also one of the first golf course developments to feature fairway-side houses.

Bernard Darwin refers to the West as the Tiger Course in his book, *Golf Between Two Wars*. He writes: "The course is intended to test that rampacious animal to the full".

At the start of the Second World War, the Army requisitioned the clubhouse and labyrinths of underground bunkers were built. Deep below the famous clubhouse lies a secret wartime HQ. It was the Second World War that gave rise to the other name for the course – "Burma Road". The course was allowed to grow wild because it was feared that enemy aircraft might land on the fairways. Towards the end of the war, German prisoners were brought in from a nearby internment camp to clear the course. One of the officers overseeing the clearance operation reputedly said: "Let this be their Burma Road".

There are many memorable holes and the 2nd is a charming, exacting short 155-yard par three; a huge sentry oak stands between two bunkers guarding the right-hand side of the plateau green. The tee is level with the green, but the tee shot must carry across a valley to find the putting surface. Don't be short. The 17th is a huge 571-yard par five that seemingly sweeps infinitely to the left – from the narrow tee there are tall trees on both sides, creating a tunnelling effect. Only the longest hitters should take the strategic line down the left side of the fairway, a solid 300-yard swish will make it to the corner of the dogleg. The approach shot is played blindly over a rise, aim for the large oak in the distance, but be aware that everything slopes onto the green and then everything seemingly slithers off again.

When you step onto the first tee, you will feel an overwhelming sense of familiarity. It is definitely a place where most people would be more than happy to call home and play the monthly medal here for the rest of their lives. The holes weave their way through sprinklings of heather and across gently undulating terrain. Mature oaks, pines and silver birch trees line each and every fairway. This is a truly classy golf course and a tough one too; at more than 7,000 yards from the back tees, it is a serious challenge.

WALTON HEATH GOLF CLUB
Deans Lane, Walton on the Hill, Surrey, KT20 7TP
England
Telephone: +44 (0) 1737 812380

Website: www.whgc.co.uk
Architect: Herbert Fowler
Visitors: Contact in advance - weekends limited

Average Reviewers' Score:

Reviewers' Comments

Quite stunning when the heather is in flower - fairways framed in purple… Should come with a government health warning for the high handicapper, largely for one reason, the heather… If you end up in the heather there's no way back but to hit a wedge to the fairway… It's certainly tough but play a good shot and it will reward you… A hard but fair course, greens are tough to read… A well designed and well maintained heathland golf course… The condition of the course was excellent… Despite its apparent openness, the holes are varied in design, yet there are three or four that have a similarity about them… The 16th is a lovely hole and very different to the rest, with a challenging second shot with disaster beckoning to the right of an elevated green… The lunch is superb… The clubhouse and staff very welcoming… A nice straight par three opening hole gives time for the extra portion of jam roly-poly… This is one of the best heathland courses… A must-play course and, combined with the New, provides a day to remember.

Walton Heath (Old) 25th

Herbert Fowler designed both courses at Walton Heath (Old & New). Fowler was related by marriage to the founder, Sir Henry Cosmo Bonsor. "It was a stroke of genius on the part of Mr Herbert Fowler to see with his prophetic eye a noble golf course on the expanse of Walton Heath", wrote Bernard Darwin. "It was in August 1902, that Mr Fowler had begun his survey. In April 1904, James Braid moved to Walton from Romford and in May the course was opened with a due flourish of trumpets," wrote Darwin in the Biography of James Braid. James Braid remained the club professional until 1950.

Surprisingly, Walton Heath was not given the royal charter, despite the fact that the Duke of Windsor was club captain in 1935. During his year as captain, he became King Edward VIII. It's the only club in history to have a reigning monarch as its captain. His term as captain probably lasted longer than his reign on the throne. King George VI was also an honorary member and Winston Churchill also played the Old course.

This is where links golf meets inland golf. There is no salty whiff of sea air, but the course plays and feels like a seaside links. A profusion of heather stripes the edge of the fairways. In the summer, when the heather is in flower, it is an absolute delight to look at, but a real challenge out of which to play. The greens are true and fast and the undulations make it tough to read the lines and the pace of putts.

Some of the carries across the heather are quite lengthy and if you don't hit the fairways, you can often wave goodbye to your ball. This is a course that favours the lower handicap golfer. There are some really strong holes – one of the best of the outward nine is the 5th, a cracking 391-yard par four that demands a solid drive that must avoid the thick, tangly heather shrouding the fairway. A mid-iron approach shot will find the green, amply guarded by bunkers left and right.

The last three holes are especially challenging, especially the 16th, a 510-yard par five, well described by Bernard Darwin in his book *The Golf Courses of the British Isles*. In 1910, it was the 17th hole and it was played as a par four. "The second shot is the thing – a full shot right home on to a flat green that crowns the top of a sloping bank. To the right the face of the hill is excavated in a deep and terrible bunker, and a ball ever so slightly sliced will run into that bunker as sure as fate".

Walton Heath has hosted many important competitions, including the 1981 Ryder Cup. Europe was thrashed 9½ -18½ by America, thanks to the likes of Watson and Nicklaus. For serious golfers, this is a fantastic venue for a golf day. Lunch in the clubhouse is simply stunning but probably worth passing on the dessert if you want to swing properly in the afternoon!

ROYAL ST DAVID'S GOLF CLUB
Harlech, Gwynedd, LL46 2UB, Wales
Telephone: +44 (0) 1766 780361

Average Reviewers' Score:

Website: www.royalstdavids.co.uk
Architect: Harold Finch-Hatton, William Henry Moore
Visitors: Current handicap required – book in advance

Reviewers' Comments

Royal St David's is the top course in this area, no question... A daunting proposition from the moment you turn up... It's a fantastic experience... The imposing Harlech Castle watches every shot, giving an eerie indication of the challenge ahead... It's a ridiculously difficult par 69 layout – more like par 73... Standard scratch is well above par... It's long and hard but oh so good... Often referred to as the toughest par 69 in the world... Two very different nines... Some breathtaking golf holes... The front nine allows you to get a score going... The back nine is possibly the toughest nine holes anywhere outside of the Open rota... 15th and 16th are truly magnificent holes, especially when the wind is up... The back nine bobs and weaves its way through sand dunes and hillocks... If the closing hole could be improved, it would have one of the finest back nines in all golf... North Wales has such a strong golfing heritage and tied in with Aberdovey, Nefyn and Conwy you are sure of a real treat... They run a junior Open every Easter and only charge £2 – what an opportunity for youngsters... Members still love to tell the tales... Harlech is a genuine must-play course.

Royal St David's

The glorious setting for the Royal St David's links at Harlech is nothing short of beautiful and romantic. The forbidding medieval Harlech castle and towering sand dunes guard the course. Behind the dunes, to the northwest, is the sweeping bay of Tremadog and to the north are views across to Snowdon and the lesser peaks of Snowdonia. "Small wonder if the visitor falls in love with Harlech at first sight," wrote Bernard Darwin in, *The Golf Courses of the British Isles*, "for no golf course in the world has a more splendid background than the old castle, which stands at the top of a sheer precipice of rock looking down over the links."

According to folklore, Harold Finch-Hatton reputedly identified the links upon his return from Australia, originally using the area for boomerang practice. Finch-Hatton teamed up with William Henry Moore and in 1894, St David's was born. It seemed poignant that Wales should have a golf club called St David's; after all, Scotland has St Andrew's and England has St George's. Edward VII granted the club royal patronage in 1908.

Locals regard Royal St David's as the world's toughest par 69. Who would argue with them? The course measures 6,500 yards from the back tees. It's not your usual out-and-back links – the holes zigzag in all directions, subjecting each shot to the vagaries of the prevailing westerly wind.

The opening dozen holes are fully exposed to the elements. They play back and forth across fairly flat and, at times, open ground. When the 13th hole is reached, the landscape changes dramatically and at last we enter rippling undulating dune land. The bunker-free par four 15th requires a long carry across dunes from an elevated tee to a narrow fairway – Mount Snowdon is in the distance. A decent drive leaves a partially blind approach shot to a raised green nestling between sand dunes. You might catch a quick glimpse of the Irish Sea from the 16th tee before turning back inland towards the clubhouse. Unusually, Royal St David's closes out with a tough 200-yard par three with the green directly in front of the clubhouse.

Royal St David's has hosted many major amateur championships over the years. There are a number of famous names on the roll of honour, including Cecil Leitch. In 1926, she beat Mrs Garon 8&7 to win the Ladies' British Amateur Championship. More recently, in 1994, Sweden's Freddie Jacobson won the British Youths' Open Amateur Championship here at Harlech.

NAIRN GOLF CLUB
Seabank Road, Nairn, IV12 4HB, Scotland
Telephone: +44 (0) 1667 453208

Average Reviewers' Score:

Website: www.nairngolfclub.co.uk
Architect: Archie Simpson, Old Tom Morris, James Braid and Ben Sayers
Visitors: Contact in advance – Not Sat/Sun am

Reviewers' Comments

There must have been some mistake – move it up the rankings immediately... My favourite links course anywhere... Best greens I have ever played on in my life... During the Kings Trophy (Nairn's Open competition) the tees are true enough to putt on, never mind the greens... The best-conditioned links imaginable, so if there's a criticism for the ultra-traditionalist it's that it's too manicured... Holes 1 to 7 are outstanding in their design and the views out to sea are classic links... Stunning views from every hole, and, just for good measure, the 13th and 14th look as if they should be at Sunningdale... Great par threes of differing distance and direction, short and long par fours and the same with the par fives... If the wind is blowing then the course changes character in a matter of minutes... Enjoyed the feeling of being so close to the sea... Generally manageable from the yellows, so it's a course the average player can enjoy as much as a low man... If in the area it's a must-play... I'd challenge anyone to find a true links course in better condition with this quality of holes... I'm contemplating retiring here so I can play it everyday – only 30 years to go.

Nairn

Nairn Golf Club is located on an elevated, rumpled piece of linksland on the Moray Firth coastline, close to the historic fishing port. It's one of Scotland's lesser-known gems.

This is a course that has been touched by many great architects. The club was founded in 1887 and Archie Simpson originally designed the course. A few years later Old Tom Morris extended the layout and, prior to the Great War, James Braid made further alterations. Directly after the Great War, Ben Sayers added his mark to the course only to find James Braid itching to polish off the design. It is no wonder that Nairn is such a detailed masterpiece.

One of the most spectacular seaside courses in Scotland, Nairn boasts sea views from every hole. If you are a right-hander and you've got a slicing problem, you could find the beach from your very first tee shot. The sea is in play on six of the first seven holes; make sure you've got an adequate supply of balls.

When the sun is low in the sky and the shadows are long, you cannot fail to appreciate the undulating, bunker-pitted moonscape that is Nairn. It's a delightful links with fast, firm but narrow fairways, a number of which are framed by gorse bushes and heather, heaping further pressure onto a nervous drive. The greens are sited in the trickiest places – some are raised and others are nestled in hollows. Most are well protected, either by bunkers or natural hazards, and all of the greens are fast and true, a Nairn trademark.

There is a plethora of good holes at Nairn. One of the best is the 5th, a great 390-yard par four called "Nets", requiring a straight solid drive which must avoid the beach on the right to leave a short approach shot to a small elevated green that is well protected by bunkers and a sharp bank sloping off to the right.

Nairn is a very long way north. However, you may be surprised to hear that despite Nairn's Highland latitude, it is located in one of the driest places in Britain. So, why not follow in the footsteps of Peter McEvoy? In 1999, here at Nairn, he led the Great Britain and Ireland Walker Cup team to a resounding 15-9 victory over the USA.

GLENEAGLES
Auchterarder, Perthshire, PH3 1NF, Scotland
Telephone: +44 (0) 1764 662231

Average Reviewers' Score:

Website: www.gleneagles.com
Architect: James Braid, Major C.K. Hutchinson and Donald Matheson
Visitors: Book at least 8 weeks in advance

Reviewers' Comments

Surely there is no finer place on earth to play golf than at Gleneagles... The setting of the hills and mountains and the quality of golf holes makes you wish your round would never end... Remember the old Pro Celebrity golf series on the BBC in the 70s... Always billed as one of the true great golfing resorts in the world and I was not disappointed... I cannot help thinking the King's course overall did not live up to what I expected it to be... Overrated and too expensive – Downfield and Blairgowrie are as good at less than half the price... Worth every penny of the green fee... Someone once said that this is 'the perfect setting for the best game in the world' – I can only agree... Preferred the Queen's... Try it for yourself and you can compare... The variety is never ending and all holes are so different... Loved the 6th, 13th and the 18th ... The halfway house is worth a stop off to gird your loins for what is a cracking finishing series of holes... A perfect venue and a perfect course in every way... Go to Gleneagles at least once.

Gleneagles (King's)

The King's course at Gleneagles is surely the finest course never to have been ranked in a world Top 100.

In 1908, the Gleneagles idea came to Donald Matheson, general manager of the Caledonian Railway Company. He had a dream to build a "Palace in the Glens" which would attract noble and wealthy railway travellers. James Braid (the five times Open Champion) was commissioned to design the King's course, assisted by Major C.K. Hutchinson and Matheson himself. In 1919, the championship King's course opened for play.

This is the perfect mountain setting for a game of golf; the King's course is surely the best moorland track in the world. The sweeping views of the Ochil Hills and the peaks of Ben Vorlich and the Trossachs are simply ravishing.

Braid was given the most perfect terrain upon which to build a golf course and he built a very special golf course. The holes blend perfectly into the landscape. The springy fairways wind their way through punishing rough, strewn with heather and gorse. Many mature pines, silver birch and rowan provide natural amphitheatres on a number of the holes.

You cannot help but be enchanted by this golf course, even the named holes are evocative: Silver Tassie, Blink Bonnie and Wee Bogle. But it's the views that will probably interrupt your concentration on the game. In *Golf Between Two Wars*, Bernard Darwin wrote: "The beauty of the place is beyond all question; the exact merits of the course perhaps more difficult to decide". Darwin went on to say that the ground was once slow; this made the course very long, even for the likes of J.H. Taylor and Sandy Herd. Then the ground hardened under the feet of thousands, and the ball ran further and further and, consequently, the scoring became lower.

The book, *Classic Golf Holes*, features the 18th hole: "From the tee boxes beside the little hut just beyond the 17th green, the drive should ideally clear the crest of the ridge over a line between the twin bunkers. It will then catch a downslope which will speed the ball on towards its ultimate destination. Thereafter, again ideally, the player will repair for the night to the splendour of the hotel."

A number of important events have been played over the King's course, including the Curtis Cup, Dunhill Trophy, Scottish Open and the WPGA Championship of Europe. Lee Trevino, standing on the 1st tee of the King's course, remarked: "If heaven is as good as this, I sure hope they have some tee times left".

SWINLEY FOREST GOLF CLUB
Coronation Road, Ascot, Berkshire, SL9 5LE, England
Telephone: +44 (0) 1344 874979

Average Reviewers' Score:

Website: None
Architect: Harry Colt
Visitors: By invitation only

Reviewers' Comments

Amazing little course if you can get on... Fantastic – this is a great golf course with a capital G... Excellent course... It simply smells of old money - just like stepping back in time... Course is pretty but just a little rough and ready around the edges... Usual quality of Surrey/Berkshire heathland is evident all around Swinley Forest and I loved my round here... All of the par threes are a picture and not easy... Three really strong par fours on the front nine (6th, 7th and 9th) – All at 400+ yards from the back tees... Tricky to read greens also go someway to protect the course par... The whole course is very pleasing to the eye... The 18th hole has a silly little bunker placed right in the middle of the fairway, so if you hit a decent drive it still goes in the sand. Otherwise, it is top-notch... There is meant to be a scrumptious lunch too - but sadly, as a non-member, I had to eat my corned-beef sandwiches in the changing room... To play, you do need an invitation – go out of your way to get one – it's worth it.

Swinley Forest

Swinley Forest is an absolutely charming golf course, situated on the famous Surrey/Berkshire sand belt, but it's a club that is frozen in time, exclusive, unusual and totally eccentric. In fact, you would be hard pressed to describe it as a conventional golf club: there is no captain and despite being in existence for nearly 100 years, no history, except in its members' heads. Only recently have scorecards been printed, holes allocated par figures, and competitions introduced for Swinley's distinguished gentlemen members.

Harry Colt designed the layout and the course opened for play in 1909, reputedly Colt's favourite and finest design. One of the many delights of Swinley is the ambience and the fact that it's unpretentious. It has none of the glamour of its near neighbours, Sunningdale and Wentworth, but what Swinley Forest does have is bags of style.

If you are lucky enough to get a game here, you will undoubtedly have the course to yourself. It's possible that Major So-and-so and his dog will be out there on the 15th and Lord Such-and-such will be having a beer in the clubhouse. Perhaps Peter Alliss will be there too. You will certainly find out who is around and about because the steward will tell you when he accepts your green fee. It's likely that you will be able to count other golfers playing the course on one hand.

We will make no bones about it – Swinley is a beautiful course. The short, one-shot holes are simply outstanding. The site/position of the greens sets Swinley apart from many other courses. Although the yardage is only a little over 6,000 yards, the par of 68 makes it a real challenge.

If you are lucky enough to play Swinley in late spring, look out for the rhododendrons (you can't miss them). They are simply breathtaking. Combine this with swathes of purple heather and lovely springy fairways winding their way through mature pines and this really is a special place. Drop a letter in the post to the secretary by way of introduction, or maybe telephone him. Who knows, he might let you play this amazing private members' course.

SAUNTON GOLF CLUB
Braunton, North Devon, EX33 1LG, England
Telephone: +44 (0) 1271 812436

Average Reviewers' Score:

Website: www.sauntongolf.co.uk
Architect: Herbert Fowler
Visitors: Book in advance – handicap certificate required

Reviewers' Comments

Saunton is amazing and it has everything going for it... A course of massive dunes hiding beautifully kept greens... Two fantastic courses, excellent clubhouse (views to die for), good food and friendly service. Perfection... Followed a seniors foursomes competition around the course as a two ball and we couldn't keep up... The East is a truly amazing links course – don't expect to play to handicap here first time round, it's tough... Raw, traditional, fascinating links with amazing dunes... Just loved the first tee shot – formidable... The 18th is particularly memorable and the first tee shot quite an intimidating start from its high tee... There are no weak holes, just true, honest, undiluted links golf... My kind of course... Must be one of the best links courses on the planet.

Saunton (East)

If there is a need for another seaside Open Championship venue, then surely the East course at Saunton is a worthy candidate. Saunton has never held an Open but it has hosted a number of other important events. Sergio Garcia won the British Boys' Championship here in 1997, beating R. Jones 6 and 5.

Saunton is located on the beautiful unspoilt North Devon coast. On the edge of Bideford Bay and the estuary of the River Taw, lie the Braunton Burrows. Unesco has designated the sand dunes at Braunton Burrows of international importance and it is the first site in the UK to become a biosphere reserve. The area is unique because there are more than 500 species of flora; many, including the water Germander, are extremely rare. This area will now rank alongside Mount Vesuvius and the Danube Delta.

The East course, laid out in 1897, runs through a small part of this amazing expanse of sand dunes. Herbert Fowler added a bit of redesign magic in 1919 and very little has since changed. Fowler took full advantage of the natural terrain, routing the holes through the dunes with skill. This is the man who was responsible for the masterpiece at Walton Heath and Saunton is his finest seaside creation.

Bernard Darwin was in love with the ancient links situated just across the Taw estuary at Westward Ho! He frequently made the "reverent pilgrimage" to Royal North Devon. Darwin had probably never played the East course at the time of writing: "Saunton looks at first glance like a fine golf course". Harry Vardon loved it. He said he "would like to retire to Saunton and do nothing but play golf for pleasure".

It's a tough golf course. The East has eight par fours over 400 yards long and only two par fives. Scoring well is very difficult, even more so now that the 2nd hole, once a short par five, has been lengthened to almost 530 yards. There are two excellent short par threes, which demand accuracy, and there's the tough 207-yard 17th hole, which often needs a decent crack with a wood.

One of the many delights of Saunton is that each fairway tunnels its way through the dunes, providing the feeling that you have each hole to yourself. Saunton has 36 of the finest seaside links holes, making an excellent venue for a golf day. Whilst the East course is the best, the West is very good too. You will need to go to St Andrews or Ballybunion to find such an outstanding collection of links holes.

HILLSIDE GOLF CLUB
Hastings Road, Hillside, Southport, Merseyside,
PR8 2LU, England
Telephone: +44 (0) 1704 567169

Average Reviewers' Score:

Website: www.ukgolfer.org/clubs/hillside
Architect: Fred Hawtree, Donald Steel
Visitors: Contact in advance – not weekends

Reviewers' Comments

Hillside is a cracker… No doubt about it, it's a BIG course… Doesn't suffer in comparison with its illustrious neighbour, Royal Birkdale… Hard to find a favourite amongst the home of golf in England, they're all such fine courses… Very effective use of the natural dunes and rolling landscapes – it provides an excellent test of golf for all… Greg Norman describes this course as having the best back nine in Britain. I'm inclined to agree… Shame to have to compare the front nine with the back, but the back is so good that it's inevitable… It's not all about the back nine - the front nine is varied and tough too, but there's no doubt, the back nine is special… I doubt whether there are three better courses next door to each other anywhere in the world. Royal Birkdale, Hillside and S&A… Amazing and thoroughly challenging experience… Par five 11th is stunning and now becomes one of my top 10 holes played… After playing the short 10th, there is a series of doglegs, right and left, elevated tees and greens amongst huge dunes… Loads of classic history in and around the clubhouse too… Do not miss a chance to play Hillside.

Hillside

There are eight superb seaside courses between St Annes and Liverpool and many people believe that this is the best stretch of linksland in the British Isles. It is certainly England's links golfing Mecca and Hillside is the best of the non-royal commoners.

Hillside is an underrated gem, separated only by a footpath, but hiding in the shadow of its noble next-door neighbour, Royal Birkdale. The railway line separates Hillside from Southport and Ainsdale, another superb but relatively unknown links.

Today's layout is very different to the original Hillside, founded in 1911. The club acquired some new land in the 1960s and Fred Hawtree extensively remodelled the course, making major changes to the back nine. The front nine has always been highly regarded and plays over relatively flat ground, but it's the homeward nine that is really special and frequently bracketed alongside Ballybunion because the holes ripple and undulate through the giant dunes.

There are many strong and individual holes but the 11th has everything going for it. A reachable par five of just over 500 yards doglegs left, the elevated tee provides a panoramic view of the hole in play and many other holes too, not only at Hillside but also at Royal Birkdale and Southport & Ainsdale. A well-struck drive to the dune-flanked fairway will tempt the big hitters to go for the raised green in two, but watch out for that cavernous bunker lurking on the right.

Although Birkdale is a regular Open host, Hillside has staged numerous major events, both amateur and professional. In the 1982 PGA Championship, Tony Jacklin tied with Bernhard Langer. Jacklin went on to win at the first playoff hole; this was to be his last professional title and Hillside's most recent major event.

COUNTY LOUTH GOLF CLUB
Baltray, Drogheda, County Louth, Ireland
Telephone: +353 (0) 41 988 1530

Average Reviewers' Score:

Website: www.countylouthgolfclub.com
Architect: Tom Simpson
Visitors: Contact in advance

Reviewers' Comments

Not many people know about Louth, presumably because the golfing masses head for Kerry. If only they knew what they were missing... Baltray is one of the true hidden gems in golf... Remote location only adds to the charm... A classic links, which will test the best golfers... There are no tricks here and few really memorable holes but there is not one single weak hole... A number of elevated tee shots and greens that are tucked away here and there... If you can avoid the bunkers and find the rolling putting surfaces and then read the greens well, you may be in for a good score... Baltray is reputed to have the best greens in Ireland and I've played here three times and I can't disagree... The only criticism is that it can be tough to get on this course due to all the competitions... Make sure you book in advance... A course to savour and enjoy... The welcome here, as you would expect in Ireland, is warm and friendly... Onsite hotel is also good value and the food is magnificent... Play here at all costs... County Louth is as good as any course in Ireland.

There is generally a certain level of anticipation when one plays a course for the first time. The approach road to the links of County Louth, or Baltray as it is better known, named after the local fishing village, is especially uplifting. This is a course that has remained relatively anonymous, except to those in the know. It is one of Ireland's secrets.

County Louth Golf Club was established in 1892. Tom Simpson designed the present course in 1938.

Darren Clarke won the East of Ireland Championship in 1989, an amateur stroke play event held at County Louth since 1941, although it is unlikely that anybody will beat Joe Carr's record. Joe Carr was the "East" champion 12 times between 1941 and 1969. Amazingly, Joe's son Roddy won the 1970 "East" championship.

Baltray has no weak holes. The course is laid out in two loops, and most holes run in different directions. However, the greens are County Louth's hallmark – they are amongst the very best in the whole of Ireland. If you can avoid three putting for 18 holes, then you have the right to claim you're a great putter.

County Louth developed two of Ireland's best lady golfers. In 1938, Clarrie Tiernan was the first Irish woman to play in the Curtis Cup. Unfortunately, the USA beat Great Britain and Ireland 5½ 3½ at the Essex County Club in Massachusetts. It was Clarrie's rival, Philomena Garvey, who was the most successful post war Irish player. Phil was five times a finalist in the Ladies' British Amateur Championship, winning once, in 1957, at Gleneagles. Phil also won a record 15 Irish Close titles in a span of 18 years from 1946.

Although County Louth is a championship links golf course, golfers of all levels can enjoy it. The back nine is especially entertaining, with a number of holes running close to the shore with distant views towards the Mountains of Mourne. It was here in 2004 that Australian Brett Rumford won the Irish Open.

SUNNINGDALE GOLF CLUB
Ridgemount Road, Sunningdale, Berkshire, SL5 9RR
England
Telephone: +44 (0) 1344 621681

Average Reviewers' Score:

Website: www.sunningdale-golfclub.co.uk
Architect: Harry Colt
Visitors: Contact in advance - Not Fri, Sat, Sun or public holidays

Reviewers' Comments

Sunningdale really has style and it doesn't really matter whether you play the Old or the New, they are both first class courses... In many ways I prefer the New to the Old. It's more challenging and plays on higher ground. Not only that, it's cheaper too... For me, the New is a far more challenging test and from a value perspective it's certainly cheaper to play here but it's definitely not pay and play golf... The New is now a tremendous test of golf... It's a real driver's course... I played both courses and I certainly prefer the New, it's a more strategic course... Either way, both Old and New are both superb, but for me, the New just has the edge... This is certainly a traditional club but somehow it doesn't have quite the same pretentiousness as some of the other clubs on the Surrey/Berks heath belt.

Sunningdale (New)

Taken together, the New and Old courses at Sunningdale represent the finest 36 holes of golf in the whole of the British Isles. The same architect who made modifications to Sunningdale's Old course, Harry Colt, designed the New, which opened for play in 1923 to meet the ever-increasing demand for golf.

This is a superb driving course for it is more open than the Old; the trees do not encroach quite so much. Having said this, the New demands long carries from its elevated tees over heathery terrain to narrow fairways. The club has been following a programme of regeneration that has involved the felling of a number of trees, thereby allowing the heather to return. In addition, this has cleared the way for long lost views to reappear across to Chobham Common in the south.

Many people will come to Sunningdale hell bent on playing the Old course, but if it's a real athletic challenge you are after, you will get severely tested on the rugged 6,700-yard par 70 New, a tougher, more rounded test of golf than the Old. So far, nobody yet has managed to better Jack Nicklaus's course record of 67, which is a testament to the technical test that the course throws up.

There are many excellent and memorable holes, perhaps not as many as there are on the Old but certainly the 5th is worthy of mention, a charming par three. The views across the treetops to the common beyond are superb.

Sunningdale is located on Surrey and Berkshire's famous, magical sand-belt, home to so many other fine golf courses. There is no better natural inland golfing terrain anywhere in the world and Sunningdale is blessed with two of the world's very best heathland courses.

FORMBY GOLF CLUB
Golf Road, Formby, Merseyside, L37 1LQ, England
Telephone: +44 (0) 1704 872164

Average Reviewers' Score:

Website: www.formbygolfclub.co.uk
Architect: Willie Park, James Braid, Hawtree and Taylor, Donald Steel
Visitors: Contact in advance

Reviewers' Comments

No sea views to drink here at Formby, but the pines make up for it… An attractive links course… A links course of high quality - as you walk around you can be transformed from classic links, to holes that would not be out of place at Woburn… Fairly short in length but with numerous good and varied holes… Holes 7, 8 and 9 are a great test and there is a big chance to ruin a good front nine card… It's a tough monster - you really need to be on your game… The middle of the back nine does become a little 'samey' but this is meant in the kindest way possible as the quality is always there… Formby recently staged the 2004 Curtis Cup… Great photos in the clubhouse including the 1984 amateur championship - José Maria and Monty looking very fresh… Watch out for the hippo… Very friendly clubhouse and members… Worthy inclusion in the British Isles Top 50… It's a must-play course if in the area.

Formby **34ᵗʰ**

Formby is the prettiest of the eight top-notch links courses located between the seaside town of St Annes and the city of Liverpool. It is bordered on three sides by pine trees, giving the links a decidedly softer, heathland feel than the others.

Founded in 1884, originally as a nine-hole course designed by Willie Park, it was extended to 18 holes by the turn of the century. James Braid remodelled the layout in the 1920s and Hawtree and Taylor added their changes in the 1930s. More recently, Donald Steel lengthened the course to almost 7,000 yards.

It's a unique course in so much as the holes are routed in a huge anti-clockwise circle around the Formby Ladies' Club which sits slap bang in the middle of the men's course. The first three holes follow the railway line, the 4th turns and heads out towards the Irish Sea and at the turn, we meander back home, zigzagging up and down along the way.

Play Formby when you have been sufficiently beaten up by the other windy links courses around Liverpool and Southport, but don't be fooled into thinking that this course is easy. It certainly is not. Bunkering is strategic, the undulating fairways are very much links-like, the rough is strewn with heather and the pines provide an element of park-like protection from the wind. This course will suit both links lovers and the player who prefers the softness of inland golf; both these camps will arrive contentedly at the 19th watering hole.

The club has hosted a number of important amateur events over the years and played host to the 2004 Curtis Cup. After an exciting finish, the United States successfully retained the trophy, winning 10-8. The Amateur Championship was played here on three occasions; José Maria Olazabal emerged as the 1984 winner.

In Bernard Darwin's book, *The Golf Courses of the British Isles*, he wrote: "The greens are beautifully green; they are likewise very true and keen enough, without ever being bare and hard. The lies, too, are excellent, and it is altogether one of those courses where the player's fate is entirely in his own hands. If he plays well everything will conspire to help him on his way, but he has got to play really well — good, sterling, honest golf: there is no mistake about that at Formby."

This is a relatively unknown course, primarily because many golfers head in droves towards the three big Royals in this area (Liverpool, Birkdale and Lytham St Annes). If you are planning a trip to the northwest and haven't already played here, we thoroughly recommend that you do. You will get a warm welcome and a unique and exciting experience.

Julie

PRESTWICK GOLF CLUB
2 Links Road, Prestwick, Ayrshire, KA9 1QG, Scotland
Telephone: +44 (0) 1292 671020

Average Reviewers' Score:

Website: www.prestwickgc.co.uk
Architect: Old Tom Morris
Visitors: Contact in advance – not Thu or weekends

Reviewers' Comments

If you like your golf old fashioned (like the Machrie) then this is the place for you… In my top three courses anywhere… Palpable history with idiosyncratic holes and awesome greens… As for the course – magnificent… Blind drives and approach shots over massive dunes… Generally small and wildly undulating greens make this a course not suited to the faint-hearted… Too old fashioned to ever be considered an Open venue again, it is a place to pay homage to the venue for those original Opens… Enjoy playing on the same holes of Open champions from over a hundred years ago… Course set up for matchplay with greens second to none… Did I forget to mention the bunkers? Many feet taller or deeper than your height, these massive sleepered craters are a sight to behold and a hazard to be avoided… I'm surprised the committee haven't stipulated the compulsory wearing of Plus-Fours… Clubhouse full of golfing artefacts and catering would put Gordon Ramsay to shame… Every golf nut should play this course at least once, as there is no other club like it.

Prestwick

In 1851, a 12-hole course was founded at Prestwick with Old Tom Morris as "Keeper of the Green". Nine years later, in 1860, the British Open Championship was born and didn't move away until it went to St Andrews in 1873. The Open has been hosted here no fewer than 24 times, although the most recent championship was held in 1925. St Andrews is the only venue to have hosted more Opens than Prestwick and obviously the Old Course is still on the Open circuit.

The first eleven Opens were contested for a red Moroccan belt, which was won outright by Young Tom Morris after he successfully won three consecutive titles between 1868 and 1870. There was no Open Championship in 1871 because there was no trophy to play for until the Claret Jug was purchased for £30 and offered for annual competition in 1872. Ironically, Young Tom Morris was the first winner of the Claret Jug. Six more holes were added to the original 12-hole layout in 1883.

The course is a traditional monument, an authentic affair with a layout of holes that snake to and fro through rugged dunes and rippled fairways. There are numerous blind holes and cavernous sleepered bunkers with wooden steps to take you down to the bottom. The greens are notoriously firm and fast – some are hidden in hollows whilst others are perched on raised plateaux. The majority are quite small and all of them have wicked borrows to negotiate.

A great strength of the course is the quality and variety of the holes. The 1st is one of the most intimidating holes in golf, a par four called "Railway". The railway tracks run all the way down the right-hand side of the hole, waiting to gobble up a right-hander's slice. The 3rd is a short par five (stroke index 1) called "Cardinal" and is famous for its deep, deep bunker, propped up by railway sleepers. The 5th is a blind par three called "Himalayas" – your tee shot must carry over a huge sand dune.

There are so many great things to say about Prestwick. The best thing to do is to play the course and judge it for yourself. Any serious golfer must tick this one off the list.

Bernard Darwin can bring things to a close much better than we can. In his book, *The Golf Courses of the British Isles*, he wrote: "So ends Prestwick, and what a jolly course it is, to be sure!"

WESTERN GAILES GOLF CLUB
Gailes, Irvine, Ayrshire, KA11 5AE, Scotland
Telephone: +44 (0) 1294 311649

Average Reviewers' Score:

Website: www.westerngailes.com
Architect: Willie Park, Fred Hawtree
Visitors: Welcome Mon, Wed & Fri – contact in advance

Reviewers' Comments

Extremely attractive, high quality links course with many varied and interesting holes... You need to know how to handle a links course to play well here... My son and I played ten of the great courses in Scotland including Turnberry, Troon, Prestwick, St. Andrews, and North Berwick. Out of all the courses we played, Western Gailes was our favourite... I was fortunate enough to play Prestwick, Turnberry (Ailsa) and Western Gailes. Out of the three I liked Western the best... A demanding course with tricky subtle greens that are well protected... A couple of excellent little par threes provides great entertainment... The run from the 6th is especially good... A true links course and one of the best on the Ayrshire coast... I thought it was fabulous... Clubhouse is an imposing but welcoming building and the staff and members are really friendly... A very hospitable members' club, well worth experiencing... We played 36 holes and would have played more if we had the time... Western will appeal to the connoisseurs because it has everything going for it, but always in an understated way.

Western Gailes

The Western Gailes golf course is wedged between Irvin Bay and the railway tracks on one of Ayrshire's narrowest strips of links land. Western and its next-door neighbour, Glasgow Gailes, are the northernmost of the exceptional links courses located on this prodigious stretch of Ayrshire coastline.

Four Glaswegians who were fed up with playing on muddy parkland founded the club in 1897. They recruited the Willie Park father and son team to design Western Gailes and the layout remained virtually untouched until Fred Hawtree revised a number of holes in the mid-1970s.

Western is an unusual layout in that the clubhouse is more or less centrally located. The first four holes head north, parallel to the railway tracks. The next nine holes head straight back along the coastline in a southerly direction, passing the clubhouse along the way, and then the closing five holes head northwards, back towards the clubhouse and once more along the railway line.

Whilst the layout, as we have already mentioned, is an unusual but ostensible nine out and nine back, the holes are wonderfully varied. The fairways undulate gently, interrupted occasionally by three meandering burns that dissect this thin strip of land. The green sites are cleverly located in naturally folded ground – burns protect some – whilst others, like the 6th, are in hollows guarded by sand dunes. All the greens are fast, firm and subtly contoured. The 14th hole, a wonderful par five which often plays downwind, provides a huge temptation for big hitters, but numerous bunkers lie in wait.

Be prepared for a westerly wind that can be undeniably ferocious and cunning as it switches direction from south-westerly to north-westerly. On occasions it can be soul-destroying. Western Gailes is a suitably fitting name for this golf course.

Western is a very stiff golfing test – expect to use every club in the bag. The layout measures 6,714 yards from the back tees and Western has hosted a number of important events, including the 1972 Curtis Cup, narrowly won by the USA, and the 1964 PGA Championship, won by AG Grubb. Additionally, the course is used for final qualifying when the Open is played at Troon or Turnberry.

OLD HEAD GOLF LINKS
Old Head of Kinsale, Kinsale, Cork, Ireland
Telephone: +353 (0) 121 477844

Average Reviewers' Score:

Website: www.oldheadgolflinks.com
Architect: Joe Carr, Paddy Merrigan, Ron Kirby, Eddie Hackett, Liam Higgins & Haulie O'Shea
Visitors: Closed Nov- Mar – book in advance

Reviewers' Comments

This absolute stunner is still my number one... The most spectacularly beautiful course I have ever played... Visual golfing feast, bar none... Stunning throughout with views across the rugged coastline of West Cork... Test of golf is relatively straightforward if there is no wind... Mixed bag of amazing holes, lovely holes and a few weaker holes but all in all a great course... Design is a bit random and doesn't flow well, but it has the wow factor... There are *twelve* holes where the sea comes into play and at the end of the round you will not find a better sea view from any clubhouse... Nature intended some areas of land to be left as they are... A number of holes require tee-shots or approaches over 200 feet drops... Don't be fooled by the straightforward 1st hole as then it's off to the cliff edge for the 2nd and 3rd... Best hole on the course is the 12th – the most intimidating tee shot in golf... Ridiculously expensive but worth remortgaging for just one round... Book direct with the club to get the lowest rates... Value for money 10/10... Each turn presents something special for all golfers... Play it to believe it.

A number of people were involved in the creation of Old Head: Dr Joe Carr, Paddy Merrigan, Ron Kirby, the late Eddie Hackett, Liam Higgins and Haulie O'Shea. The course opened for play in 1997.

Laid out on a narrow headland, jutting out for two miles into the Atlantic Ocean, this has to be one of the most exhilarating sites in the world on which golf is played. You feel as though you are on the edge of the world and if you suffer from vertigo, some of the tees might present a problem. Three hundred feet up, looking over the edge of the cliff, you will notice seagulls gliding below you. Atlantic waves crash onto the rocks, booming and echoing as they smash into the cave tunnels. It certainly takes your breath away.

Take some extra golf balls; you may well lose a few unless you are really on top of your game. There is little margin for error along the edges of the holes bordering the cliff-tops. The signs should be adhered to; they warn you off looking for balls for obvious reasons! Take note of the marker posts, or should we say "Stones of Accord" (the club's logo) – they give you the right line for your tee shot.

This really is a very special place indeed. The peninsular tells a lamentable tale, perhaps mourning the loss of life (many vessels sank in this vicinity). The Lusitania went down here too, in 1915, not because of the rocks, but courtesy of a German torpedo.

There are many memorable holes and none more so than the 17th, called "Lighthouse", a long par five. It requires a bold second shot to the right-hand side of the fairway; anything to the left will leave a blind approach to the green, which nestles in a punchbowl on the edge of the cliffs. The 18th is a dramatic closing hole but our favourite is the do-or-die par five 12th – it's one of the most outrageous holes in golf – whatever you do with your tee shot, don't bite off more than you can chew.

We think that Old Head is probably the most dramatic course in the world.

ABERDOVEY GOLF CLUB
Tywyn Road, Aberdovey, Gwynedd, LL35 ORT, Wales
Telephone: +44 (0) 1654 767493

Average Reviewers' Score:

Website: www.aberdoveygolf.co.uk
Architect: Herbert Fowler, Harry Colt and James Braid
Visitors: Welcome - contact in advance

Reviewers' Comments

Dovey is a real treat… Lives in the shadow of Harlech but it needn't, it's a great course in its own right… Not as tough as some of the other links courses in North Wales… It's a bit of a trek to get here but it's worth every ounce of effort… You are assured of a fair test of golf here… Holes are varied and therefore interesting… Opens up with a gentle par four… Par three 3rd is a real tester, a semi blind tee-shot into a heavily guarded green – make sure your game is tuned in from the off… The other par threes all offer up a different examination of your golf game… 12th is a stunning par three and a par here will feel like an eagle… Short par four 16th is a true classic, skirting the railway line. It's a brave golfer who attempts to hit this sloping green from the tee… Greens are reputedly the best in Wales… Must be the friendliest members' club in the world and they've got one of the best links courses too… Recently refurbished clubhouse is a fitting end to this gem in the Dovey estuary… It has to be played.

Aberdovey

"If one dare write about Aberdovey at all," wrote Patric Dickinson in his book, *A Round of Golf Courses*, "one must begin by letting Bernard Darwin through on the way to the first tee. For this links is 'his', and it is all and more than one would expect from a writer and golfer of such style; for it is both a 'classical' and 'romantic' links."

Aberdovey is set enchantingly within the Snowdonia National Park at the mouth of the Dovey Estuary, and the links are wedged between the Cambrian Mountain range and the shore. "I can just faintly remember the beginning of golf at Aberdovey in the early eighties," wrote Darwin in his 1910-book *The Golf Courses of the British Isles*. "Already rival legends have clustered round that beginning, but the true legend says that the founder was Colonel Ruck, who, having played some golf at Formby, borrowed nine flower pots from a lady in the village and cut nine holes in the marsh to put them in." A great deal has changed since then and the hands of many great architects have touched Aberdovey: Herbert Fowler, Harry Colt and James Braid. It is not surprising that it is such a revered links.

Despite its old age, it's no shorty, measuring over 6,500 yards from the back tees. It will test, and has tested, the very best golfers, playing host to a number of amateur championships over the years and it was here as a youngster, that Ian Woosnam developed his craft. It isn't the hardest links course in the British Isles by any stretch of the imagination, but when the wind blows, it can throw the ball off line and into the punishing rough. Only the skilful will score well.

There is so much history here that you cannot help but fall in love with the place. Running alongside this classic out-and-back links is the railway line, reminding us of the days when the trains were full of travelling golfers. Darwin's short story entitled "Aberdovey" tells an enchanting, romantic and amusing tale about his many pilgrimages to this Welsh links and how he used to love writing down the names of the stations as they passed by. Or as Patric Dickinson said: "A round at Aberdovey is always a brave and gay adventure, whatever the wind's quarter."

THE K CLUB
Straffan, Co. Kildare, Ireland
Telephone: +353 (0) I 6017200

Average Reviewers' Score:

Website: www.kclub.ie
Architect: Arnold Palmer
Visitors: Contact in advance

Reviewers' Comments

The K Club is a very special place and you can tell as soon as you approach the estate, the grounds are just unbelievable... Fantastic conditioning and a very good golf course... Better than Loch Lomond and Gleneagles but too expensive... The round cost a king's ransom but it was worth every cent... One of my favourite days on a golf course ever... Would barely make my Top 15 parkland courses played around the world but good for the British Isles... It's a tough course, you just need to glance back at the championship tees, but playing it off the yellows is a manageable test... I really didn't want the round to end, oh to be a millionaire.

K Club (Palmer)

The K Club is probably the most opulent resort in the whole of the British Isles. To put the resort into context, this is where an Irish piper will greet you as you switch off your helicopter. You'll then be whisked away to "The Island" in the middle of the River Liffey for a quick BBQ lunch. We can't cope with this much excitement before a round of golf.

The K Club, or to give its full title, the Kildare Country Club, is located in 550 acres of rolling County Kildare countryside and the North course, or rather the Palmer course, as it is now called, was deigned by Arnold Palmer, opening for play in 1991. The River Liffey meanders through the course and becomes hazardous on a number of holes, especially the 8th, where it runs all the way down the left hand side of the fairway.

There are four teeing areas to choose from and we recommend that you select the right one carefully because the course measures a whopping 7,337 yards from the blues which should really be left for the very best golfers, the likes of Phillip Price, Michael Campbell, Darren Clarke and Lee Westwood. The aforementioned gentlemen are the most recent winners of the European Open, held at the K Club for the last nine years. Clearly they will also be proud to host the 2006 Ryder Cup; this will be first time that the competition goes to the Emerald Isle and we have no doubt that a great deal of Guinness will be consumed that particular weekend.

You will either love the course or hate it; you might hate it if you are off your game because it will beat you up viciously, and you'll love it if your game is on song. Either way, no one could dispute that it's a challenging test of golf and will most certainly provide some entertainment during the Ryder Cup.

The holes are designed to shock and, in some cases, they are intimidating. The 7th is a monster par five, measuring over 600 yards from the blue tees; the hole double doglegs past all types of hazards, including trees, water, bunkers and punishing rough, and then you have to find the green, fiercely protected on both sides by the River Liffey. Even more difficult than the 7th is the stroke index one par four 16th measuring less than 400 yards. It's a potential card wrecker that requires an accurate approach shot to another green guarded by water. These are just two examples of what to expect during your adventure.

In many ways, the K Club is reminiscent of the Belfry. Firstly, it's a tournament course. Secondly, it's a resort course. Thirdly, it's dominated by water. Fourthly and finally, it is tough. Having said this, the Palmer is an aesthetically pleasing and immaculately maintained course and one you'll never forget.

THE BERKSHIRE GOLF CLUB
Swinley Road, Ascot, Berkshire, SL5 8AY, England
Telephone: +44 (0) 1344 621495

Average Reviewers' Score:

Website: None
Architect: Herbert Fowler
Visitors: By prior arrangement

Reviewers' Comments

Wonderful course but it needs to be played more than once… The Red is definitely the better of the two courses, which are tough to spilt after the first visit… After first time of playing all 36 holes I couldn't tell the Red from the Blue… The Red is tighter and more intimate, with each hole shielded from the next by the magnificent trees… Many people claim that the Red and the Blue make up the finest 36-hole heathland combination in the world - for me, the Old & New at Sunningdale are far better bet… The combination of six par threes, fours and fives is entertainment but it's the outstanding par threes which will stick in the mind… If you only have time for one round - make sure you play the Red rather than the Blue. The Red is a classic.

Berkshire (Red)

Many people say that there is nothing better than a day's golf amongst the forest, heather and springy turf of the Berkshire. Both the Red and the Blue courses are charming. The Red course is considered to be the more senior of the two, but frankly there is little to choose between them. Indeed, it is likely that they will both merge into one unless you have been sufficiently fortunate to play them more than once.

Herbert Fowler, who had a gift for blending golf courses into their natural surroundings, laid out both courses in 1928. Fowler clearly did a great job because only minor changes have since been made to his original design. The land was once the hunting forest of the royals and dates back to the reign of Queen Anne. Each hole is played in seclusion, the mature sycamore, birch, chestnut and pine trees providing majestic tunnels for the rippled fairways.

The Red acquired its name from a military analogy, with the Blue taking the opposite side. The Red course is highly unusual in design. The configuration of six par threes, six par fives and six par fours provide for much interest, variety and entertainment.

You need a straight and steady game to score well here otherwise you can very quickly become accustomed to chipping sideways out of the trees or hacking out of the heather. Needless to say, accuracy rather than length is all-important. The Red, measuring 6,369 yards from the white tees (5,733 from the reds) is the longer of the Berkshire's two courses and it plays over slightly higher ground than the Blue.

The Berkshire is closely linked with amateur golf; its own Berkshire Trophy has produced some famous winners, including Nick Faldo and Sandy Lyle. Numerous ladies' amateur competitions have also been held at the Berkshire.

There are many great holes but the best is probably the 6th, a short par four measuring 360 yards from the white tees. This hole doglegs to the right and requires an accurate drive to the left hand side of the fairway in order to leave a short approach shot to a raised green.

The hallmark of the course is the six par threes – they are all superb in their own right. Actually, we think that this a fantastic golf course, which will provide a memorable day out for any serious golfer.

NORTH BERWICK GOLF CLUB
Beach Road, North Berwick, East Lothian, EH39 4BB
Scotland
Telephone: +44 (0) 1620 892135

Website: www.northberwickgolfclub.com
Architect: Unknown
Visitors: Contact in advance

Average Reviewers' Score:

Reviewers' Comments

Would rather play North Berwick than Muirfield… It was a delight to play… This is thoroughly entertaining golf… The start is mildly reminiscent of St Andrews… Berwick has more than its share of quirkiness but the routing is superb and the holes call for a variety of shots… Greens not up to traditional, slick, links standard but what they lacked in presentation, they made up for in layout, with some wickedly sloping surfaces… A fantastic collection of memorable holes… Some great holes in an out and back configuration with some playing close to the water, especially the 2nd – a classic bite-off as much of the water as you can chew par four… Last six holes, in particular, are an absolute joy to play (especially Pit, the 13th with a low wall protecting the green, the famous 15th – Redan and the last hole; which was reminiscent of St Andrews from an elevated tee)… I loved this course. It's the sort of place I could happily play every week for the rest of my life… Traditional Scottish links golf at its best… Most enjoyable course in the area… It easily gives the more famous courses a run for their money.

North Berwick (West) 41st

The West Links at North Berwick is an immensely enjoyable golf course, located on the Firth of Forth with stunning sea views across to Craigleith Island and Bass Rock. The equivalent of Turnberry's "Ailsa Craig", Bass Rock is a huge volcanic lump, rising up over 300 feet from the Firth of Forth. It's the closest seabird sanctuary to the mainland and home to 80,000 nest sites; approximately 10 per cent of the world's population of Atlantic Gannets stay here.

This is a course that is extremely close to the origins of golf. It's the thirteenth oldest golf club (founded in 1832) and the second oldest course in the world still playing over its original fairways. Only the Old course at St Andrews is more senior.

The original architect is unknown. We do know that North Berwick started out in life as a 6-hole course and was extended to 18 holes by 1877. Around the turn of the 19th century, the course was stretched out to a little over 6,400 yards. There are two reasons why North Berwick is such an enjoyable course: firstly, the land is raised above sea level, affording those excellent views, and secondly, it has a superb collection of holes, a number of which have been replicated at other courses the world over.

The par three 15th is the most copied hole in the world and it's called "Redan" (a military term meaning "guarding parapet"). Bernard Darwin referred to this hole in his book, *The Golf Courses of the British Isles*: "a beautiful one shot hole atop a plateau with a bunker short of the green, to the left, and another further on to the right, and we must vary our mode of attack according to the wind, playing a shot to come in from the right or making a direct frontal attack".

One of the many beauties of the course is that you can play without being punished brutally by penal rough. They like a round to take no more than three hours and consequently, the rough is kept relatively short to speed up play. It's not the longest links course in the world but it's sheer fun and a unique experience to boot. You'll need to negotiate stone walls, deep bunkers, all kinds of humps and hollows and burns. You'll need to hit blind shots and you'll need to hit shots out over the beach. Fantastic stuff.

It's not often that we thank politicians, but in this case, we should take our hats off to golf-mad former Prime Minister Arthur J. Balfour, immortalised as "The Golfour" by Punch magazine. He was once captain of North Berwick and took every opportunity to popularise golf. So, what are you waiting for? If Arthur liked North Berwick, then surely you will too.

ROYAL ABERDEEN GOLF CLUB
Balgownie Links, Bridge of Don, Aberdeen, AB23 8AT
Scotland
Telephone: +44 (0) 1224 702571

Average Reviewers' Score:

Website: www.royalaberdeengolf.com
Architect: Robert and Archie Simpson, Tom Simpson, J.H Taylor, James Braid, Donald Steel
Visitors: Contact in advance – restricted at weekends

Reviewers' Comments

Classic, ancient, historic, natural - a complete joy to play this old beauty… A course for big boys, believe me… Every hole provides a different test, from the first tee shot with the members' lounge close at hand, to the long iron or wood into the last… We played the front into a good wind and were humbled… A lot of blind shots from undulating fairways… Tough as Carnoustie in the wind but more unfair with too many blind shots and lost balls with great shots… It can be intimidating… You really must stay on the fairway and if you do, you will love this stern test of golf… Massive greens will give you plenty of putting practice… The gorse is severe and penal… I didn't come expecting a stroll in the dunes and neither should you when the wind is up… You can sense tradition, quality, grace but maybe a little of a lesser welcome than at close-by Cruden Bay and Murcar… Clubhouse was not as crusty as expected… Don't be put off by the segregated clubhouses… It oozes character and tradition - wonderful to sample… Royal Aberdeen should not be missed… Balgownie is a jewel.

Royal Aberdeen (Balgownie)

Originally known as the Society of Golfers at Aberdeen, founded in 1780, this is the sixth oldest golf club in the world. They originally played over a public strip of common land between the Don and the Dee. In 1815, the society changed its name to the Aberdeen Golf Club. The common land was becoming over-crowded, so in 1886 they moved to their present home, the Balgownie links, north of the river Don. Royal title was finally applied in 1903, despite the fact that Prince Leopold granted patronage more than 30 years earlier.

A trio of Simpsons had a hand in fashioning this course, brothers Robert and Archie and then the flamboyant Tom Simpson. J.H. Taylor, James Braid and, most recently, Donald Steel, also made revisions.

Royal Aberdeen is a traditional out and back links running along the shore of the North Sea and is regarded by many as having the finest first nine holes in golf. The first tee is under the clubhouse window and the fairway heads straight for the sea. The next eight holes run parallel to the shore, weaving their way through towering sand dunes. You then turn back, heading for the clubhouse. The back nine plays on higher ground and provides stunning North Sea views.

Whilst the front nine holes are undoubtedly excellent, the back nine holes are probably harder. They are more exposed to the elements, and consequently, bear the full brunt of the wind. The par threes are also first class, as is the finishing hole, a brutal par four, in excess of 400 yards. A good tee shot will finish in a hollow in the fairway, leaving a long second shot across a swale to an elevated green perched in front of the clubhouse.

This is an excellent traditional links course, so remember to take your jacket and tie if you want to use the lounge or the dining room. Make sure you haven't spent too much time looking for your ball in the rough though; the five-minute rule was made here back in 1783.

CRUDEN BAY GOLF CLUB
Aulton Road, Cruden Bay, Aberdeenshire, AB42 0NN
Scotland
Telephone: +44 (0) 1799 812285

Average Reviewers' Score:

Website: www.crudenbaygolfclub.co.uk
Architect: Old Tom Morris, Archie Simpson, Tom Simpson, and Herbert Fowler
Visitors: Welcome weekdays – advisable to contact in advance

Reviewers' Comments

One of Scotland's most picturesque links courses... Good old-fashioned links golf from a time gone by... It's a delight to play and the scene is set from the moment you pull into the car park... Elevated clubhouse provides a wonderful 360 panorama of the course falling away beneath... A unique 'Figure 8' design and probably the best 14 holes one could wish to play but the first two and last two are a bit of a let-down... Golf here brings the fun back into playing the game... A few quirky blind shots, including a blind par three... Holes are varied and exciting... The 4th has an idyllic setting and is one of the best par threes in the UK and the 15th is similar to the 'Dell' at Lahinch - only 85 yards longer... Chill out and see the future of links golf encapsulated in the past... More than a little over-rated... This course is severely under-rated and one of my favourites in the UK... Hire a caddie the first time... Slains Castle (purportedly of Dracula fame) is a backdrop to the course... Shed your golfing inhibitions on the first tee and you will step off the 18th as a born-again links golfer.

Cruden Bay

Some say golf was played at Cruden Bay way back in the 18th century, but the club wasn't formed until at least 100 years later. Old Tom Morris and Archie Simpson were commissioned by the Great North of Scotland railway company to design the course and it opened for play in 1899. In 1926, Tom Simpson and Herbert Fowler remodelled the layout. Little has since changed.

The railway company used pink granite to build a luxurious hotel at Cruden Bay, which was nicknamed "the Palace in the Sandhills". They hoped for the same success as at Gleneagles, but sadly, in 1952, the hotel was demolished. Money was tight in the 1950s and the club and course almost fell by the wayside until three local businessmen stepped in to save Cruden Bay from extinction. A new clubhouse was built in 1961 on the same spot as the hotel but that, too, has disappeared, making way for the present 1998 clubhouse.

It's an inspirational golf course, regarded by some as quirky and considered by others as a masterpiece. Either way, this is a thrilling place to play golf because the designers used the original lie of the land to fantastic effect. Rugged linksland, pebble-dashed with sand dunes as high as three-storey buildings. Elevated tees cut high into the dunes, humped and hollowed fairways bumping their way along to punchbowl greens, nestled in attractive dells. And all set against the backdrop of the steely North Sea.

The 500 World's Greatest Golf Holes features the 4th hole, a par three measuring 193 yards. It is described delightfully: "Cruden Bay's routing takes golfers to many gorgeous expanses of dunes, but the elevated fourth tee is cited as the prettiest spot on the course. It offers the first true glimpse of the North Sea, with the old Port Erroll fishing cottages standing guard on the left. Crossing the white footbridge on the way to the green, one can smell the salt air, an enticing foreshadowing of the seven seaside holes to come."

Cruden Bay winds its way in a figure of eight through towering dunes. Many of the holes are secluded from each other by the sandhills, enabling that wonderful feeling of intimacy. There are panoramic sea views, a stunning beach, drivable par fours, blind drives, back-to-back par threes. That's entertainment.

MOUNT JULIET
Thomastown, County Kilkenny, Ireland
Telephone: +353 (0) 56 777 3064

Average Reviewers' Score:
⚫⚫⚫⚪

Website: www.mountjuliet.com
Architect: Jack Nicklaus
Visitors: Welcome – contact in advance

Reviewers' Comments

You have to admire what Nicklaus did at Mount Juliet – he's created a fun and challenging golf course... If you like excellent service, superb facilities and Americanised golf, then you'll love Mount Juliet. If you want history and tradition, you are at the wrong place... It's not the most natural course in Ireland, the mounds provide good perspective and dimension but it feels rather artificial... I thoroughly enjoyed it and the condition is faultless... I can't fault the greens, they are fabulous and some of the best putting surfaces I've played on, there's no chance of avoiding a three putt here... The greens are enormous and undulating - take plenty of club to avoid coming up short... You have to nip the ball off the surface otherwise you struggle with the contact... A memorable day's golf at an outstanding resort.

Mount Juliet

The course at Mount Juliet is set in lush, rolling parkland, part of a 1,500 acre Irish country estate with an 18th century mansion as the clubhouse. Magnificent mature trees line the fairways. The River Nore cuts through the course, popular for salmon fishing. This is the place to allow the Walter Mitty in you to daydream about having your very own private course. But wake up, because this is the best inland course on the Emerald Isle.

Jack Nicklaus must have been delighted when he was asked to build a course on this beautiful country estate. He created a manicured parkland gem. In 1991, he opened the course with an exhibition match against Christy O'Connor Snr. It is not surprising that there is a distinctly American feel to this layout, with numerous teeing areas, plenty of bunkers and water hazards. The course even has concealed drainage and irrigation systems. Thankfully, the buggy paths are absent; it would be sacrilege to drive on these immaculate fairways.

This is a course which can cater for the very best golfers, measuring well over 7,000 yards from the back tees. Three of the world's best have already won the Irish Open here: Faldo (1991), Langer (1992) and Torrance (1993). Another golfer won the American Express Championship here in 2002, someone called Tiger Woods. The course, however, is eminently playable for the handicap golfer from a choice of forward tees.

Nicklaus has designed a fun golfer's golf course. Water is the main hazard but if you can avoid it, you will have a great time. It is also worth checking out the putting green, the venue for the National Putting Championship. It's impressive. 18 holes, par 53, with bunkers and water hazards – are you sure this isn't America?

MACHRIHANISH GOLF CLUB
Machrihanish, Campbeltown, Argyll, PA28 6PT, Scotland
Telephone: +44 (0) 1586 810213

Average Reviewers' Score:

Website: www.machgolf.com
Architect: Old Tom Morris
Visitors: Welcome – no restrictions

Reviewers' Comments

Surely Machrihanish would be in the top 20 if it was less remote... Well worth the six-hour round trip by road from Glasgow... What an absolute gem... Whatever you do, make sure you set two days aside for this corking crackerjack of a course... Found it a very fair course with not too many blind shots... I've been lucky enough to play some 50 of the Top 100 and for me this is Scotland's best course... The site is truly magnificent and it has an overwhelming feeling of space for an old fashioned links... Kept thinking they could have built another course within the acreage, as there's plenty of land to spare amongst the dunes... It's doubtful that I could play a more enjoyable track... You get a feeling of stepping back in time to when golf was a simple, uncomplicated game... And what a great little clubhouse... This playing experience is worth every minute of the full day needed to savour its delights... I simply loved it here and if I had my own private helicopter I'd become a member of this delightful links at the tip of the world...Wow!

Machrihanish

The small village of Machrihanish is situated on the western side of the remote Kintyre Peninsula; this is where the sky is big, the sunsets are dramatic and the air has been warmed by the Gulf Stream. Nearby Campbeltown was once the whisky capital of the world, but today only the Springbank distillery remains in full operation.

In 1876, the Kintyre Golf Club was founded; it's unclear who originally laid out the course, so we'll put it down to Mother Nature, but we do know that Old Tom Morris left his stamp on the links in 1879. The members felt that Kintyre was too ordinary a name for such a special golf course, so they changed it to the resonant Machrihanish in 1888.

This links must be one of the most natural, romantic and most enjoyable places to play golf in the whole of the British Isles. It's not long, grand or a championship course, but it is sheer fun. It's got an outstanding front nine and a thrilling start. The first, called "Battery", is regularly voted as one of the best opening holes in golf, a teasing 423-yard par four with an elevated tee on the edge of the shore. The fairway hugs the beach and we must drive diagonally across it. How heroic can we afford to be with our very first tee shot? The beach is in play, not out-of bounds. But dare we play our second shot from amongst the seashells?

Machrihanish is not just about one great opening hole – the front nine is exceptional and the entire experience magical. The greens are firm, fast, true and are positioned in the most varied of locations. Some are sunk in punchbowls whilst others are on a raised plateau or flattened dune tops. There are blind tee shots, fabulous sea views, undulating rippling fairways and exciting rugged dunes.

You have to make an extra special effort to get to Machrihanish, but it is worth it. The welcome is extraordinarily friendly and the golf is extraordinary. Expect to leave this place with a broad smile on your face.

ASHBURNHAM GOLF CLUB
Cliffe Terrace, Burry Port, Carmarthenshire,
SA16 0HN, Wales
Telephone: +44 (0) 1554 832269

Average Reviewers' Score:

Website: www.ashburnhamgolfclub.com
Architect: J.H. Taylor, Fred Hawtree and Ken Cotton
Visitors: Welcome – no restrictions

Reviewers' Comments

This is a man-sized test of golf and memorable too… Ashburnham taught me the true meaning of an "out-and-back" course… The course provided a good variation in hole types – each one was enjoyable… The par three start was a little daunting – it got me paying attention from my first swing… The holes improve as you make your way round… The greens are tough to hold and even tougher to read… The greens were in superb condition and it took a while for me to get used to greens running as true as these… It is obvious that the greenkeepers spend a lot of time looking after the greens whilst overlooking the tees, especially the 16th… The par threes face the same way, therefore the wind will be key on the short holes… The 18th has a great uphill approach to the green, a par will be a great way to end your round…Staff were friendly and helpful in the pro shop and around the course… I'd love another round just to see if the wind would be more friendly… This is a really superb links golf course.

Ashburnham is one of the finest and oldest golf courses in Wales, founded in 1894. It's located close to the Burry Estuary and Worm's Head, with fine views over Carmarthen Bay. A number of important events have been hosted here, including the PGA Championship. Bernard Gallacher picked up his first pay cheque at Ashburnham, when he won the 1969 Schweppes PGA Championship. Sam Torrance and Dai Rees were also victorious here.

Ashburnham originally started out in life as a nine-hole course and was extended in 1902 to 18 holes. Today's course, which measures 6,630 yards from the back tees, is the result of alterations by J.H. Taylor in 1914, Fred Hawtree in 1923 and then Ken Cotton (himself a member at Ashburnham). These three great architects have created a classic out-and-back links course, rolling gently through the dunes.

Unusually, the round begins with a downhill par three, where out-of-bounds lurk menacingly at the right of the green. In fact, the course is a nightmare for the right-handed slice, as there is invariably trouble beckoning to the right on many holes. The first two holes and the closing two holes are somewhat out of character with the rest, having an inland, almost park-like feel. But the holes in between are the real thing – undiluted and undulating linksland. By the time we reach the 3rd hole, we're running parallel to the sea and often into the teeth of the prevailing wind. At the turn, we head back, wind assisted but a little further inland.

According to local Ashburnham folklore, an extraordinary tee shot was struck on the 18th. During the Home Internationals, an amateur event, England's John Davis struck his drive from the 18th tee directly onto the clubhouse roof. The ball ricocheted off and landed to the left of the green, pin high! Admittedly, the wind was from behind, but the ball must have travelled at least 400 yards.

After a game, make sure to have a drink in the welcoming clubhouse. The members are friendly and often willing to tell a yarn or two. Above all, ensure that you don't miss playing this historic links. It's an absolute delight and guaranteed to put a smile on your face, making you want to come back for more.

ST ANDREWS LINKS
St Andrews, Fife, KY16 9SF, Scotland
Telephone: +44 (0) 1334 466666

Average Reviewers' Score:

Website: www.standrews.org.uk
Architect: Old Tom Morris and W. Hall Blyth
Visitors: Book at least one month in advance

Reviewers' Comments

St Andrews. Just the mention of the name fills you with a mixture of excitement and apprehension of treading the hallowed turf... It doesn't have the aura and famous landmarks of the Old, but the New is a fantastic course in its own right... For me, like many others, it's probably better than the Old course... The design feels as though more effort, thought, and most importantly, imagination has been put into this neighbour of nostalgia... Definition supplied by nature and the finishing touches added by man... The 10th is fantastic, a golfer and designer's hole... There were not enough memorable holes but the experience of being out on the links land of St Andrews is a privilege... The New course for me was a wonderful example of how golf was played... If this was not the so-called home of golf, I don't believe it would rank so highly, but that said, what are we without tradition and history? There is plenty of gorse around but you have to be errant to get penalised here... Put this top of your list of the St Andrews trio, you'll get the same challenge without the hole in your wallet.

In the late 1800s, the Old Course was getting too popular, largely due to the extra visitors flocking to St Andrews on the trains. The R&A decided to pay for the New course to be built in return for allocated tee times on the Old. These rights are still enclosed in an Act of Parliament passed in 1894, the precursor to the current Act of 1974, which specifies how the public St Andrews links courses are managed.

The New course was designed by Old Tom Morris and W. Hall Blyth and opened for play in 1895. This makes it one of the oldest "new" courses in the world!

Situated adjacent to the Old course, the New is often referred to as the local's favourite because it is tighter and more defined than the Old. It possesses some similarities to the Old, shared fairways, a double green at the 3rd and 15th and the traditional out and back layout. In many ways it plays and feels better than the Old – it's certainly less quirky and prettier too, with swathes of dense gorse providing brilliance of seasonal colour.

The fairways are undulating, but they don't have the same slopes and curves as the Old. Consequently, there are fewer hanging lies. There are some great holes on the New, especially in the dunes around the turn for home. The 10th hole, a tough 464-yard par four was one of Bernard Darwin's favourites. In *The Golf Courses of the British Isles*, he wrote: "This is nevertheless a really fine one, running down a narrow gorge between two ranges of hills, with a fine, slashing second shot with the brassey, albeit more or less a blind one".

We think that if the New Course could be transported to virtually any other coastal stretch of the British Isles, away from the shadow of its auld mater, it surely would have a higher reputation and be recognised as the excellent links course it is. Who knows? If the course had not been in the shadows for so long and perhaps updated to a similar extent as many other links courses, it might well have played host to an Open Championship.

In 1910, Darwin wrote: "Still there occasionally comes a time when we grow sick to death of the crowding and waiting on the old course, and then we are glad enough to steal away on to the new course and have a round, which will probably be at any rate a comparatively quick one." Could this really be the reason why the locals prefer the New?

ST GEORGE'S HILL GOLF CLUB
Golf Club Road, St George's Hill, Weybridge, Surrey
KT13 0NL, England
Telephone: +44 (0) 1932 847758

Average Reviewers' Score:

Website: www.stgeorgeshillgolfclub.co.uk
Architect: Harry Colt
Visitors: Contact in advance – handicap cert required

Reviewers' Comments

A sweeping statement, but I think that St George's Hill is the pick of the courses on the Surrey/Berkshire sand belt... The course is magnificent, probably the prettiest I have ever played... If you've not played this course, put it at the top of your list immediately... The holes are cut like valleys through very undulating terrain - very often teeing off from a raised area and playing into a raised green... Probably the most enjoyable inland course I have played after Woodhall - it is prettier than Woodhall but nowhere near the same test of golf... I cannot fault this place... The sense of occasion and grandeur never leaves you from when you enter the estate... Wonderful traditional club... The clubhouse is stunning... Everyone is extremely friendly and it has the edge on its Ascot neighbours... What lucky members... Best of the outstanding Surrey heathland courses... I will be making a booking next year.

St George's Hill

St George's Hill is the prettiest of the many heathland courses on the Surrey/Berkshire sand belt and, in our opinion, one of the very best. In 1911, a local builder came up with an original idea, to build luxury fairway-side houses and by chance, Harry Colt was the chosen architect. The course opened for play in 1913 and it is considered to be Colt's greatest work.

The most notable difference between St George's Hill and the other heathland layouts in this area is the terrain. The land here sweeps and undulates like a rollercoaster and Harry Colt used these dramatic elevation changes superbly in his design.

At this stage, it is worth pointing out that there are three loops of nine holes, called Red, Blue and Green. At one time, St George's Hill was a 36-hole complex but sadly, no longer. The main course comprises the Red nine and the Blue nine, the Green nine is somewhat shorter.

The spectacular panorama from the front of the clubhouse, or the pavilion as it was originally called, totally whets your appetite. It is one of those views that grabs you and makes your heart pound in excited anticipation. You cannot help but want to get out onto the first tee as quickly as possible.

Opening up is a super 384-yard par four played from an elevated tee. A good drive will leave your tee shot at the bottom of a valley, your approach will then need to be struck steeply up the hill to an inviting green that waits patiently at the top. The 2nd is even better, a brutal 458-yard par four, a blind drive over the brow of a hill will leave a tough approach shot from a hanging lie which must carry a stream on its way to a distant raised green. And so it goes on, with many more memorable holes, especially the par threes. In fact, there isn't a single weak hole at St George's Hill.

Within the grandiose setting is inherent charm and beauty. The houses beside the fairways have style and never impose and are complementary, adding to the amazing St George's Hill experience.

SILLOTH ON SOLWAY GOLF CLUB
Silloth on Solway, Cumbria, CA7 4BL, England
Telephone: +44 (0) 1697 331304

Average Reviewers' Score:

Website: www.sillothgolfclub.co.uk
Architect: Davy Grant, Willie Park Jnr.
Visitors: Contact in advance

Reviewers' Comments

A seriously wind-blasting course - tests you to the very limits... If there is a better value course in the Top 100, I would be extremely surprised... Glorious course with a lovely natural flow to the holes... Very natural, very tough but leaves you with an amazing sense of achievement once you've played it - and plenty of memories too... Immaculately maintained and an absolute delight to play... Outstanding links course with many interesting and testing holes... Accuracy is everything on many of the holes with sunken greens and big trouble off to the sides... Not a course for the faint-hearted... OK, it's remote - but the drive from the M6 is gorgeous... I would travel a long way to play this course again... Great views across the Solway Firth... A clubhouse with plenty of history... Probably the best course I've played - and a bargain... Links golf at its most supreme.

Silloth on Solway

At last, Silloth on Solway's reputation is becoming recognised more widely, thoroughly deserving its position in the Top 50. It is currently ranked as the 8th best links course in England.

Founded in 1892, with the help of Railway Company money, it was originally designed by Davy Grant (with a little help from Willie Park Jnr.). Silloth is famous for its affiliation with ladies' golf.

The famous Leitch sisters learnt to play golf on the Silloth links. Charlotte Cecilia Pitcairn Leitch (or Cecil as she became known), went on to be the best lady golfer in the world, winning a record four British, five French, two English and one Canadian titles. In 1910, Cecil played a match against Harold Hilton (one of the greatest male golfers of the time) over 72 holes, 36 at Walton Heath and 36 at Sunningdale. Sportingly, Hilton gave Cecil nine shots per 18 holes and found himself five holes up in the last round, with only the last 15 holes to play. Cecil, showing true grit, fought her way back and ended up winning on the 71st green, 2 up and 1 to play.

Silloth has parliamentary connections too. Viscount Willie Whitelaw was the President of Silloth on Solway Golf Club until his death in 1999.

You have to make an extra special effort to get to Silloth because it is located in one of the most remote and isolated places in England, at the mouth of the Solway Firth. When you get to Silloth, it's a surprise to see the nearby industry that slightly blots an otherwise perfect landscape.

With heather and gorse adding brilliant splashes of seasonal colour, this is a cracking links golf course. When the wind blows, it's unlikely that you will play to your handicap. Even on a calm day, you'll find it tough. Finding the tight greens is no mean feat and when you do, they are tough to read with their subtle borrows.

It's well worth the time (and the money) to get to Silloth and once you get there, you won't want to leave. You are at one of the best value golf courses in the whole of the British Isles.

GLENEAGLES
Auchterarder, Perthshire, PH3 1NF, Scotland
Telephone: +44 (0) 1764 662231

Average Reviewers' Score:

Website: www.gleneagles.com
Architect: James Braid
Visitors: Book 8 weeks in advance

Reviewers' Comments

The Queen's makes you glad a) to be alive and b) that you're a golfer... Such an enjoyable experience... The views are simply stunning and the whole layout blends in beautifully with its surroundings... If you plan to make a day of it and play two of the three courses, make the Queen's one of your choices... The views, wildlife and course design are incomparable - how you play is almost secondary... Great hotel and nice views but the courses are average and terribly overpriced... It's a touch less than 6,000 yards from the medal tees, so not too long... The condition of the course from tee to putting surface is so good - everything is well manicured and presented... You'll find a huge difference between the nines in terms of difficulty – back nine about six shots easier – but you will never regret anything about your day... Far better experience than the one I'd had at the King's... Course to savour in beautiful surroundings... Pricey but how often do you play at a venue like Gleneagles? An honour and a delight to play the Queen's.

Gleneagles (Queens's)

The Queen's course is the pretty little sister at Gleneagles. The holes are set within an altogether softer landscape than the King's and PGA Centenary courses. She's only a short course and not the most challenging, but she is exquisitely delicate and stunningly beautiful. Patric Dickinson summed up Gleneagles in his book, *A Round of Golf Courses*: "So let us be fair from the very start; or even before the start, Gleneagles is something that was created, and exists, sheerly to please; if I may take a simile from the theatre, it is glorious musical comedy."

Designed by James Braid, the Queen's course opened for play in 1917. From the medal tees, the course measures less than 6,000 yards, but with a lowly par of 68, it represents an immensely enjoyable challenge. This is one of the finest parcels of golfing land in the British Isles. The holes weave their way across undulating moorland, through charming woodland, to greens set in pretty glades. The ball sits proudly on the springy fairways, inviting the most solid strike. The greens are true and ideal for bold putting and this really is an enchanting and exhilarating place to play golf.

Gleneagles is unusual in that it has three different golf courses and it's also unique because it's the only place in Scotland to have three inland courses and they have all appeared in recent ranking lists. This is a place to enjoy the entertainment and have some fun. Or as Patric Dickinson said: "Gleneagles is one of the wonders of the golfing world, a kind of Hanging Garden of Babylon on a Scottish hillside, and if you marry Golf, here's the place to spend your Hinny Mune!" [1]

[1] Honeymoon.

NOTTS GOLF CLUB
Hollinwell, Kirby-in-Ashfield, Nottinghamshire
NG17 7QR, England
Telephone: +44 (0) 1623 753225

Average Reviewers' Score:

Website: www.nottsgolfclub.co.uk
Architect: Willie Park Jnr. and J.H. Taylor
Visitors: Contact in advance – weekdays only – handicap cert required

Reviewers' Comments

Not a weak hole on the course and excellent value for money… Played it in the winter and it was a dream… 2nd and 3rd holes are the pick of the front nine with the 3rd green by the clubhouse… One or two of the holes on the front nine remind me of Woodhall Spa… Some great looking holes and each one felt well defined… I did not have a drink in the holy well, as it looked a bit dirty. However, this is an excellent short par four… Back nine has a moorland feel to it… The course was presented very well… Greens in fabulous condition and dry underfoot for winter… Greens were as good as any I have played but beware of the speed – they are very fast and undulating… A dream for very good putters but average putters would struggle… I thought this was a very fair test of golf… A course I'd love to go back to in the summer… The clubhouse is one of the best I've been in, very old and spacious with plenty of interesting photos and trophies… Highly recommended and reasonably priced.

"After being too long away I lately went back to Hollinwell, which, as all the golfing world knows, or ought to know, is the course of the Notts Golf Club," wrote Bernard Darwin in an article for Country Life. "On one side of it, there runs a pleasant wooded path by a series of lakes, and by this path Byron used to walk from Newstead to see Mary Chaworth at Annesley. Behind the course stands a hill covered with bracken from which Robin Hood used to watch for signals at Nottingham warning him that the Sheriff was setting out in pursuit. These are romantic circumstances, and I thrilled as I was told of them."

Hollinwell is so called because there is a holy well located amongst the trees close to the 8th fairway. Water from the well is said to lend much needed strength to the golfer, especially during the heat of summer. One of the British Isles' finest inland golf courses, Notts opened for play in 1887, originally designed by Willie Park Jnr. Modifications (primarily to bunkering) were later made by J.H. Taylor, whom the Club paid the princely sum of five guineas for his services! The bunkers at Notts are relatively shallow, unlike some of the cavernous bunkers found at Woodhall Spa or Ganton. Perhaps the price of sand was factored into Taylor's wages!

The land is wonderfully undulating and some of the fairways sweep through wooded hillsides and others run through heather, fern and gorse-clad valleys. Unusually, there are a number of varieties of gorse and even in the depths of winter, you will find some in flower.

Notts feels very much like heathland (the soil is sandy and the turf is spongy), but it also has a moorland flavour and a touch of woodland. Despite the varied landscape, this attractive course comes together really well and actually gets better and better as you progress from hole to hole. It is also worth mentioning that a great deal of effort is being put in to encourage the heather to return to its former glory.

Over the years, Notts has hosted a number of professional and amateur events. The 1970 John Player Classic (won by Christy O'Connor Senior) was probably the most notable, with a world record first prize of £25,000. It's also a monster of a course (at more than 7,000 yards long) and it is probably capable of hosting a modern tournament.

Keep an eye out for the fabulous 13th hole; six bunkers surround the green. It's a downhill par three (228 yards from the back tees) with stunning views.

PENNARD GOLF CLUB
2 Southgate Road, Southgate, Swansea, SA3 2BT
Wales
Telephone: +44 (0) 1792 233131

Average Reviewers' Score:

Website: www.pennardgolfclub.com
Architect: James Braid and Ken Cotton
Visitors: Welcome, contact in advance

Reviewers' Comments

This unusual course is absolutely enchanting and exceptionally tough... They don't make 'em like this any more... If you're a visitor from abroad used to playing immaculate courses then do yourself a favour and play Pennard and see what you've been missing... The electrified fences are an added hazard in their own right and can prove a useful distraction if your opponent gets zapped... Sloping lies make things very tricky... Spectacular design from nature with stunning cliff top views and medieval castles... You simply can't criticise any element of this course... The course is carved into some of the best land I have seen... The 10th, called Three Cliffs, has to be one of the best short par fives in Wales... The 13th, called Colonel, is one of the principality's toughest par threes... Not an easy walk (a lot of ups and downs) but miss playing at Pennard at your peril... The one course in Wales I'd travel from London to play again... A breath of fresh air... A stunning course, totally different, but just as good in its own way as Royal Porthcawl... If you're only slightly interested in golf you should do yourself a favour and play here.

Pennard

52nd

Although Pennard Golf Club is located only a few miles southwest of Swansea, it's set on the rugged Gower Peninsula, amongst one of the most dramatic landscapes in Britain. Its cliff-top site provides an ideal vantage point – from the heights, the views across to the beautiful sandy beaches of Three Cliff and Oxwich Bays are simply arresting.

This is one of the oldest golf courses in Wales and reputedly, golf has been played here since 1896, although the Pennard Golf Club was not founded until 1908. It's often called "the links in the sky", because the holes play across links-like ground, full of dunes, humps and hollows but the land is 200 feet above sea level.

The great James Braid originally designed it, and, some years later, he returned with Ken Cotton to implement certain revisions. For many years, the unusual course was relatively anonymous until the great American architect, Tom Doak, declared that Pennard "is one of my all-time favourites – the site is one of the most spectacular I've ever seen." Since Doak's comments, the course is continuing to enjoy a renaissance. The ruins of a 12th century Norman Castle stand guard over the course, which measures a modest 6,329 yards from the back tees. It's by no means a championship test, but there are 18 wonderful holes and Pennard has hosted a number of important amateur events. This is where the inspirational Curtis Cup player, Vicky Thomas, honed her game.

When the strong winds funnel up the Bristol Channel, it will pose a stern challenge to the very best golfers. Don't let your concentration be affected by the wild ponies and cattle, which graze on the links. Additionally, expect a few blind shots and don't expect too many flat lies – it's seriously hilly, with more ups and downs than most links courses.

Each and every hole has character and there are at least nine great holes. The four par fours from the 6th to the turn are simply tremendous. The short par four 7th, aptly called "Castle", will remain etched in the mind for a long time – from the elevated tee, the drive must bravely cross a deep chasm to find a distant undulating fairway. The ruins of Pennard Castle watch in silence. A semi-blind approach shot is to a sunken green, which is protected by dunes – fantastic stuff! High up in the dunes once again, the tee shot from the 493-yard 16th, called "Great Tor", is also nerve-jangling. A solid drive to the rippled fairway below will leave a short, but blind, second shot across a ridge. The approach shot must find the green, perched on the cliff-top, which slopes wickedly from back to front. Don't leave a downhill putt, or you may find yourself pitching back on to the green.

It's is a delightful old-fashioned affair and without doubt, this is one of the very best links courses in the British Isles. No trip to South Wales would be complete without tasting the sheer delight of Pennard.

BLAIRGOWRIE GOLF CLUB
Golf Course Road, Rosemount, Blairgowrie, Perthshire
PH10 6LG, Scotland
Telephone: +44 (0) 1250 872622

Website: www.theblairgowriegolfclub.co.uk
Architect: Old Tom Morris and James Braid
Visitors: Mon, Tue & Thu – contact in advance

Average Reviewers' Score:

Reviewers' Comments

Blairgowrie is a unique and valuable Scottish asset… The course was in great shape for the time of year and I remember I didn't remove the driver from my golf bag once all day as it is so important with trees lining most holes to keep the ball in play on the fairway… Fun to play parkland track but not as good as Downfield… Easy to walk… Course presentation and drainage are first-class and beautiful late autumn colours everywhere but the course still leaves me underwhelmed… Decent golf course and well manicured… A very pleasant and enjoyable course, but I was expecting more… Green fees were overpriced for what was on offer… Every tee offers a similar challenge (thread drive between tall trees) and the flatness of it all gives a sameness to the experience… Well worth playing… The best holes are 1, 16 and 17… It's a delightful place to spend some time, let alone play golf.

Blairgowrie (Rosemount)

Blairgowrie is charmingly situated at the feet of the Grampian Mountains amongst glorious pine, birch and heather. It was founded in 1889, originally as a nine-hole course.

There is an element of controversy as to who extended the course to 18 holes. Keith Mackie intimates (in the Strokesaver) that it was Dr Alister MacKenzie who performed the work, with the new course eventually opening for play in 1927. James Braid is suggested to have "revamped the course just seven years later". However, in the biography of James Braid, Bernard Darwin wrote: "When it came to turning the old nine-hole course into one of eighteen and the taking in of new land in consequence, James was called in; he and Millar, the professional there, planned it out between them and without apportioning exact shares there is credit and to spare for both of them, for this is a lovely course".

Regardless of who really did what in terms of design, Blairgowrie is definitely a very pretty and classy inland course, the crisp turf has a moorland feel to it with the fairways pitching and rolling through avenues of trees. Each hole is carved through the trees, which provide a natural amphitheatre for a calm and tranquil round of golf.

From start to finish the holes are good and varied but the best holes are left until last. The 17th is especially noteworthy; it's a lovely par three called "Plateau" with a two-tiered green. The pro's tip is to take plenty of club, to get on the right level and avoid three putts.

The Rosemount is regularly voted in the top twenty Scottish courses and it does deserve its plaudits for it is an excellent course. There is nothing dramatic or significantly difficult about this layout. You can open your shoulders, as the fairways are generously wide. The course is maintained to a very high standard and all this makes for good, honest and enjoyable golf. Perhaps it's a course to which you might want to retreat after you have had enough buffeting at the seaside.

THE BERKSHIRE GOLF CLUB
Swinley Road, Ascot, Berkshire, SL5 8AY, England
Telephone: +44 (0) 1344 621495

Average Reviewers' Score:

Website: None
Architect: Herbert Fowler
Visitors: By prior arrangement

Reviewers' Comments

It's hard to split these two courses; they are both excellent heathland layouts... The Blue's a good course but not as good as the Red... The opening hole is an absolute brute of a par three... Not the easiest opener after lunch and a couple of beers... The Blue has a more open feel to it and it's certainly more forgiving than the Red... There are a number of holes on top of the busy road and these detract from the overall enjoyment... In my view, the Berkshire comes up just short of Wentworth's original 36-hole combination (East & West)... A bit stuffy in the clubhouse... If you can, play the Blue first and leave the superior Red until last... Certainly worth playing as a 36-hole package.

Berkshire (Blue)   54th

Sunningdale and Wentworth are the only clubs in the whole of the British Isles other than the Berkshire that can boast about having two heathland golf courses positioned in the Top 100. It's an amazing surprise that so few people know how charming the Berkshire experience really is.

The Blue course is the Red's more conventional and slightly shorter sister. A more standard four par threes, three par fives and eleven par fours make up the configuration for this delightful par 71 course. In Bernard Darwin's book, *Golf Between Two Wars*, he wrote: "The other, the Blue, which some people prefer, a little less 'big', but by no means a secondary course. The country is essentially undulating and interesting and full of natural beauty…The Berkshire courses have more of charm perhaps and less of austere grandeur than Walton Heath."

Herbert Fowler was the Berkshire's architect and the Blue course opened for play in 1928. Fowler was actually very good at designing excellent twin golf courses. Not only did Fowler design both courses here at the Berkshire, but he also designed the superb intertwined courses at Walton Heath, the Old and the New.

Both the Berkshire courses have the same natural hazards, although the Blue plays over flatter ground than the Red. Cruelly, the Blue opens up with an exceptionally tough par three, with the tee directly in front of the clubhouse window. The green sits on a distant plateau. Not the easiest hole on which to start a round of golf – play the Red course in the morning to prepare for it!

There are many other notable holes on the Blue course but it's the closing sequence of five holes that make this a tough but special course. All five are par 4s and three of them are more than 400 yards long. It could be argued that the Blue has a similar but less acute weakness than her brother the Red – the three par 5s on the Blue course are very short indeed, the longest measures only 477 yards.

However, short par fives aside, the Berkshire is the most delightful place to play 36 holes of golf, perhaps only surpassed by the pairing of Sunningdale's Old and New courses.

PYLE & KENFIG GOLF CLUB
Waun-y-Mer, Kenfig, Bridgend, Mid Glamorgan
CF33 4PU, Wales
Telephone: +44 (0) 1656 783093

Website: www.pandkgolfclub.co.uk
Architect: Harry Colt and Philip Mackenzie Ross
Visitors: Welcome, contact in advance

Average Reviewers' Score:

Reviewers' Comments

Pyle and Kenfig is undoubtedly a heroic links... The back nine is dazzling, set amongst towering dunes... Two distinct nines with the second half the better of the two... Truly magnificent experience... The 11th and 14th being all that links holes should be, in fact the 14th goes into my top 20 holes played... Greens on all holes are in tiptop condition and the Pyle and Kenfig experience is a must when in the area... The greens are as true and as fast as those at Burnham & Berrow - and that's saying something... If they could somehow utilise some of the virgin dune land and move the front nine, this would be the Ballybunion of Wales and it would put Porthcawl firmly in its shadow... Great welcome from the members but a little colder from the bar staff and catering staff... Very, very tough course... Would like to see this course rated higher... Oh to be a member here... This is a Top 100 course, no question.

Pyle and Kenfig

Pyle and Kenfig, commonly known as P&K, is one of Wales's finest links courses. Its famous regal neighbour, Royal Porthcawl, lies next door. But make no mistake, Pyle and Kenfig is almost as great as the mighty Porthcawl.

Breathtaking views of Welsh mountains, Rest Bay and the Bristol Channel can be seen from this old links course, which was founded in 1922 and originally designed by Harry Colt. Nine holes were commandeered by the military during World War II, but after the war, it was decided to extend the course to 18 holes once again. With great foresight, some wild linksland was identified, which lay closer to the sea. Philip Mackenzie Ross (the architect behind Southerness) was asked to design the new holes...and what a job he made of it. Colt's front nine is good, but Mackenzie Ross's back nine, routed through the dunes, is simply outstanding.

Unusually for a links course, it's laid out in two loops of nine. The original front nine is where to make a score because the back nine is a very stiff test, especially when the wind is up. The 11th hole, a 525-yard par five known as the Valley Hole, is where the dunes come in to play – from here on in, it is sheer entertainment. Drink in the view from the 14th tee, a 416-yard par four – the panorama towards the Gower Peninsula is stunning. The last three holes (all long par fours) are amongst the best closing holes in golf. They will severely test the mettle of the very best golfers.

Solid driving is key to a good round and if you can avoid the trouble and find the fairways, scoring well will be a real possibility. From the regular tees, the course measures a lowly 6,122 yards against a par of 71. Step back onto the medal tees and it's a different proposition – 6,728 yards and the par is still 71. The club has hosted a number of important events, including the Amateur Championship in 2002 (with Royal Porthcawl) and the Girls' Home Internationals in 2003. Additionally, in 2006, they will play host to the Men's Home Internationals.

Good shot-making will be rewarded because it's a fair golf course without any unforeseen tricks up its sleeve. Additionally, it's a fine traditional links, believed by many to be an epic. Ensure that P&K is included on any golfing itinerary to South Wales – we guarantee you'll thoroughly enjoy this overshadowed gem.

John Moody

COUNTY SLIGO GOLF CLUB
Rosses Point, County Sligo, Ireland
Telephone: +353 (0) 7191 77 134

Average Reviewers' Score:

Website: www.countysligogolfclub.ie
Architect: George Combe, Willie Campbell, Harry Colt and Charles Alison
Visitors: Welcome, contact in advance

Reviewers' Comments

There's just one thing to say about County Sligo – outstanding... Rosses Point is one of the best and fairest links courses I've had the pleasure to play... One of the most memorable courses I've played... Ben Bulben seems to watch you all the way round and the ocean views (due to the fact that there no huge dunes in the way) are a complete joy... After a gentle start and a somewhat out-of-character 2nd, the course really gets going, and when you get out to the turn, the feeling of peace and quiet is truly fantastic... The best holes are in the middle of the round... The 14th is as tough a par four as you can get and the 17th is one of my all-time favourite golf holes... To finish, you need a cracking drive just to reach the fairway across all sorts of trouble – it's a wonderful conclusion to a remarkable course... If you get lucky with the weather, this is just about as close to links golfing heaven as you can get... Make the journey and sample it for yourself – you won't be disappointed... The whole experience is simply divine.

County Sligo (Championship)

County Sligo – or Rosses Point, as it is better known – is an exhilarating west coast links, situated in the heart of Yeats country. W.B. Yeats won the Nobel Prize for Literature in 1923.

Rosses Point started out in life as a nine-hole course, designed by George Combe, and opened for play in 1894. At the turn of the 20th century, Willie Campbell extended the course to 18 holes. The famous Colt and Alison partnership remodelled the course in 1927.

There are many spectacular golf courses in Ireland and County Sligo is no exception. The views of the Darty Mountains and Benbulben, Sligo's limestone "Table Mountain", are simply beautiful. Drumcliffe Bay sweeps around the golf course. Its fine long sandy beaches, the Atlantic and the harbour are often in full panoramic view. The Ox Mountains – Knockalong the highest peak – add a further dimension to the already stunning vista.

In the same vein as the scenery, the course is a real joy. With dramatic undulations, raised plateau greens, high ground, low ground, cliffs, burns and dunes, County Sligo has it all. The back nine, especially the 11th to the 17th, played on the headland, are truly magnificent. The sheer individuality of holes and the varied terrain make County Sligo an absolute must-play golf course.

County Sligo is the home of the West of Ireland Amateur Championship and host to other important amateur events. It was here, in 1981, that Declan Branigan won the Irish Amateur Close Championship, becoming the first Irishman to win three major Irish amateur titles in the same year. Earlier that year, Branigan won the West (also at County Sligo) and the East (at County Louth).

DRUIDS GLEN GOLF RESORT
Newtownmountkennedy, Co. Wicklow, Ireland
Telephone: +353 (0) 1 287 3600

Average Reviewers' Score:

Website: www.druidsglen.ie
Architect: Pat Ruddy and Tom Craddock
Visitors: Book in advance

Reviewers' Comments

Only one word for this place – stunning... Take your camera, it's simply beautiful here and there is no doubt that this course is as good as some of the world's best inland tracks... Comparisons are being made to parts of Augusta - well, they are not wrong... An absolute beauty... The whole experience is not to be missed and right from the off, the staff treat you perfectly... New course but it looks perfect... It's great to see a new course following the general curvature of the land without the architect doing all that earth moving and mounding - everything is so natural here... Attention to detail is very high and it is a real joy to play golf here... Greens are some of the best I've putted on... The course seems to focus your mind to the extent that you concentrate on your game... Difficult and too tough from the back pegs for the average handicap golfer... Could play here hundreds of times without being bored... If you are in the Dublin area, don't pass this one by... Make sure you book in advance... Highly recommended - goes into my personal Top 5.

Druids Glen 57th

Druids Glen is the kaleidoscope of golf courses, for there is more colour here than at any other course in Ireland. With its colourful flora and the card-wrecking stretch of holes from the 12th to the 14th, called "Ireland's Amen Corner", it is no surprise that it is genuinely regarded as the Augusta National of Ireland.

Located in the heart of County Wicklow, to the south of Dublin, in a stunning, rolling, manicured landscape, Druids Glen feels more like a classy American Country Club than an Irish Golf Club. The course opened for play in 1995, designed by Pat Ruddy and Tom Craddock, and they immediately impressed the European Tour. The PGA selected the course to host the 1996 Irish Open and it remained here for the next three years. It's a course that Colin Montgomerie remembers fondly because he won the Irish Open here in 1996 and 1997, in the middle of Monty's domination of the European Order of Merit.

It's a unique golfing experience, derived from Ruddy and Craddock's inspired design. The ambience is distinguished and distinctly Irish, including an ancient druid altar behind the 12th green. The views are pretty pleasing too and the challenge is not insignificant, but if you can keep on the immaculate and generous fairways, scoring well will become a real possibility. This is target golf country, from the perfect fairway lie to a huge soft green where putting on the immaculate surface is an absolute joy. But don't be fooled by this, there are many varied challenges, not least the threatening water, which seems to be everywhere. If you're not on top of your game, it can be a brutal course.

After a strong start and a tough Amen Corner after the turn, Druids Glen closes in a blaze of glory. The 17th will put fear into all but the most confident golfer. It's a 203-yard par three to an island green – let's hope it's not too windy. The closing hole measures 450 yards and there's water all around the approach to the green.

There is no doubt that Druids Glen will remain etched in the memory for a long time. Make sure that you take enough golf balls with you.

HUNSTANTON GOLF CLUB
Golf Course Road, Old Hunstanton, Norfolk, PE36 6JQ
England
Telephone: +44 (0) 1485 532811

Average Reviewers' Score:

Website: www.club-noticeboard.co.uk/hunstanton
Architect: George Fernie, James Braid and James Sherlock
Visitors: Contact in advance – must be a golf club member – not weekends

Reviewers' Comments

Traditional links... Total entertainment... To use a football phrase, Hunstanton is definitely a game of two halves. After six holes I was wondering what all the fuss was about because the strong wind was at our back. After the turn, this course decided it was time to bite back and the prevailing wind made the journey to the clubhouse a totally different game... Have played here on numerous occasions and the greens are consistently fast and true... Greens second to none... Superb undulating fairways... Couple of blind shots... Fascinating traffic lights... Back at the clubhouse the bar food was excellent and the members and staff very friendly and welcoming... Very friendly club... The course is good honest fun.

Hunstanton 58th

Hunstanton is the ancestral home of the le Strange family. Hamon le Strange invested £30 to get the original nine holes ready for play; George Fernie was the architect. The club was founded in 1891 and Hamon became the inaugural club president. In 1907, James Braid revised the existing layout and extended the course to 18 holes, alterations that cost a total of £25! James Sherlock made further subtle modifications in the 1920s and little has changed since.

This natural course is a simple out and back affair, interrupted only briefly in the middle of the outward and inward nines by a few short holes that zigzag at right angles across the central dunes. The River Hun and the Wash frame this narrow strip of links land, but only a few glimpses of the sea are on offer from the course itself.

This is the premier golf course in East Anglia, just ahead of its nostalgic neighbour, Royal West Norfolk at Brancaster. But, when Darwin wrote about Hunstanton in his book, *The Golf Courses of the British Isles*, things were different: "Hunstanton is very amusing golf; it is more than that, for it is for the most part very good golf. Perhaps it is a little unfairly overshadowed in public estimation by its near neighbour Brancaster, which is altogether on a rather bigger and grander scale." Nevertheless, it's a connoisseur's golf course, jammed full of memorable quality golf holes. The members are quite rightly proud of the greens, they are tricky to read, fast, hard and true. The rippling fairways are tightly mown and gently undulating.

Two of the world's best lady golfers have played and won here at Hunstanton. In the year before the Great War, Cecil Leitch beat G Ravenscroft 2 and 1 to win the Ladies' British Amateur Championship and in 1921, the great Joyce Wethered beat J Stocker to win the English Ladies Close Amateur Championship. More recently, in 1972, Hunstanton hosted the Ladies' British Amateur Championship; when Mickey Walker went on to win, beating Claudine Rubin of France.

A feat of incalculable odds also occurred at Hunstanton. In 1974, the amateur Bob Taylor holed in one during a practice round for the Eastern Counties Foursomes. The following day in the actual competition he again holed in one. The very next day in the same competition, he once more holed in one. If a hole in one on three consecutive days is not enough, you'll be amazed to hear that it was achieved each time on the same hole, the 16th, a 191-yard par three!

This is a full-blown championship golf links; an absolute must-play for serious golfers. Make your score on the outward nine, the back nine is much more difficult, except for the par three 16th, a simple hole in one opportunity.

KILLARNEY GOLF & FISHING CLUB
Mahony's Point, Killarney, County Kerry, Ireland
Telephone: +353 (0) 64 31034

Average Reviewers' Score:

Website: www.killarney-golf.com
Architect: Eddie Hackett, Billy O'Sullivan and David Jones
Visitors: Contact in advance

Reviewers' Comments

Killeen is definitely the best of the three Killarney courses, but I'm left wondering what might have been had they left the original course intact… Fantastic scenery, and of course, the lakeside location is truly stunning, but if you take that away and focus on the course I'm not sure the Killeen is Top 100 material… I believe that the course is undergoing complete refurbishment and I hope that when it reopens it will be somewhat better than it was before… You certainly need a strong accurate game to score well on this course, otherwise the trees will stymie you… Killarney is not the cheapest… I'm personally a links lover, so parkland courses need to be exceptional to get my pulse racing and unfortunately Killeen comes up short… I can't wait to see what it's like when it reopens.

Killarney (Killeen)

There are three courses at the Killarney Golf & Fishing Club and the Killeen course is considered to be the best. Killarney is set in its own National Park within the famous Ring of Kerry. Here we have some of the most magical and enchanting scenery in Ireland, the Killeen course being set on the banks of Lough Leane, the largest freshwater lake in the southwest. The backcloth is the majestic Carrauntoohil, the highest mountain in Ireland, one of the many peaks of the Macgillycuddy's Reeks, and this is the most mountainous region in the Emerald Isle.

Golf at Killarney dates back to 1891, but the Killeen course is relatively young, opening for play in 1971. It was originally designed by Eddie Hackett and Billy O'Sullivan and updated in 1991 by David Jones ahead of the 1991 Irish Open, which was won by Nick Faldo. In 1992, the Irish Open returned to the Killeen course and once again Faldo triumphed.

Despite the proximity of the mountains, the Killeen is set on flat ground. The lake comes into play immediately and remains a hazard until the 5th hole, which turns inland. The course then plays in more traditional parkland surroundings until the 7th hole, which once again plays alongside the lake.

The tree-lined fairways appear narrower than they really are, especially from the back tees; keeping the ball in play is the order of the day. Scoring well will be a challenge for the very best golfers. The course is over 7,000 yards long from the back tees. There are three other tees available, so choose carefully to ensure the maximum enjoyment, but remember that everything is measured in metres here, so take at least one club more.

The fantastic experience at Killarney is made up from many factors – the setting is breathtaking, the conditioning of the course is first class, the holes are varied and exciting and, last but not least, the Irish welcome is warm and friendly. The Killeen course is currently undergoing refurbishment by Donald Steel and will be closed until June 2006.

ST ENODOC GOLF CLUB
Rock, Wadebridge, Cornwall, PL27 6LD, England
Telephone: +44 (0) 1208 862200

Average Reviewers' Score:

Website: None
Architect: James Braid
Visitors: Contact in advance – handicap certificate required

Reviewers' Comments

Probably the most varied and interesting course I've ever played… Great condition and fantastic coastal views… Some fantastic sea views all around with absolutely superb opening and closing holes… There are some cracking holes, a gorgeous par three, that bunker, the church hole… That bunker is simply the biggest I've ever seen…My favourite as usual was a short par four, the 4th, with out of bounds very close on the right and behind the green - a cracker… The holes around the church are a little disappointing compared to the rest of the course… The finishing holes are tremendous… Great 18th with an elevated tee down to an undulating fairway that finishes in front of the clubhouse… Well worth the green fee to play here… Even in March the course was in great condition… Beware - you will not get on without a handicap certificate… Oh to be a member here… Enjoy it!

Some Cornish people regard Cornwall not as a county of England, but a Celtic independent province. Not wishing to offend anybody we will simply say that Cornwall is a beautiful part of the British Isles, a place where the influence of the sea is everywhere. The golf course at St Enodoc is no exception. It's located at the royal sailing town of Rock, the links overlooking the Camel Estuary and the picturesque harbour of Padstow beyond. The Church course takes its name from the tiny 13th century place of worship that stands to the right of the 10th green. In the middle of the 19th century, a fierce storm completely covered the church in sand and it was eventually extricated in 1863.

Although St Enodoc Golf Club was founded in 1891, it didn't really become a good golf course until James Braid did a proper design job on it in 1907. In his 1910 book, *The Golf Courses of the British Isles*, Bernard Darwin wrote: "Cornwall has several pleasant courses…of these, St Enodoc is a course of wonderful natural possibilities". Braid returned to update St Enodoc in 1936 and today's layout hasn't changed much since.

St Enodoc is certainly a quixotic links, set amidst towering sand dunes clad with tufts of wild sea grasses. The fairways undulate and ripple just as if the sea had ebbed only moments ago. The terrain is entirely natural and dunes are so pronounced that you cannot help but feel humbled, the holes are varied and charming and finally, so much of the experience is memorable.

There are many great holes, but the 6th is a bit of a collector's item, a hole of absolute uniqueness, a blind drive followed by a blind mid-iron second shot which must carry over a confrontational sand dune called "Himalayas" that stands some 100 yards out, guarding the hidden green. Let's be honest, this is an enormous dune, worthy of its name, rising up over 75 feet high. Make sure you get your club selection right and that you strike the ball cleanly! The 10th is also a great hole, apparently one of Peter Alliss' favourites. It follows a natural ravine and requires a solid drive from an elevated tee across a valley to a lovely rippling fairway below. There is a hint of moorland to some of the holes, especially those surrounding the church, but this simply provides variation.

We could go on, but we wouldn't want to spoil all the other lovely surprises that are in store for you here at St Enodoc.

GULLANE GOLF CLUB
Gullane, East Lothian, EH31 2BB, Scotland
Telephone: +44 (0) 1620 842255

Average Reviewers' Score:

Website: www.gullanegolfclub.com
Architect: Unknown
Visitors: Book in advance

Reviewers' Comments

Stark, natural links course, very exposed so expect to get those cobwebs blown away... I couldn't get my head round the idea of a Top 20 Scottish links course rising and falling so high up Gullane Hill... Unique terrain, and at the high point of the course, the views are tremendous... There are some great holes, a real links fan's course with open and panoramic views... Some locals will tell you that No.2 is better but for me No.1 is by far the best... No.1 is overpriced and not as good as No.2... For the extra £20 it's worth including No.2... You'll love them both but I know which one I prefer... Fast greens and an abundance of newly riveted bunkers throughout... Excellent greens and difficult to read... The 'proper' clubhouse is only open to visitors playing No.1 and you need a jacket and tie for lunch... This, my golfing friends, is a golfing Mecca... It's a very enjoyable experience.

"Gullane Hill, with the sun shining and the wind blowing, the black clouds banked beyond the Forth, and just a glimpse in the distance of the mighty tracery of the Forth Bridge, is one of the most beautiful spots in the world," wrote Bernard Darwin in an article for Country Life called, *On Gullane Hill*, which was reprinted in his book, *Playing The Like*.

Gullane is a small town that lives and breathes golf; there are five superb golf courses in this locale, including the mighty Muirfield. The Gullane No.1 course was laid down in 1884 and is the most senior of a triumvirate of courses at this golf club. Records dating back to 1650 show golf being played over these links, though it is unclear who originally designed the No.1 course. Therefore until we can establish otherwise, we must put it down to Mother Nature.

Gullane is blessed with the most exquisite turf – winter rules are not needed here. If you hit the fairways, a perfect lie awaits, even in the depths of winter. The opening hole, cunningly called "First", is a relatively gentle short par four. The 2nd called "Windygate" begins the march up Gullane Hill. The 3rd is called "Racecourse", a short par five which plays along what was once an old 18th century racecourse and it continues to take you onwards and upwards, now at a canter, until you reach the 7th tee and the 200-foot summit of Gullane Hill.

The 360-degree views from the vantage point of the 7th tee are simply breathtaking. In the foreground, all around are the fluttering flags of Gullane, Muirfield and Luffness New. The Lammermuir Hills lie to the south, while the Firth of Forth wraps up the panorama to the north, west and east. And now, it's time for the 7th hole and its inviting downhill drive and the scurry home down Gullane Hill.

If you have read up to here and you haven't yet played Gullane No.1, it will come as no surprise to you that there is the requirement for varied uphill and downhill shot-making. This in itself is quite unusual for a links course and makes it all the more fascinating. Don't be misled into thinking that Gullane is a quirky old-fashioned affair; this is a high class golf course, host to many important competitions, including the Open Championship Final Qualifying.

To complete the Gullane experience, visit the club's fascinating museum, put together by past Gullane captain, Archie Baird. Archie is a golf historian and collector who wrote *Golf on Gullane Hill*.

WENTWORTH CLUB
Virginia Water, Surrey, GU25 4LS, England
Telephone: +44 (0) 1344 842201

Average Reviewers' Score:

Website: www.wentworthclub.com
Architect: Harry Colt
Visitors: Handicap certificate required - contact in advance - not at weekends

Reviewers' Comments

I'd rather play the East than slog round the West - it seems more natural and definitely prettier... Enjoyed the East recently - best way for me to describe it is that it is a mini version of the West... The East course lacks the fame of the West, but in its own right it's a little beauty... Definitely easier and more suited to the handicap golfer... Shorter than its illustrious counterpart but still as tight, just as pretty and a lot less busy... For me the East is not as good as the West... Fairly short in places - had many approaches less than a full wedge into the greens... Par threes are superb... It's hard to believe when you play it that there are two other courses so close by... Add the East to your list of courses to play as in its own right it's a memorable course sited in the beautiful leafy Wentworth estate... Don't rush to Wentworth and make straight for the West, this course is equally worth the money.

Wentworth (East)

The West is the course that everybody rushes to play, but the East is more enjoyable for the average player. It is also more sandy, intimate and charming. This was the first course Harry Colt built at Wentworth and it was born in 1924, two years earlier than its bigger and brasher younger brother.

The first unofficial match between the American and British/Irish professionals, "which was the begetter of the Ryder Cup," wrote Bernard Darwin in *Golf Between Two Wars*, took place on the East course in 1926, one year prior to the inauguration of the Ryder Cup. The match heralded a landslide victory for Great Britain and Ireland (GBI 13½, USA 1½). In the foursomes, Abe Mitchell and George Duncan beat Walter Hagen and Jim Barnes 9 and 8.

In terms of length, the East is relatively short, measuring 6,200 yards from the back tees, but it's an exceedingly pleasant walk on the springy turf and the lowly par of 68 will make playing to handicap a serious challenge. There's only one par five, but there are five par fours measuring in excess of 400 yards. It's the East's collection of five short holes that stand out; they are simply outstanding par threes. Only the delightful West Sussex course at Pulborough can perhaps claim to have a finer assemblage of short holes.

The East course occupies the central area of the Wentworth estate with the newer Edinburgh course now sitting on the eastern side. It is a very special and intimate experience, as many people will already know. The enclosed woodland setting confuses your sense of direction – where only one hole is generally in view and they seem to zigzag all over the place. It always comes as a pleasant surprise when we reach the halfway house where we can have a drink and draw a deep breath before we take on the 7th, an appealing, but challenging, long par three.

It's a shame the West overshadows the East but it's understandable that golfers want to play the championship course. There is obviously only one thing to do – get here early and play them both.

ROYAL WEST NORFOLK GOLF CLUB
Brancaster, Norfolk, PE31 8AX, England
Telephone: +44 (0) 1485 210223

Average Reviewers' Score:

Website: None
Architect: Holcombe Ingleby
Visitors: Contact in advance – restricted at weekends

Reviewers' Comments

This could be the course that time forgot... The epitome of golfing tradition... The soul of this course is hard to define but easy to feel. Magnificent... This course is unique within the British Isles with its 'tidal' entrance... One of the most peaceful and natural links courses that I have ever played... Course and clubhouse are locked in a timewarp and they have benefited immeasurably from this... The course is great too - right from the small walk across the beach to the first... You would never get bored playing this course... Deep, deep bunkers and shots over partially flooded tidal plains at the 8th and 9th... Smaller and greens more lush than expected but this is real golf at a real course that does not need changing to cope with modern equipment... Loved the par three 10th - would not look out of place on the Open circuit... The clubhouse is a labyrinth of old wood panelled corridors with 'dressing rooms' rather than changing rooms - real charming tradition... Very traditional but not stuffy... It's a real golfer's course... A complete delight... Do play Royal West Norfolk - I will again.

Royal West Norfolk

Founded in 1892, Royal West Norfolk is a classic links course. Nothing much has changed here for 100 years. Squeezed beautifully between Brancaster Bay and the salt marshes, Royal West Norfolk truly is a peaceful golf links, except when the wind blows and boy, is the wind bracing here!

Check the tide times before you plan your trip, the course plays on a narrow strip of links-land which gets cut off at high tide, turning it into an island. If you are lucky enough to play the course during high tide, you are in for a real treat; the downside is that you will need plenty of golf balls.

Prior to your game, grab a quick drink in the oak-panelled Smoke Room inside the Victorian clubhouse and check the wind speed on the gauge next to the bar. If you want to eat after your round, make sure you order before you play, otherwise you will only be offered a choice of delicious cakes.

"In the days of the gutty it was most emphatically a driver's course," wrote Bernard Darwin in his book, *The Golf Courses of the British Isles*, "since nobody could get over the ground without exceptional hitting. Even now, when the pampering Haskell has noticeably reduced its terrors, it is still a driver's course, in the sense that it is one on which one derives the maximum of sensual pleasure from opening one's shoulders for a wooden club shot."

Out on the course, you feel delightfully isolated; often all you can hear is the seductive sound of the wind, the seagulls, the clinking of stays and the flapping of boat sails. Essentially, the course is a traditional out and back links; huge sleeper-faced bunkers, fast greens and that beautiful links turf, a magical place to play golf. However, three-ball play is only allowed at the discretion of the Secretary and four-ball play is forbidden.

"Few things are more terrifying than the first hole at Brancaster on a cold, raw, windy morning," wrote Darwin, "when our wrists are stiff and our beautiful steely-shafted driver feels like a poker. There is a bunker – really a very big, deep bunker – right in front of our noses."

Beware the weather at Brancaster though; it can take you by surprise. The last time we played was a late spring day and we ignored the black clouds to the west. After all, we were on the 15th and the sun was shining. By the time we reached the 17th it was raining and by the 18th, we faced a full-blown tempest. When, soaked to the skin, we arrived to knowing smiles in the clubhouse, the wind gauge was fluctuating between 50 and 55mph.

ROYAL CINQUE PORTS GOLF CLUB
Golf Road, Deal, Kent, CT14 6RF, England
Telephone: +44 (0) 1304 374007

Average Reviewers' Score:

Website: www.royalcinqueports.com
Architect: Henry Hunter, James Braid and Sir Guy Campbell
Visitors: Contact in advance – Not Wed am or at weekend

Reviewers' Comments

When the wind is blowing, you'll not find a harder back nine anywhere this side of Scotland... Back nine is a real test with a number of 400-yard plus par fours, all playing into the prevailing wind... With a little TLC this course could host an Open... More interesting than its near neighbour, Royal St. George's... Needs something more if it's either going to get an Open or catch up with its more famous neighbour... Fantastic elevated tee positions ensure great views towards the undulating fairways... Serious rolling fairways and wonderful greens... Without doubt it's a great links course – the design is masterful and bunker placement cruel... Greens and the approaches to the greens are alarmingly undulating... Dozens of elephants have surely been buried here... Everything you'd expect from a classic British links golf course... Without some of the aesthetic charm of other courses... First impressions are that it's stark and cheerless... New tees have done wonders to several of the holes... What lets it down is the condition, it generally looks unloved... What a delight it was. Greens were in great shape and the overall condition was good... A fantastic golf course... All in all great fun!

Royal Cinque Ports

64th

Royal Cinque Ports, or Deal as it is more commonly known, was founded in February 1892. Henry Hunter, Deal's first greenkeeper was appointed shortly afterwards and three months later, a nine-hole course was ready for play. A second nine was soon added. The First and Second World Wars did their level best to obliterate the links, but James Braid restored the course and it reopened in 1919. Sir Guy Campbell later performed a similar role and once again, in 1946, the course reopened. Donald Steel is engaged in an advisory capacity at Royal Cinque Ports. His company is renowned for making sympathetic changes to traditional links courses.

Deal is an absolute brute of a links course. Its back nine, or rather the last seven holes, are relentless, invariably playing directly into the teeth of the prevailing southwesterly wind. The layout is stark and cheerless – only the sandhills and wild dune grasses provide this narrow out-and-back layout with any real definition. You can expect tight and hanging lies from the fairways, making stances awkward. Let's make no bones about it – this is a tough course. Make your score on the front nine, otherwise Deal can make even the very best golfers look like weekend duffers.

In 1909, J.H. Taylor one of the Great Triumvirate, proudly won the first Open ever played at Royal Cinque Ports. The Open returned to Deal in 1920 and made Walter Hagen look decidedly useless. In the lead-up to the Open, Hagen had boasted that he was unbeatable. He eventually ended up in 55th place! The real story behind the 1920 Open focused on two Brits, Abe Mitchell and George Duncan. It's a story that is beautifully documented by Bernard Darwin in his book *Golf Between Two Wars*. In those days, the Open was played over two days with 36 holes played each day. After the first day, Mitchell had a six shot lead over his closest pursuer; Duncan was even further adrift, a massive 13 strokes behind. The first round of the final day saw Duncan card a 71 while Mitchell could only manage an 84. Darwin wrote: "His lead had vanished like a puff of smoke". In the final afternoon round, Duncan consolidated his 71 with a 72, Mitchell could only manage a 76. Darwin's moral of this story is "that the man to back on the last day of a championship is he who gets his blow in first".

1920 was to be the last Open held at Deal, despite the fact that it was planned to return in 1949, but sadly the sea breached its defences and flooded the course.

We'll let Darwin draw things to a close: "Golf at Deal is very good indeed – fine, straight-ahead, long hitting golf wherein the fives are likely to be many and the fours few".

ROYAL CINQUE PORTS

NEFYN & DISTRICT GOLF CLUB
Morfa Nefyn, Pwllheli, Gwynedd, LL53 6DA, Wales
Telephone: +44 (0) 1758 720966

Average Reviewers' Score:

Website: www.nefyn-golf-club.com
Architect: J.H. Taylor and James Braid
Visitors: Contact in advance

Reviewers' Comments

You have to pinch yourself to believe it's really true. It's everything the previous writers have said and more... WOW. The club is friendly, the views are breathtaking and the golf is simply stunning... Fantastic clifftop course around the Lleyn peninsula... Scenery is something out of a film set, looking out over the bay to massive volcano like mountains climbing out of the sea... 2nd hole gives a true taste of what's to come - a drive out over the rocks and the sea to a fairway that snakes along the cliff edge. This is one of, if not the most spectacular tee shot in Wales... Some wonderful holes especially the first four – no, in fact, all of them... 13th, which involves a 200-yard shot across the cliffs, is alone worth the trip... 12th and 17th on the peninsula are awkward to play if there are holidaymakers walking... What an amazing place... It's just so different... Every golfer should treat themselves to a trip to Nefyn but make sure you book for the Old course... When you've finished the golf, the hospitality is second to none... Truly awesome, unique, spectacular and the most memorable course I've ever played.

Nefyn is dramatically located on the clifftops at the foot of the Porthdinllaen headland, a tiny promontory that juts out from the Lleyn Peninsula into the Irish Sea. In terms of sheer exhilaration, this is Wales's equivalent of Ireland's Old Head of Kinsale. This is literally golf on the edge of the world and it makes the adrenaline pump.

Nefyn and District Golf Club was founded in 1907, originally as a nine-hole course and in 1912, it was extended to 18 holes. Two of the great triumvirate, J.H. Taylor and James Braid were commissioned in 1933 to add a further nine and to revise the existing course.

Today's layout at Nefyn is extremely unusual because only 26 holes are now in play. We have a feeling that one of the holes fell into the sea. The course now comprises 10 outward holes and two separate inward 8 holes. They call the two courses the Old and the New. This strange configuration makes it exceedingly difficult to say which layout is in the Top 100. There is certainly a lack of clarity. Either way, it doesn't really matter – both courses are fantastic in our view.

There are only a few seaside courses where you can see the sea from every hole, but you sure can at Nefyn. Not only is the sea in view, but also on a clear day, you can spot peaks of the Wicklow Mountains across the Irish Sea. The opening hole takes you away from the clubhouse to a series of clifftop holes on the edge of the headland. There's heather, blind drives, strategically placed pot bunkers and thick rough to contend with.

For us, the Old course is the one. The back eight holes play along the peninsular, providing spectacular views across the cliffs and the bay. After the par five 12th, you'll find a footpath down to the Ty Coch Inn, located on the beach at Porthdinllaen. A quick beer here on the pub's famous wall, with the soothing sound of the sea and the glorious view across the bay to Mount Snowdon, will set you up nicely for the closing six holes.

RYE GOLF CLUB
Camber, Rye, East Sussex, TN31 7QS, England
Telephone: +44 (0) 1797 225241

Average Reviewers' Score:

Website: None
Architect: Harry Colt, Tom Simpson and Sir Guy Campbell
Visitors: By invitation only

Reviewers' Comments

Rye is a 'quirky' little links course and it definitely has the feel of a walk back in time... Old fashioned links as it was meant to be... Tough to get on, but it's worth persevering because it's a joy to play... Combination of rock hard undulating fairways and wispy rough ensures the driver stays in the bag most of the day... Super slick greens and in great condition throughout... Some of the fairways are pencil thin, especially on the dune tops... The 4th is a fantastic 400+ yard par four with a 'table-top' fairway and a WW2 bunker overlooking the green... Traditional through and through, but somewhat spoilt at the turn with holes 10 and 11 which are more parkland-like and 17 which is a nothing hole... 11 is a hole that's a little out of character with the rest of the course, but strong holes like 17 (long par three) and 18 (long par four) underlay its tough under-belly... It's a pity that it's not a little longer but I'm sure that the members are happy with things just the way they are... A wonderful experience and well worth a visit... An amazing course... What lucky, lucky members.

"Rye - and there are surely few pleasanter places to get to," wrote Bernard Darwin in *The Golf Courses of the British Isles*. "It looks singularly charming as the train comes sliding in on a long curve, with the sullen flat marshes on the left and the tall cliff on the right, while straight on in front are the red roofs of the town huddled round the old church. We have only a few yards to walk along a narrow little street; then we twist round to the right up a steep little hill and under the Land Gate and we are at the Dormy House, old and red and overgrown with creepers."

So, we've arrived at Rye, but will we get a game? Well, it's so very private that it is exceedingly difficult to secure a tee time. It is easier to get a game on the Old course at St Andrews. You never know your luck. Or, as James W. Finegan wrote in *All Courses Great and Small*: "...with the planets properly aligned, you may just find yourself on the 1st tee, under the warning eye of the clubhouse clock, ready to embark on the splendid adventure."

Rye was founded in 1894 and a young 25-year-old Harry Colt laid out the course - surely one of the most impressive debut designs in history. Colt later became Rye's secretary. Today's layout bears the hallmark of Tom Simpson and Sir Guy Campbell, though the Second World War almost obliterated the links and a flying bomb almost destroyed the clubhouse. But, thanks to the faithful few, Rye rose up like a phoenix.

"The two great features of golf at Rye are the uniformly fiendish behaviour of the wind and the fascinating variety of the stances," wrote Darwin. "If you suffer from a lack of balance," wrote Patric Dickinson in *A Round of Golf Courses*, "this is not the course for you, it is seldom that you get a flat stance, this is one of Rye's real tests. The fairways nearly always undulate and you will find you must play a full shot from the side of a miniature down and one foot on a level with your nose."

With a measly par of 68, and a course that measures over 6,300 yards, it has to be one of the toughest courses in the British Isles. The one and only par five hits us straight away and it comes too early in the round to take too much advantage. The five short holes are outstanding but brutal, with alarmingly elusive elevated greens. The remaining twelve par fours are there for the taking - well, three of them at least. Nine others, yes nine, measure more than 400 yards in length.

In 1954, following the death of his wife, Darwin moved into the Dormy House at Rye. On the 18th October, 1961, in the room overlooking Land Gate (Rye's medieval entrance), he died, aged 85. His leather armchair now rests close to the window of the men's bar.

DOONBEG GOLF CLUB
Doonbeg, Co. Clare, Ireland
Telephone: +353 (0) 65 905 5246

Average Reviewers' Score:

Website: www.doonbeggolfclub.com
Architect: Greg Norman
Visitors: Welcome, with restrictions, contact in advance

Reviewers' Comments

Having played all but a couple of the links courses in the UK & Ireland, I have a fair number of courses to make comparison. Doonbeg is right up with the leaders - a stunning start, some classic holes… You are taken by buggy to the practice ground where logoed balls are waiting for you… Great hospitality, which definitely has to be noted… It soon became clear that Greg Norman knew what he was doing… Incredibly challenging course… Great layout with some wonderful holes - the 1st and 14th come immediately to mind… 14th 111 yards off the back tees – eight tee shots and no-one hit the green… A cliché but a must for everyone who loves links courses… Really high-class… The course itself is tremendous… Overall a great course with some great holes… Bit pricey but very friendly… By the way, I am going back there in June!

Doonbeg

The name Doonbeg is derived from 'Dun Beag', which, roughly translated, means small fort. So it's no surprise that this pretty seaside village grew up beside a castle, which was built in the 16th century for the Earl of Thomond. You'll find Doonbeg 30 minutes or so due west of Shannon airport. Just keep going until you reach the Atlantic. You can't miss the golf course, just look out for the mountainous dunes and keep your eyes peeled and somewhere around these spectacular 100ft high sandhills, you might get a glimpse of the Great White Shark. Because this is the course that Greg Norman built - his one and only architectural ensemble in the whole of the British Isles.

Apparently Norman made 23 visits to this amazing piece of links-land, which curves and tumbles for a mile and a half around the crescent-shaped Doughmore Bay. "When I first looked at this site, I thought I was the luckiest designer in the world," Norman said. "If I spent the rest of my life building courses, I don't think I'd find a comparable site anywhere." Norman's design is totally in tune with nature - 14 greens and 12 fairways were simply mown - not much earth moved here for Greg. The look and feel of the layout is old-fashioned and the routing follows an out-and-back style, synonymous with traditional links architecture. Not bad for a course which opened on July 9, 2002, marked by an exhibition match between Padraig Harrington and the Great White Shark.

According to legend, officers of the Scottish Black Watch Regiment planned to turn these dunes into a golf course in the early 1890s, but they settled on Lahinch because it's located closer to the railway station. When Norman got his hands on this land a century or so later, he said: "I'm not going to Americanise this golf course - not one single foreign blade of grass". He remained true to his word.

The layout is unusual in that it has a combination of five par threes and five par fives - the par 72 course measures 6,885 yards from the back tees. The signature hole is probably the 14th, a par three and one of the most sensational short holes in Ireland, although there are many memorable holes on this remarkable course. The 14th measures a mere 111 yards, but hitting the green is easier said than done because there are numerous distractions... the Atlantic stretches out beyond the green and the wind will dictate your club selection. Expect to take anything from a sand wedge to a 3 iron and hope for the best.

The Doonbeg project is believed to be the largest single investment in this part of Ireland and this amazing golf course has a magnetic appeal for thousands of golfers. It's a priceless jewel between Lahinch and Ballybunion and one that simply must be played.

BURNHAM & BERROW GOLF CLUB
St. Christopher's Way, Burnham-on-Sea, Somerset
TA8 2PE, England
Telephone: +44 (0) 1278 785760

Average Reviewers' Score:

Website: www.burnhamandberrowgolfclub.co.uk
Architect: Herbert Fowler, Hugh Alison, Harold Hilton, Dr Alister MacKenzie & Harry Colt.
Visitors: Handicap certificate required – contact in advance

Reviewers' Comments

Burnham is perhaps the most underrated course in England... A cracking course, a little out of the way but well worth stopping off for... It has all the elements of classic golf – true greens, a great set of short holes, blind shots and plenty of dunes... The greens when I played were unbelievable - quick, true and tricky, and all this in spring... Played Burnham in early March and the greens were simply superb, as good as the very best greens in summer... There are a few great holes in the opening nine with a couple less so at the turn, but overall the quality shows through... There are several holes, which any club would love to claim... The holes in the dunes are amazing... Friendly clubhouse to boot... This course made our trip really special.

Burnham & Berrow

"Hole succeeds hole, and still the endless range of hills goes on, and from the summit of each one we get the most lovely views, with the Cheddar Gorge in the distance; to the left the Bristol Channel, with the islands of Steep Home and Flat Home and an expanse of dim country on the other side. When we turn for home at the ninth, we see the sandhills stretching tumultuously away towards Weston, with their range of fantastic shapes and occasionally a narrow, meandering ribbon of turf in between." Burnham in "Somersetshire" was a favourite course of Bernard Darwin, and so it seems fitting to allow him the introduction.

The club was founded in 1890 and soon after, they hired a youngster called J.H. Taylor. His task was to be the club's first professional and keeper of the greens. One of the great triumvirate, Taylor went on to win the Open Championship five times. It is unclear who originally designed the links, but according to the book by Phillip Richards, entitled *Between the Church and the Lighthouse*: "The development of the course took thirty years to reach today's shape and just about every one of the leading course designers during that period had an input into the course architecture. Herbert Fowler and Hugh Alison were members of Burnham and both had an important part to play in improving the links. So to a lesser extent did Harold Hilton and Dr. Alister MacKenzie but the shape of today's course is mainly due to Harry Colt." There is a church in the middle of the course and that in itself is unusual. Consequently, over the years, changes have been made to the layout to ensure that the faithful congregation does not get injured by wayward shots; additionally, some of the blind drives have been designed out.

Burnham is a traditional out-and-back links course and as per Darwin's introduction, taken from his 1910 book, *The Golf Courses of the British Isles*, Burnham is "ringed round with sandhills", gigantic ones too. It's a challenging layout with the tumbling fairways laid out in narrow valleys, protected by deep pot-bunkers and thick rough. The greens are fairly small, requiring precision approach shots and once you are on the putting surface, the fun really begins. Burnham's undulating, slick greens are amongst the very best in the British Isles.

There are many notable and varied holes, with a strong collection of par threes. The first six holes are especially good and the back nine is magnificent. Burnham closes with a classic 18th, one of the best finishing holes in golf, a dogleg left over dunes and an intimidating long second shot across another ridge of dunes towards a green protected by deep threatening pot-bunkers.

Burnham has played host to many important amateur championships over the years and the course is regularly used for Open Championship qualification. A round is an absolute must for links purists and comparatively good value too for such a fantastic course in these times of escalating green fees.

TENBY GOLF CLUB
The Burrows, Tenby, Pembrokeshire, SA70 7NP, Wales
Telephone: +44 (0) 1834 842978

Average Reviewers' Score:

Website: www.tenbygolf.co.uk
Architect: James Braid
Visitors: Contact in advance

Reviewers' Comments

An enjoyable but unusual course, which is a real pleasure to play... Terrific course and a good test... Tenby is a classic links course... In my opinion this links is neither charming nor classic... There are too many holes and greens on top of each other... Other parts of the course are memorable for the right reasons... Ideally suited to short, straight hitters... As tough an opening four as I have come across... The course is a test... Let down a little by only having a couple of sea views, but with a good variety of holes. You cannot relax for one minute... Holes on the other side of the railway are not in keeping with the others... 12 and 17 - both par threes - are good holes and the last hole is great from the back tees but your approach to the green is blind, even if you hit 300 yards down the middle... It's a relatively weak finish... A little bit out of the way, but worth every effort to get there... Feel this course is very overrated... Great clubhouse feel and genuinely warm Welsh welcome... It's worth playing if in the area.

Tenby

Tenby is the oldest course in Wales, established in 1888, originally as a 9-holer. James Braid was commissioned to extend the course; 18 holes opened for play in 1907.

This charming, classic links is situated on the beautiful Pembrokeshire coast, affording superb views across to one of Britain's most fascinating and holiest of islands. Caldey Island has experienced more than one thousand years of Cistercian prayer. A pleasant summer boat trip from Tenby harbour will take you to the island where you will receive a warm welcome from the various orders of monks.

It is here you will find links golf at its most natural. There is nothing modern about Tenby, but it's an amazing experience. Many shots are blind, the contoured greens are hard and fast, and there are snaking hog's back fairways, dense gorse, cruel pot bunkers and rugged dunes. It's not a long course by today's standards at a little over 6,300 yards, but the opening four holes (three of which are over 400 yards long) will challenge the very best golfers.

It would be easy to dismiss it as a holiday golf course or as unfair, eccentric or quirky. We think it's sensational; playing here is always a truly memorable experience and you'll probably end up playing shots from positions you've never faced before. What an absolute delight.

Don't tell too many people, but the green fee is tremendous value too, and what's more, you'll be given a very warm Welsh welcome.

ALWOODLEY GOLF CLUB
Wigton Lane, Leeds, Yorkshire, LS17 8SA, England
Telephone: +44 (0) 113 268 1680

Average Reviewers' Score:

Website: www.alwoodley.co.uk
Architect: Alister MacKenzie and Harry Colt
Visitors: Contact secretary in advance

Reviewers' Comments

Alwoodley can be summed up in one word – fantastic… A top quality course, which is playable all year round… Only Ganton can better this course in Yorkshire… Probably gives Ganton a run for its money… It's certainly one of the best courses I've played in Yorkshire… It's a MacKenzie classic… Distances are tough to judge, even with a yardage chart… It's a tough no-frills heathland/moorland test and it's always a delight to play here… A golfer's golf course that will test the best and you'll need to have your swing intact if you plan to score well… It's very much a member's club but it's accessible and well worth the green fee… The clubhouse is very unusual – a similar design to that at Ballyliffin and a really great atmosphere inside… Simply tremendous and I can't wait to return to try and improve on my last feeble score… If I lived in or around Leeds, this is where I'd want to play… Stunning.

Alwoodley

Alwoodley is certainly one of the finest and most subtle inland courses in the British Isles, located in a secluded spot. In many ways, it is reminiscent of Woodhall Spa's Hotchkin course, which is very high praise indeed.

Founded in 1907, Alwoodley is the cream of a cluster of excellent courses stretching across the moors just north of Leeds. The great Alister MacKenzie (a doctor at the time) joined forces with the already renowned architect, Harry Colt, to fashion Alwoodley. This was Dr MacKenzie's first dabble with golf course design. Clearly inspired, he went on to become a full time golf course architect and later went on to design the great Augusta National, home of the Masters.

The course is a combination of heathland and moorland with rippling fairways and fine, crisp, springy turf. There is plenty of heather and gorse, which provides glorious seasonal colour and punishes the wayward shot. There are few trees, other than the occasional cluster of pines and silver birches on this glorious, windswept heath.

Essentially an out and back course, the front nine is generally regarded as the easier of the two nines (the only two par fives are on the outward nine). The back nine invariably plays into the prevailing winds coming off the Yorkshire moors.

Alwoodley possesses some great and supremely challenging holes and the 3rd is typical. It's a very subtle straight par five measuring 510 yards and on the surface, it appears open and devoid of definition. The only visible hazard, apart from the rough on the left and the heather on the right, is a lonesome bunker on the left-hand side of the fairway, some 200 yards from the tee. Find the fairway and you might be tempted to go for the green in two, but you'll need to play your approach towards the right-hand side of the green because it slopes steeply from right to left. We also love the 17th hole, an excellent driving hole if you can avoid the out-of-bounds on the left. It's a 434-yard par four where a reasonable drive will leave a blind approach to a hidden green nestling some 30 feet below.

Make sure that you bring your full compliment of golf clubs. It is likely that this hard but fair course will force you to use every club in the bag. Alwoodley has played host to many important amateur events over the years and it regularly tests the pros when the course is used as a Regional Qualifier for the Open.

SAUNTON GOLF CLUB
Braunton, North Devon, EX33 1LG, England
Telephone: +44 (0) 1271 812436

Average Reviewers' Score:

Website: www.sauntongolf.co.uk
Architect: Frank Pennink
Visitors: Book in advance – handicap certificate required

Reviewers' Comments
Saunton is the perfect place for a full day of golf, it's a fantastic club and I doubt if a day here could be beaten anywhere in England... Not quite up to the standard of the truly fantastic East course... The wild and rugged sand dune setting make this an inspirational place to play golf... From an interest perspective, I think the West has an edge over the East... It's not of championship length, but it has everything going for it and it's an exacting test of golf... The West has some classic and memorable holes and it will test the best golfers just as much as its big brother, the East... Don't expect to play to handicap first time round... There are plenty of nuances here... With two courses of this quality, Saunton should be at the top of any serious golfer's must-play list... The West is a wonderful classic links... It's fabulous and a must for links lovers.

Saunton (West)

Saunton is located on the beautiful unspoilt North Devon coast. On the edge of Bideford Bay and the estuary of the River Taw, lie the mountainous Braunton Burrows – one of the largest systems of sand dunes in England.

The West is the second course at Saunton and was originally laid out in the mid-1930s. The land was used as a training ground during the Second World War and it lay dormant for over 40 years. Frank Pennink brought the West back to life and the course opened for play in 1975.

It's shorter than its older sister – the East – but, nonetheless, the West represents a fine test, measuring 6,403 yards from the medal tees. The West challenges the very best golfers, playing host to a number of County Championships and the EGU Seniors Championship. It's a worthy understudy to the East, requiring accuracy from the tee. Both courses at Saunton have par set at 71, but the configuration of holes on the West's inward nine is unusual. Three back-to-back par fours in the middle and three par threes and three par fives interspersed at the beginning, and then again, at the end.

A number of narrow streams (if we were in Scotland, we'd call them burns) come into play and many of the holes feature doglegs. Apart from the opening hole, which plays directly through towering dunes, the rest of the course plays over pleasant undulating links land, where the dunes are far less imposing.

Possessing some of the best putting greens in England, the West is an excellent course. But alongside the mighty East, the West will always play second fiddle but always in perfect harmony.

WEST SUSSEX GOLF CLUB
Golf Club Lane, Wiggonholt, Pulborough, West Sussex
RH20 2EN, England
Telephone: +44 (0) 1798 872426

Average Reviewers' Score:

Website: www.westsussexgolf.co.uk
Architect: Sir Guy Campbell and Major C.K. Hutchinson
Visitors: Contact in advance – Not Fri Sat or Sun

Reviewers' Comments

Totally beautiful, traditional and a thoroughly enjoyable test of golf… West Sussex is quite beautiful and there's nothing wrong with the course, just the fact that the club imposes playing restrictions – it's a "two ball club" and visitors are expected to play singles or foursomes… What happens if you're a group of three visitors? I thoroughly enjoyed my round on the pure heathland layout… It's hard to imagine a better course… If only they could find another 300-400 yards then they would have a fine Championship layout… Its difficulty definitely belies the Par 68 on the scorecard… What it lacks in length is more than made up for by strategic placement of heather and bunkers (especially on the doglegs)… I was impressed by the renowned 6th but also long par three 12th… The course was well presented… The par threes are brilliant and the course has a really strong finish… Only hole, which I thought was 'lacking something', was the 1st which is a 'soft' opening hole… Keep your eyes open for the gliders overhead… A classic heathland course… On a par with St George's Hill… One of the best, if not the best heathland course in the land.

West Sussex 72nd

West Sussex is one of our favourite inland courses. It is sheer delight to play golf on this charming sandy outcrop of heathland. The course occupies a priceless, stunning, undulating site on the northern edge of the South Downs.

In the scheme of things, West Sussex is a relative youngster, dating back to 1930. Commander G.W. Hillyard, who moved down to Sussex from Leicestershire, originally discovered the site. Sir Guy Campbell and Major C.K. Hutchinson designed the course; these two architects created one of the most natural and aesthetically pleasing golf courses in England.

On the surface of it, West Sussex is a short course, measuring 6,200 yards from the back tees. The first hole, a short par five, is the only easy birdie opportunity. After that, you'll have to negotiate seven par fours measuring over 400 yards. You will do very well to play to your handicap and it's unlikely that you will get the impression that the course is short.

Clearly, this isn't a championship golf course but it will provide a challenging and thought-provoking round for the very best golfers whilst remaining enjoyable for the higher handicapper. The holes wind their way through enchanting woodland, with oak, silver birch and pine providing a pretty backdrop and the heather and the cunning bunkering providing the definition. The colours, especially in autumn are breathtaking.

Each hole demands thought and holds attention. There is a great deal of variation to the holes and many are memorable. There isn't a signature hole as such, but we especially like the 6th, a 224-yard downhill par three with a pond lurking 40 yards in front of the green. To make matters worse, the whole area of pond is out-of-bounds.

In *Golf Between Two Wars*, Bernard Darwin wrote the following: "The day on which to see Pulborough, if not to play our best on it, is one when the wind is blowing hard, for the sand is wafted in great puffs, like white clouds across the course, so that we can scarcely believe that the sea is not round the corner... it is a little sandy jewel set in the Sussex clay... What more can anyone desire?"

MARRIOTT ST. PIERRE HOTEL AND COUNTRY CLUB
St. Pierre Park, Chepstow, Monmouthshire
NP16 6YA, Wales
Telephone: +44 (0) 1291 625261

Average Reviewers' Score:

Website: www.marriott.co.uk
Architect: C.K. Cotton
Visitors: Welcome. Book in advance

Reviewers' Comments

The Old Course is fantastic... It's a cracker but very long and tough and oh so difficult to make a decent score... Manicured condition each time I played and some of the best greens around... The greens when I played were fabulous, which is saying something as every time I go it seems to rain... It's a strategic course and you need to be in the right position off the tee to have any chance of getting near the pins... In a nutshell, this is a real golfer's course and you can see why the pros have been tested here... 1st and 9th on the right hand side of the driveway are good holes... The drive from the elevated 7th is tremendous... 15th and 17th are made by their greens which back out into the lake... The 18th is, in my opinion, one of the most challenging closing holes in British golf... They have another course here called the Mathern but nearby Rolls of Monmouth is a much better bet... You can now get some great stay and play deals, so it's not as expensive as it used to be... Well worth shopping around and well worth playing the Old course.

St Pierre (Old)

Just across the Severn Bridge is the resort of St Pierre, set in 400 acres of rolling South Wales countryside. The graceful 14th century manor house doubles up as an impressive clubhouse and a comfortable hotel. For safekeeping, the Crown Jewels were kept in the manor house during the Battle of Agincourt. The hotel sits alongside the St Pierre church, which dates back to Norman times. It's a majestic setting.

The Old course, which occupies a mature, former deer park, opened for play in 1962, and was designed by C.K. Cotton. It was here, in the 1980 British Masters, that Bernhard Langer became the first German to win a major tournament. In total, St Pierre hosted the British Masters no fewer than eight times. Amongst the winners were Tony Jacklin, Bernard Gallacher and Greg Norman. Norman found the putting surface on the 362-yard 10th with a 3-wood on his way to victory in 1982. Ian Woosnam, "Woosie", was St Pierre's last Masters' champion, claiming the title in 1983.

Huge, mature sentry trees lie in wait to stymie the errant tee shot and a lake covering more than ten acres poaches many golf balls. The 6,750-yard par 71 layout is certainly no pushover – accurate positioning from the tees will pay dividends. Without doubt, the most famous and dramatic hole on the Old course is the 18th – a 230-yard par three – which, unusually, is completely devoid of trees. A solid tee shot across the edge of the lake is required. The elevated tee provides an ideal vantage point to celebrate glory... or to commiserate as the ball finds dry land or a watery grave.

The amateur Arwyn Griffiths will certainly remember the infamous closing hole at St Pierre. He walked on to the tee requiring a par three for an incredible course record gross 63. Sadly, he putted out, having taken eleven strokes. The good news was that his score of 71 was good enough to win the event.

St Pierre is a quality resort, now owned by Marriott. The shorter second course, the Mathern, is pleasantly challenging and complements the Old admirably. A visit to St Pierre will certainly be memorable, especially if you see the ghosts. Allegedly, a grey lady spectre and the ghost of the "laughing gardener" haunt St Pierre. The gardener apparently walks through the gate, into the walled garden and then disappears into the churchyard, roaring with laughter all the way.

TRALEE GOLF CLUB
West Barrow, Ardfert, Tralee, Co. Kerry, Ireland
Telephone: +353 (0) 66 713 6379

Average Reviewers' Score:

Website: www.traleegolfclub.com
Architect: Arnold Palmer
Visitors: Handicap certificate required – contact in advance

Reviewers' Comments

Perhaps the least prominent of the southwest Ireland courses, but probably my favourite... Tralee is a good links golf course set in a most spectacular setting.... The scenery is a whisker below Pebble Beach with tremendous views of the ocean and beach below... As enjoyable as Ballybunion, Waterville and Doonbeg, which we played during the same trip... Mr Palmer appears to have made the best use of a very natural piece of land adding a lovely dash of green placement to keep all golfers on their toes... Irish golfers rate this course, which for me says something... Fabulous back nine... There are some good holes especially 2, 3, 8, 11, 12 and 17... And so, so beautiful is the beach that runs along the edge of the course... The holes are varied... Excellent greens and a friendly place to boot... Great hospitality too... Be sure to put Tralee on your list... I will return on a sunny day...definitely!

Tralee 74th

"I have never come across a piece of land so ideally suited for the building of a golf course," said Arnold Palmer. Tralee was his first Irish endeavour and it opened in 1984; it's a rugged and exhilarating creation. Now, let's be honest, Kerry is a very special county, the 'Lake District' of Ireland, an unspoilt, quiet and romantic place. Surely anybody could design a golf course in these surroundings? Well, first of all we might need to remind ourselves that Palmer wasn't exactly a run-of-the-mill golfer and when he turned his attention to design, he always wanted to choreograph a links course in Ireland. When the opportunity arose, he wasn't going to mess it up, was he?

Palmer has designed a course that will stimulate the senses every bit as much as the enchanting and breathtaking scenery. According to folklore, Palmer created the first nine and Mother Nature did the rest. The front nine plays across fairly level links land, but the majority of the holes hug the coastline and the ground is elevated, affording magnificent views from the cliff top across Tralee Bay to the Atlantic Ocean beyond. The back nine plays through mountainous dunes with fearsome carries across ravines to plateau greens.

The combination and variety of the holes make the entire experience captivating and exciting. There are only a few courses that grab your attention from the first tee shot, keeping hold of it until the very last putt drops. The links at Tralee is one of those few captivating courses. There are so many great holes that it is almost impossible to single one out, although the 3rd, called "The Castle", is considered to be the signature hole, a par three measuring almost 200 yards from the back tees. Scenically, it is glorious and reminiscent of the 7th at Pebble Beach. Take a line on the ruined castle which stands sentry to the left and behind the green – anything hit to the right of this green will be eaten by the rocks and the sea. The 17th is called "Ryan's Daughter" because the landscape was dramatically filmed in the award-winning movie. It will stick in the memory for a very long time; an elevated tee shot on this 355-yard par four must carry across a ravine to a craggy fairway, leaving an approach shot to a tiny raised tabletop green.

We always say that the measure of a good golf course is that the holes stay in the memory forever. There are so many memorable holes at Tralee that you might need to throw away some lesser memories from other courses to make room for the experience.

MACHRIE GOLF LINKS
Port Ellen, Isle of Islay, PA42 7AT, Scotland
Telephone: +44 (0) 1496 302310

Average Reviewers' Score:

Website: www.machrie.com
Architect: Willie Campbell and Donald Steel
Visitors: Welcome - no restrictions

Reviewers' Comments

It's hard to put the experience into words... The island is magical and the people are so courteous and genuinely friendly... Flew in and we were collected and dropped back off at the airport by hotel staff who could not have been more helpful... I was the only player on the course in a gale, and began by wondering how many balls I might need... I managed quite well, and enjoyed the solitude, and isolation... We battled against the elements to savour a fantastic old-fashioned course, which has many elements of Cruden Bay and Prestwick... Blind shots galore, imaginative shots being called for... Stay on the line of the marker posts, you won't go far wrong... Holes 7, 8 & 9, which run alongside Laggan Bay, are tremendous... Only weak hole was the nondescript par three 10th... This is uncomplicated golf from a bygone era when it was *fun* to play... Putting surfaces are not the biggest... Silky smooth greens... Not a long course but well worth a visit... They have a wonderful menu with many traditional Scottish items, all washed down with a dram or two of their famed Islay malt whisky... You could easily be in your perfect heaven.

Machrie 75th

Machrie is a wonderfully nostalgic links course located on the beautiful Hebridean island of Islay, famous for its distilleries and the fabulous rich and "peaty" single malt whisky, such as Laphroaig and Bruichladdich.

This is the remotest of the remote links courses, laid out in 1891 by Willie Campbell. Donald Steel was brought in to make minor modifications to the layout in the late 1970s; thankfully, Steel has retained much of the charm and surprise of Campbell's original design, including the numerous blind shots.

In 1901, James Braid overcame his fear of the sea to compete in the Islay Open. The other two members of the "Great Triumvirate", John H Taylor and Harry Vardon, were also there, attracted by £100, the highest prize money of that time. At the last hole, Braid had a putt to share the prize money with Taylor. According to a report in The Scotsman, Braid's putt was deflected from "dropping" in the hole by a piece of sheep dung!

The Machrie is laid out across magnificent terrain, dominated by varied and imposing sand dunes. On a clear day, the views across Laggan Bay from the elevated parts of the course are simply breathtaking.

The most surprising aspect of the layout is that the greens are in all sorts of locations – some are raised and some are in sunken punchbowls. The amazing position of the greens has virtually negated the need for bunkers and there are very few sand traps. The sum of this variation makes for an enjoyable, challenging and interesting round of golf. If you do get the chance, take the opportunity to play the course more than once.

Pray for the weather to be kind. Although Islay is in the Gulf Stream, the weather can be horrible and, on occasions, the course can quickly become totally unplayable. When the rain is falling sideways, we recommend a large single malt whisky next to a warming peat fire, or a trip to the famous Bowmore distillery.

WISLEY GOLF CLUB
Mill Lane, Ripley, Surrey, GU23 6QU, England
Telephone: +44 (0) 1438 211022

Average Reviewers' Score:

Website: www.wisleygc.com
Architect: Robert Trent Jones Jnr.
Visitors: Members and their guests only

Reviewers' Comments

I can remember playing here as though it was yesterday... The conditioning was simply stunning and I have yet to play a course in the UK that matches the Wisley for quality... Will probably be a fair job to get a game as you need to play with a member but whatever it takes I would say it's worth doing as this is a glorious golf venue... Most noticeable for me was the absolute definition between the cuts of grass, and the rough was penal... I couldn't personally split the three nines, except in character... It's a bit too Americanised for my liking... There's a lot of water, which comes into play so often and with a higher than normal degree of difficulty... It's a tough track... My favourite holes are the 3rd on the Garden and the 9th on the Mill... Customer service is so high that you have a feeling of being in another world... The thing that sticks in my mind the most was the attentive but understated service... This is a quality venue and if you get the chance to play it, even as a second reserve, jump at it.

Wisley (Garden & Mill)

Concealed behind the Royal Horticultural Society's gardens at Wisley lies one of the most delightful private members' clubs in the British Isles. There is a strong partnership between the RHS and the Wisley Golf Club and it's apparent from the moment you arrive at this prestigious venue. The RHS provides advice and guidance to the Golf Club on shrubs and flowers and, in turn, the Golf Club helps the RHS with turf grass issues. It's a beautiful partnership.

With 27 secluded holes, set out across more than 200 acres, the Wisley is a big golf course. It opened for play in 1991, the first course in the UK to be designed by Robert Trent Jones Jnr. The Trent Jones design philosophy is to preserve the natural beauty of the site while creating a playable course rich with strategic variety. His objectives have been fully met, with many holes offering a wide selection of risk and reward choices, thanks to extensive landscaping.

A straw poll across the full complement of 700 members at the Wisley will reveal that the jury is out in terms of which of the three nine-hole loops is best (Church, Mill or Garden). We, too, are unsure which combination makes the best collection of 18 holes, but we can say that each nine is of equal standard, although subtly different in character. A prolific number of water hazards and bunkers are scattered throughout the 27 holes and there's more water in play here than at just about any other course in the British Isles – the River Wey and strategically-placed lakes come into play on no fewer than eight of the Garden's nine holes.

There are so many memorable holes that it is almost impossible to single any out, but the 6th on the Mill is one of our favourites. Here, the River Wey must be crossed twice, once with the tee shot and once approaching the diagonal green. It's a cracking 520-yard par five, which poses similar challenges to the 17th at Carnoustie. The 7th hole on the Mill is also unforgettable – a do or die par three which measures 223 yards from the back tees, where there's an amazing double water hazard to carry before the kidney-shaped green – also well protected by four bunkers – is reached.

The Wisley is certainly world-class and if you are given the opportunity to play here, take it immediately. It's easy to see why top professionals such as Colin Montgomerie, Paul Casey and Niclas Fasth are Wisley members... 27 superb holes and probably the best practice facilities in the British Isles.

SOUTHERNESS GOLF CLUB
Southerness, Dumfries, DG2 8AZ, Scotland
Telephone: +44 (0) 1387 880677

Average Reviewers' Score:

Website: www.southernessgolfclub.com
Architect: Philip Mackenzie Ross
Visitors: Contact in advance – handicap certificate required

Reviewers' Comments

Played on a blustery day and found the course a delight to play... Southerness is a delightful links course. We played it in poor weather but still thoroughly enjoyed it... Unlike some links courses (notably nearby Silloth), it's a course which high handicappers can enjoy while still providing a worthwhile test for good golfers... Liked the wee bucket of sand given to you at the starter's hut to repair divots on the way round... We had the place to ourselves apart from some Scandinavians who we talked to back in the clubhouse - they, like us, were enchanted by the location and layout... Strange having what amounts to a big sheep pen in the middle of the course... Hole number 12 was memorable, a right dogleg slightly downhill towards the beach... We also liked the markers in the distance at the side of the fairways, which were to guide your line off many of the tees - handy when playing for the first time... The clubhouse is pretty basic and showing its age a little but we were made most welcome and enjoyed our day out... Very good value for money... Well worth a detour.

Southerness

Southerness is aptly named because it's the most southerly golf course in Scotland featured on our Top 100 website. The course is set on the edge of a remote headland on the peaceful Solway coast and is virtually unknown by the golfing masses. The mountains of the Lake District are clearly visible on the opposite side of the Solway Firth and, just across the water, about five miles away as the seagull flies, is the other excellent links course at Silloth on Solway.

A lighthouse was built not far from here to guide shipping entering the River Nith and they have used the lighthouse as Southerness Golf Club's emblem. A panoramic view of Criffel peak (the highest of the local fells) is also on offer from this classic and natural links course, but it's a relative juvenile in the scheme of things. The club was founded in 1947 and it's one of Britain's last genuine championship links developments since the Second World War. Philip Mackenzie Ross, a former partner of Tom Simpson, laid out the course and Southerness is considered to be Ross's most respected composition. Ross went on to become the first president of the British Association of Golf Course Architects.

On the surface of it, the course appears to be relatively short, measuring a little over 6,500 yards, but with a lowly par of 69, it's one of the toughest golfing tests in the land. The standard scratch score of 73 suggests that par is extremely challenging. On occasions, no doubt, the competition scratch score is even higher. There are two short par fives which offer realistic birdie opportunities, but there are eight par fours measuring over 400 yards and this is where shots will be dropped. The fairways always seem to be generous and inviting, but there's gorse and heather waiting to catch wayward shots. Let's be honest – with so many 400-yard plus holes, you can't afford to leave the driver in the car.

Probably the best holes run along the shore, starting with the 8th, and the line to take is the lighthouse in the distance. The 12th and 13th are particularly strong holes.

Dumfries might not feature as a golfing venue of first choice, but if you include Silloth on Solway and Powfoot alongside the mighty links here at Southerness, you will be hard pressed to find better golfing and you will certainly get outstanding value for money.

WOBURN GOLF & COUNTRY CLUB
Little Brickhill, Milton Keynes, Bucks, MK17 9LJ
England
Telephone: +44 (0) 1908 370756

Average Reviewers' Score:

Website: www.woburngolf.com
Architect: Charles Lawrie
Visitors: Contact in advance – midweek only

Reviewers' Comments

There is a very specific sound that accompanies a round on the Duke's and it is the sound of Pinnacle on Pine… A true favourite of many with some great holes… Pines surround this beautiful course and an errant shot will find your ball bouncing between the trees… Each hole is well concealed from the other and it feels as if you are playing alone in a corridor of greenery… Shrewd positional play is recommended… Great feeling of privacy amongst the forest… Duke's is so familiar because of the TV coverage… There are at least four really memorable holes on this course, which makes the trip worthwhile… The 18th hole (fairly short par four) anywhere else on the course would be a weak hole - but as the last it has the habit of being a hole where games are won or lost in dramatic fashion - and I should know – ouch… Geared up for societies and corporate days… Pricey for what you get… Well worth the green fee… Best course in the area by far. You will *not* be disappointed playing here… Never turn down a trip to Woburn.

Woburn (Duke's)

Television has turned Woburn into one of the best-known golfing venues in the British Isles. But in the scheme of things, golf here is still in its infancy. On the other hand, the famous Woburn Abbey has been home to the Bedford family for almost 400 years.

It was Lord Tavistock's brilliant idea to bring golf to Woburn. He commissioned Charles Lawrie of Cotton & Pennink, to design the Duke's. After two years, and much tree-felling, the first course at Woburn opened for play. It didn't take long for it to be recognised. In 1979, the Dunlop Masters was hosted, and, since then, the Duke's has never looked back – playing host to the English Strokeplay Championship, the British Masters and the Women's British Open. The young and successful English golfer, Ian Poulter, is now officially attached to Woburn Golf Club.

With fairways flanked by glorious pine, birch and chestnut trees, it's an intimate golf course. Each hole is played in splendid isolation. It's a serious challenge too, measuring almost 7,000 yards from the back tees and 6,550 from the regular tees. Straight and long driving is the order of the day. This is not a course for the novice golfer – it will beat you up and spit you out.

There are some fantastic holes on the Duke's but the pick of the bunch is the famous par three 3rd. Framed by rhododendrons and gorse, it's a genuinely delightful golf hole. The green is 100 feet below the tee, and the hard green slopes violently from back to front. Measuring only 125 yards, a short iron must be played to the heart of the green, otherwise, the ball is likely to scuttle off, pronto. The 5th is a wonderful, short par five – a well-struck drive down the right, as close as you dare to the trees, will provide a chance to reach the green in two – anything struck too far left, will scamper down a slope towards the trees.

The Duke's is an outstanding course, but Woburn's young upstart, the Marquess, is threatening it. There is a benefit to this – the Duke's will be less busy – perhaps.

BALLYLIFFIN GOLF CLUB
Ballyliffin, Inishowen, Co. Donegal, Ireland
Telephone: +353 (0) 7493 76119

Average Reviewers' Score:

Website: www.ballyliffingolfclub.com
Architect: Pat Ruddy and Tom Craddock
Visitors: Welcome - contact in advance

Reviewers' Comments

First off, a couple of words about the location – it's arresting, wild, charming and stunningly beautiful... Comparisons with Ballybunion and Dornoch must be seen as compliments but Ballyliffin is a name to remember in its own right... A good number of holes have been carved into the towering dunes... It's a rollercoaster and long, too, if played off the black tees... You can tell that it's new, but that really doesn't matter... Holes are laid out intelligently, making good use of the natural lie of the land... What a tough start – three par fours more than 400 yards and uphill directly away from the wonderful new clubhouse... Two par threes at the top of the dunes are wonderfully exhilarating... A favourite of mine is the long par five 13th, uphill all the way to a wickedly contoured green guarded by a bunker that gobbles up imprecise third shots... It's a manageable test but play off the black tees only if you're feeling masochistic... Welcome in the clubhouse is exceptional, it's very informal and the craic will flow over a pint or two of Guinness... I really loved this course and it's a real credit to golf in Ireland.

Ballyliffin (Glashedy) 79th

Ballyliffin is Ireland's most northerly golf club, located off Tullagh Point on the Atlantic edge of the Inishowen Peninsula. It's difficult to pin a date on the earliest origins of the game of golf at Ballyliffin, but it is clear that the Ballyliffin Golf Club was founded in 1947. The Glashedy links is, however, much, much younger.

In 1991, the Captain of Ballyliffin, Cormac McDonough, put a proposal to the committee to alleviate pressure on the overplayed Old course. The result was that Pat Ruddy and Tom Craddock were commissioned to design a new course on the finest links land they had ever seen. Work started in spring 1993, and after significant earth moving, the Glashedy links (pronounced Glasheedy) – named after the Glashedy Rock, Ballyliffin's equivalent of Turnberry's Ailsa Craig – opened for play in the summer of 1995, to much acclaim.

Ballyliffin is often described as "the Ballybunion of the North" or "the Dornoch of Ireland" and the reason is simple; all the aforementioned are set amidst towering natural sand dunes. This youngster is no exception, except that this links has been flattened out, ensuring that the fairways are relatively even and capable of hosting a championship.

The Glashedy layout is intertwined with the Old course, the holes weaving their way through the wild dunes. It's a supremely challenging golf course, which stretches out more than 7,200 yards, with nine brutal par fours in excess of 400 yards. You really do need to be on top of your game to play to handicap. The huge greens, with some frightening undulations, are well protected by bunkers; three putting can be alarmingly frequent.

The Glashedy links is certainly good enough and long enough to hold important championships and already it has hosted the North West of Ireland Open. It would be fascinating on a windy day to watch the very best professionals stretched to their absolute limit on this wild and challenging links course. Surely this course must be a contender for a future Irish Open Championship.

SOUTHPORT & AINSDALE GOLF CLUB
Bradshaws Lane, Ainsdale, Southport, Merseyside
PR8 3LG, England
Telephone: +44 (0) 1704 578000

Average Reviewers' Score:

Website: www.sandagolfclub.co.uk
Architect: James Braid
Visitors: Welcome except Thu, Sat & Sun morning

Reviewers' Comments

S&A is a thoroughly enjoyable and entertaining links… It adds to the run of brilliant courses on this stretch of coast… It's certainly not long, but in a way, it's all the better for it… Used for many high class competitions now and once the venue for two Ryder Cups in the 1930s… It's used as an Open Qualifier… The greens are excellent and, on our trip, even better than Formby and Hillside… This is no poor relation to the other 'bigger' names in the area… Good golf is rewarded and poor shots are punished… Not a long course… No way is it a pushover… Deep bunkers surround most of the quality greens… The par three opening hole is an absolute cracker… Best hole for me, probably the par five 16th, known as "Gumbleys" – the tip here is to aim further right than you think when playing your blind approach over the railway sleepers – could save a shot or two … Very friendly place and the clubhouse extension will add even more to the overall delight of Southport & Ainsdale… Hope to return soon… Well worth playing.

Southport & Ainsdale

Only the Belfry has hosted more home soil Ryder Cups than Southport & Ainsdale. But everybody flocks to play the royal neighbour, Birkdale. If only they knew what they were missing a couple of miles down the road.

Southport & Ainsdale Golf Club was originally founded in 1907. At that time, golf was played across a stretch of links land between the railway line and the main Liverpool road. In 1922, the council decided to build another road into Southport and they decided to route it across the links, splitting the course in two. Fortunately, some new land was identified and James Braid, the greatest golf course revisionist of all time, was called in to sort things out. By 1924, Braid had built six new holes and updated the remaining twelve.

It's therefore a relative youngster and it's set amongst exhilarating dunes and tangly heather. There's a very natural feel to the layout, although it is somewhat old-fashioned with some blind drives and obscured approach shots. It's not your traditional out-and-back layout. The course is laid out in two loops, the first seven holes forming the inner loop. The fairways wind their way through gaps and valleys between the dunes and many of the greens are raised on tricky-to-hold plateaux. It's a serious golfing test, the layout measures over 6,600 from the back tees with par set at 72 and from the yellow tees, the length drops to 6,250 yards, but the par also drops down to 70.

There are many memorable holes and the 8th is a bunkerless par three, measuring 157 yards. The green is sited on a raised table and only the best tee shot will stay on the putting surface. The 16th, measuring 506 yards, plays directly into the prevailing wind and when the wind's up, three solid strikes will be required to reach the green. It's called "Gumbley's" and it has a fine example of a sleeper-faced bunker. It's a monster, set into the face of a large, tussocky sand ridge. Avoid this one like the plague.

S&A has hosted many important amateur events over the years and the Dunlop Southport and Swallow Penfold professional competitions were held here in the 1940s and 1950s with Max Faulkner, Fred Daly and Christy O'Connor emerging victorious. But the club will be remembered for the 1933 and 1937 Ryder Cups. The 1933 event went down to the very last match between Easterbrook and Shute and it turned out to be a putting contest on the final green. Shute had a six-footer for the USA to retain the Ryder Cup, but he missed. The 1937 Ryder Cup was less eventful: the score was USA 8 GB&I 4. 1937 was the first American Ryder Cup victory in the British Isles, but it wasn't their last because the USA retained the Ryder Cup for the next 20 years.

Southport & Ainsdale should be played not only from a historic perspective but because this is a very natural and challenging links course, one of Braid's finest seaside examples.

CELTIC MANOR RESORT
Coldra Woods, Newport, NP18 1HQ, Wales
Telephone: +44 (0) 1633 413000

Average Reviewers' Score:

Website: www.celtic-manor.com
Architect: Robert Trent Jones Jnr.
Visitors: Book in advance

Reviewers' Comments

With the exception of Kingsbarns and Old Head, Wentwood Hills is the best new course I've played in recent years... Resort is somewhat overwhelming but the service makes up for it... It's as tough as nails and a hard walk too but I prefer to walk rather than taking a buggy... Take a buggy, there are huge walks between greens and tees and it's hilly... It's a course for good golfers and not the novice... It's a serious course, you need to plot your way round and hope for the best... Even single figure boys will find this a bit of a slog, especially from the back tees. If you're a high handicapper, enjoy the walk... Undoubtedly laid out to test the pros, I found it too tough... Conditioning was good and the greens were superb – fast and true... This type of course is not my personal cup of tea and it seems somewhat contrived and all too Americanised... Layout is dramatic and some of the holes are really memorable... Views of the rolling countryside are very pleasant... It seems unnatural to me... I look forward to seeing how well the Ryder Cup boys get on with this monster.

The resort at Celtic Manor was conceived and developed by Sir Terence Matthews. In the late 1970s, Matthews bought a near-derelict manor house and turned it into a small hotel. The hotel became popular and successful, winning the Egon Ronay Best Hotel in Wales award five years on the trot. Matthews's long-term vision was a golfing complex; and the piece de resistance is the Wentwood Hills course, which opened for play in September 1999, designed by Robert Trent Jones Jnr.

The Wentwood Hills' mettle was shown in June 2000 in the shape of the Wales Open. The European Tour clearly liked the course because the Wales Open is now called the Celtic Manor Wales Open. Ian Poulter led from start to finish to win the 2003 event. Wentwood Hills is also the course chosen to stage the 2010 Ryder Cup – an incredible achievement for a youngster.

A bit of Augusta, a bit of Florida and a lot of Wales, is how they refer to Wentwood Hills. They are absolutely right: there's a coalition of British and American features. Robert Trent Jones Jnr has described it as "a true championship course that combines a hilly landscape with the more traditional links-like features of an estuary. There's great variety here."

Undoubtedly, it's a championship layout. The course measures a massive 7,403 yards from the back tees. It's still a challenging 6,661 yards from the regular tees so, unless your game is on fire, we suggest you choose your tee boxes carefully. The holes are varied and exciting, but the 2nd is considered to be one of the very best – a spectacular par five – the pitch into the green needs careful judgement as the green is surrounded by bunkers and perched on the hillside.

If you are a lover of all things traditional, then Wentwood Hills is probably not for you. If you are seeking an exciting and tough challenge, then this course will fit the bill perfectly. Either way, it's an excellent golf course, backed up by excellent Celtic service.

CARNE GOLF LINKS	Average Reviewers' Score:
Carne, Belmullet, Co. Mayo, Ireland	
Telephone: +353 (0) 97 82292	

Website: www.carnegolflinks.com
Architect: Eddie Hackett
Visitors: Welcome – contact in advance

Reviewers' Comments

Mr Eddie Hackett – thank you. Carne is the most wonderful golf experience, bar none... Eddie Hackett's design mantra is never truer than when considered alongside Carne, he just worked with "what the good Lord presented to him"... I find it hard to believe that there are 81 courses better than Carne... As he worked on the routing for this course he first decided where the greens would go and only once this job was done did he then try to find tees... Play it, rave about it and be amazed that this course is not in the Top 20, never mind the Top 100... The dunescape on this links is "Himalayanesque" and really must be seen to be believed... By far and away the most memorable course that you will play... The course throws everything it has at you... The wind is a relentless twitcher to any swing... I would rather play Carne than nearly all of the Open venues... A truly magnificent setting and a golf course to more than match it... I believe Carne to be the second best links course in the Isles... Jaw-dropping golf from 1 to 18... Links golf on steroids.

Carne

The Carne links at Belmullet is the late Eddie Hackett's swan song and many reckon it's his finest design. The course sits in splendid isolation on the Atlantic edge of County Mayo. It lies on a peninsula, amidst gigantic dunes with far-reaching views across Blacksod Bay to the Atlantic islands of Inis Gloire and Inis Geidhewild. And it's absolutely charming.

"I am thrilled with the way the dramatic Belmullet course has turned out," said Hackett, "and again, I reiterate my first opinion that ultimately there will be no better links course in the country, or, I doubt, anywhere." It's impossible to disagree – the course is wild, and natural. It's difficult to believe that the course only opened for play in 1993. It feels as though it's been here forever. Many of the greens and tees are sited naturally and, for such a modern course, very little earth-moving was required during the construction. From spring to late autumn, the course is alive with harebells, sea holly and wild thyme.

Carne is owned and operated by a community-owned company called Turasoireacht Iorrais Teo. Primarily, the course was developed to attract tourism to an isolated, but beautiful area of western Ireland. If you haven't heard of it, this could be your golf course find of the century. You'll certainly remember the lunar landscape and the towering sand dunes – we're in the same league as Ballybunion here at Belmullet.

This 6,700-yard links is not a simple out and back affair. Each nine wends its way back to the clubhouse – the holes snake up and down through the dunes in all directions. As with any coastal course, the wind always plays its part. On a calm day you might play close to your handicap, but when the wind is up, hold on to your hat. Undoubtedly, Hackett has created a high-spirited golf course and it's a layout that you cannot help but enjoy. "It would be great to believe that we could all leave as beautiful a signature on the world when we depart as Eddie Hackett managed to do," said Michael Pask from Golf International after playing Carne.

A trip to Ireland's beautiful west coast would not be complete without playing here. Include County Sligo, Enniscrone and Connemara on your itinerary, alongside Carne, and you've played four of the most naturally beautiful links courses in the world.

TREVOSE GOLF & COUNTRY CLUB
Constantine Bay, Padstow, Cornwall, PL28 8JB, England
Telephone: +44 (0) 1841 520208

Average Reviewers' Score:

Website: www.trevose-gc.co.uk
Architect: Harry Colt and Sir Guy Campbell
Visitors: Welcome – contact in advance

Reviewers' Comments

Trevose has recently been lengthened and having played off their back tees, it is probably one of the best tests of golf I've played... Greens were excellent and extremely fast... A classic natural links in a divine setting... I've played the championship course three times in all weather and it's always been in excellent condition... An enjoyable course, good value for money and great facilities... You don't see too much of the sea... It was expensive when I played and I think Perranporth is a more interesting course... I think you'll find this course rapidly rising up above St Enodoc in the Top 100... Don't dismiss as holiday golf - this is the real thing... There is a great atmosphere at this club... A very welcoming club... Definitely the best course in Cornwall.

Trevose (Championship)

On the north Cornwall coast lies the olde worlde fishing village of Padstow and Rick Stein's famous seafood restaurant. There's plenty of action going on in this neck of the woods, including offshore shark fishing. And, there's also plenty of excitement at Trevose Golf and Country Club, located a little further south along the Atlantic coastline at Constantine Bay. With dramatic views across the golden sandy shore of Bobby's Bay to the rugged coastline of Trevose Head, it's sheer drama.

Founded in 1926, the great Harry Colt designed the course, and Sir Guy Campbell made minor revisions just before the Second World War. It's an exhilarating windswept links where little other than dune grasses survive in the bleakness.

Trevose is a stern test of golf, especially when the wind is up. There are four teeing areas to choose from, and the par 71 links stretches out to 6,600 yards from the back tees. The crumpled fairways are generous in width and the rough is kept short to keep the speed of play up and prevent too many lost balls. Some regard Trevose as holiday golf, but the course is technically challenging and will test the very best golfers. The course record is 66 and stands as a testament to its level of difficulty. Birdie opportunities are there for the taking on the three short par fives, but make the most of it because many of the par fours are aggressive and supremely challenging. Five of them stretch out over 400 yards.

The short holes are also memorable and exciting, especially the 3rd, measuring 166 yards and the 199-yard 11th, with its two-tiered plateau green.

Some excellent facilities accompany the superb Championship course and there's a very pleasant nine-hole course, designed by Peter Alliss, called the New. This shorter course is an excellent warm-up ahead of the real Championship challenge.

ADARE MANOR HOTEL & GOLF RESORT
Adare, Co. Limerick, Ireland
Telephone: +353 (0) 61 396566

Average Reviewers' Score:

Website: www.adaremanor.ie
Architect: Robert Trent Jones Snr.
Visitors: Contact in advance

Reviewers' Comments

Not quite what you'd expect for an Irish course but also not a course to be overlooked when in Ireland... If you can get over the artificiality of the course then you will get to love it... If it wasn't for the Irish weather and the beautiful hotel and buildings, then you could easily be on the continent... Adare is an exacting test of golf and certainly one of Trent Jones' better designs... Everything about Trent Jones is bold and whenever I play his courses I'm desperate for some subtlety... Take your bucket and spade and a snorkel, it's a sand and water heaven or hell... It's also a really tough course and playing to handicap is near on impossible unless you're a bandit... As a resort course Adare is excellent, very close to the K Club in all departments: style, condition, quality and service... You can't fault the facilities and the service - second to none... A top-class resort and there's also plenty here to keep the non-golfers happy... Well worth playing.

Adare Manor

The Adare golf course is set in more than 800 acres of beautiful parkland and formal gardens. The 18th century Adare Manor, located alongside the River Maigue, is an architectural masterpiece of towers and turrets. It was once the ancestral home of the Earls of Dunraven. Now it's an opulent, luxury resort.

The course opened for play in 1995 and was designed by Robert Trent Jones Snr. It's a classic Trent Jones design, stretching out a massive 7,138 yards from back tees to a more modest 5,082 yards from the forward tees. The course bears all Trent Jones's hallmarks - cloverleaf bunkers, American-styled mounding, and lots of water. The result is rather un-Irish, but extremely exciting and challenging. Having said this, there are plenty of natural features and hazards, including the stately trees and the River Maigue, which meanders nonchalantly through the course.

Adare is certainly a dramatic golf course. The drama builds throughout the front nine with some excellent holes, but things really get going at the 11th, a tough 187-yard par three. Bunkers surround the green and the river beckons to catch anything but the perfectly struck tee shot. Still building, the drama reaches a crescendo at the last, a par five, considered by Trent Jones to be the greatest finishing hole in golf.

A number of important events have been hosted at Adare, including the Irish Seniors Open, held here for three consecutive years, most recently in 2004. Additionally, Adare hosted the 2003 Irish PGA Championship. Paul McGinley emerged victorious.

Undoubtedly, Adare Manor is a dashing, stylish resort, with an excellent championship course attached – one of the best inland tracks in Ireland.

WORPLESDON GOLF CLUB
Woking, Surrey, GU22 0RA, England
Telephone: +44 (0) 1483 472277

Average Reviewers' Score:

Website: www.worplesdongc.co.uk
Architect: John Abercromby
Visitors: Weekdays only - contact in advance

Reviewers' Comments

One of the best golf clubs in the world... The best of the three W's, altogether prettier, more strategic and generally a sterner test of golf than Woking and West Hill... Right from the inviting opening tee shot played from an elevated position, Worplesdon oozes quality through and through... Front nine is played across pleasantly undulating/rolling ground and the back nine is flatter... Bunkering is pronounced and the faces are quite steep and punishing, often resulting in at least one lost shot... Keep the ball in play otherwise it bites... The rough, especially in summer, is penal... Greens are always fast and true and I've certainly not mastered reading them... Great greens - always in immaculate condition... There are no weak holes, or at least no holes that are uninteresting... Par threes are just superb... Plateau green on the 4th is a gem and the tee shot on the 10th is stunning and the green is a nightmare to read... It is in the top five of the numerous heathland courses in this area of west London... A divine place to play golf... It's a joy to spend time both on and off the course... Clubhouse is hospitable and full of interest.

Worplesdon

Worplesdon is one of the prettiest and most delightful of Surrey's many heath and heather courses and it's arguably the best of the trinity of "Ws" (West Hill and Woking being the other two); all three courses virtually border each other. It is set amongst glorious heather, chestnut and pine trees. John Abercromby's inaugural design dates back to 1908 and little has changed after almost 100 years.

It's not a long course at just less than 6,500 yards, but it's supremely challenging and driving accuracy is far more important than length. The front nine plays across stunning undulating terrain, so expect some awkward stances. The back nine is sited on relatively even ground. The greens are always in fabulous condition and are lightning fast with some subtle borrows and undulations.

Every autumn since 1921, the celebrated Mixed Foursomes competition takes place at Worplesdon. Joyce Wethered won this event no fewer than eight times between 1922 and 1933, with seven different partners. Bernard Darwin lists Joyce's victorious partners in his book, *Golf Between Two Wars*: "Mr Roger Wethered, Mr Tolley (twice), Mr J.S.F. Morrison, Mr Michael Scott, Mr R.H. Oppenheimer, Mr T. Coke and an elderly gentleman whose name for the moment escapes me". In 1933, Darwin (aged 57) partnered with Wethered and won!

The 11th is featured in *The 500 World's Greatest Golf Holes* and it's a 520-yard par five: "Surrounded by brilliant heathland, this interesting hole has seen its challenges change with the times, but its supreme strategic character remains." The par threes are especially strong and the 175-yard 13th is an absolute cracker, surrounded by bunkers and often rated as one of the best par threes in the UK.

It's a real privilege to play this quiet and elegant course. The springy fairways roll gently up and down, flanked by many mature trees. The profusion of heather provides stunning seasonal colour and a real challenge in finding the wayward golf ball. The clubhouse is one of the most pleasant in all the land and very welcoming.

"And so farewell to Worplesdon," wrote Darwin, "but not I hope for long. If I can once again see the dahlias in the garden by the side of the fifteenth fairway and once again read The Moonstone under the kind roof which has so often sheltered me, I shall be almost perfectly happy."

WOBURN GOLF & COUNTRY CLUB
Little Brickhill, Milton Keynes, Bucks, MK17 9LJ
England
Telephone: +44 (0) 1908 370756

Average Reviewers' Score:

Website: www.woburngolf.com
Architect: Charles Lawrie
Visitors: Contact in advance – midweek only

Reviewers' Comments

A crackerjack that deserves to be much higher in the rankings... Shorter than the Duke's, but still retains the beautiful pine wood surroundings that really are such a great feature here... It doesn't have the big tricky greens like its brother the Duke's but it more than makes up for it with its utter charm... Makes you think that little bit more... The greens are small and well protected... A truly beautiful golf course... I defy anyone to not fall in love with this place... One of the very best inland courses... Tight narrow fairways the order of the day... Leave your driver in the car; you can get into serious trouble... Scoring well on the Duchess is a real test... This course has got be one of the most picturesque in the country... Highly recommended... One of my personal favourite courses.

Woburn (Duchess) th

th

The Duchess is the shortest and prettiest of the three Woburn courses. Major competitions, accolades and honours are usually heaped on the Duke's, and more recently, the Marquess courses. Nevertheless, the Duchess is delightful in its own right, and a serious challenge.

Charles Lawrie designed the Duchess, and the course opened for play in 1979. It measures a respectable 6,651 yards from the back tees and it's tighter, and perhaps less forgiving of the wayward shot than the Duke's. But all the same, it's a fine undulating woodland course, carved through pine trees. It will require the full repertoire of shots and, finding the small greens in regulation, is very challenging.

This is definitely a course where you must keep your ball in play. If you manage to do this from the tee, then the rewards can be great. Use your driver sparingly because this is a real thinker's course. The towering pine trees make each hole appear exceptionally tight. However, on occasions, you will need to go for distance.

There are some great holes, especially the par threes. The 4th, stroke index 2, is a par four, which begins with a long, narrow chute off the tee. Halfway down, everything begins to kick left. The green, a stingy little thing, is close to the trees on the right and fronted by a nasty bunker on the left.

Most of the par threes are quite long and challenging, demanding very straight tee shots. The unusual, 203-yard 7th has a huge bunker, front and right, and danger to the left. An historic ridge – the remains of an ancient Danish settlement – runs diagonally across the hole and will push anything short and left into the forest.

The 15th, a 485-yard doglegged par five, is a typical Duchess shot-maker's delight. Anything other than an arrow-straight drive ends up in the trees. A short drive leaves a blind second shot. The left-sloping fairway runs downhill, then rises sharply to a two-tiered green.

The Duchess fits into the Woburn family exceptionally well – it's a real gem. In our opinion, the Duchess is as good, if not better, than the Duke's and the Marquess.

ENNISCRONE GOLF CLUB
Enniscrone, Co. Sligo, Ireland
Telephone: +353 (0) 96 36297

Average Reviewers' Score:

Website: www.enniscronegolf.com
Architect: Eddie Hackett and Donald Steel
Visitors: Book in advance

Reviewers' Comments

Enniscrone was good but now it's excellent... It's now a superb course and one that should be more highly recognised... A fantastic course - we loved it here... It's a serious test from the back tees but it is enjoyable from any of the tees mainly because the tee shots are elevated and thrilling, which entice us to open our shoulders... Steel added six new holes in the dunes but at the same time he's left Hackett's best holes intact... One of the best things about the new 18 is that they are so varied and enjoyable... The opener looks straightforward from the tee, but you'll need a good uphill approach to a well bunkered green that's sandwiched between the dunes... This is a great golf course and so much fun... It's oh so tough when the wind blows... I'm not sure what the club intends to do with the other nine holes, but if you are travelling all this way why not play them anyway? Enniscrone is the complete package.

Enniscrone

Enniscrone started out in life in 1918 as a modest nine-hole course. But it was the prolific Irish architect, Eddie Hackett, who put Enniscrone on the map, when, in 1974, he extended the layout to 18 holes. Donald Steel has recently extended the configuration to 27 holes by using new land and adjoining dunes. He has also changed the original flat opening holes, which were out of keeping with the rest. The main course now plots its way through the gigantic dunes and across the folded rippled links land. But with 27 holes, there are now a number of playing options.

The location is ravishing; Enniscrone is set on a promontory, which juts out into Killala Bay at the mouth of the Moy Estuary. Scurmore one of Ireland's most beautiful beaches, borders the links, whilst the moody Ox Mountains provide a stormy backdrop to the east and the Nephin Beg Range dominates the westerly skyline.

The course itself complements its surroundings. The fairways pitch and roll between towering shaggy dunes. Greens are raised on plateaux and are protected by deep valleys and ravines, whilst others nestle at the feet of high dunes. There are elevated tee shots and panoramic ocean views. Enniscrone really is a breathtaking golf course with a serious challenge attached.

Stretching out to almost 6,900 yards, it calls for some solid driving. There is nothing unnatural about Enniscrone; it's in tune with its surroundings, where there is this ever-present sense of space and freedom.

You must expect a bit of wind here, and that will naturally bring another dimension to the challenge. If you are feeling weary and windswept after your round, why not visit Kilcullen's Seaweed Baths in Enniscrone village? Guaranteed to provide relief from the rigours of the round. Or try to unravel the giant and rampageous Enniscrone black pig myth. But whatever you do, take the time to play this course before it gets too well known and becomes the Ballybunion of the Western Seaboard.

CASTLETOWN GOLF LINKS
Derbyhaven, Isle of Man, IM9 1UA
Telephone: +44 (0) 1624 822220

Average Reviewers' Score:

Website: www.castletowngolflinks.co.uk
Architect: Old Tom Morris and Philip Mackenzie Ross
Visitors: Welcome - contact in advance

Reviewers' Comments

Castletown has it all... Wild, natural, breathtaking views, tricky greens deep bunkers... Undeniably a true and undiluted test of links golf... If you like links golf in the raw, this is the place to come... Played here in what was considered locally to be a gentle breeze, where I come from, the wind was gale force... The course is virtually surrounded by the sea and boy does the wind blow here... You need to master the bump and run shot to score well... Condition was superb with greens true and fast... Stay in the hotel for the complete experience... I'll be back to see whether my nerve has improved and with some more golf balls to make up for all those that I left behind... Entertainment right from the off but this beauty saves the best till last... Castletown has the best collection of finishing holes anywhere... This is one of my favourite links courses in the whole of the British Isles and I never tire of playing it.

Castletown

88th

The Isle of Man is very different from anywhere else in the British Isles. It doesn't belong to the UK, or the EU. It's self-governing, with its own currency, culture and postage stamps. During the first two weeks of June, the place goes motorcycle mad. The T.T. – the world famous motorcycle event – is staged on the island's mountain circuit.

The links is located at the southeastern tip of the island, on the rocky Langness Peninsula, better known locally as Fort Island. On a clear day, the distant Cumbrian Mountains can be seen. The peninsula is designated as a Site of Special Scientific Interest, with a number of formally listed ancient monuments, including an Iron Age fort. The triangular headland is bordered on three sides by the Irish Sea and is connected to the mainland by a thin strip of rocks. It's breathtaking.

Old Tom Morris originally laid out the course back in 1892 and Philip Mackenzie Ross revised it after the Second World War. Little has changed since. Castletown is full of natural hazards – wild rough, rocky beaches, gorse and, of course, the wind. The course is laid out high above sea level and, with no sand dunes, there is no protection from the elements. The upside to this are the unrivalled, panoramic views of the Irish Sea. It's hard to imagine that any other course could possess more coastal frontage.

There are many great golf holes but one of the best, and most memorable, is the par four 17th. The tee-shot must carry across a deep rocky gorge. Try not to let the sea – crashing into the rocks below – disturb your concentration.

Some people draw a parallel between Castletown and Turnberry. Mackenzie Ross is certainly a common denominator, as is the dramatic rocky coastline. Turnberry is perhaps a sterner test, but we think Castletown is more thrilling, dramatic and much better value for money.

MOORTOWN GOLF CLUB
Harrogate Road, Leeds, LS17 7DB, England
Telephone: +44 (0) 113 268 6521

Average Reviewers' Score:

Website: www.moortown-gc.co.uk
Architect: Dr Alister MacKenzie
Visitors: Contact in advance

Reviewers' Comments

Even in the winter, the class of this lovely course shone through... The winter green fee made it excellent value too... Varied and interesting layout that provides a testing challenge... You are presented with a variety of challenges and all aspects of your game need to be in order if you are to play to your handicap... Par threes are especially strong and the greens are simply superb... Play it in the summer and be prepared for plenty of three putts... We were made to feel welcome by the staff and members... Very friendly members' club... Moortown has it all, it's a great course with plenty of history.

Moortown 89th

Fred Lawson-Brown, a non-golfer, was inspired by the beauty of Ganton and decided that Leeds should have an equivalent golf course. 175 acres of potential golfing terrain were acquired from the landlord of the Bramham Park Estate, and, as luck would have it, Dr Alister MacKenzie was in the area, busily working on nearby Alwoodley. And so, in 1910, seven years after Lawson-Brown's visit to Ganton, the Moortown golf course on Black Moor was ready for play. To mark the occasion, an exhibition match was staged between James Braid and Harry Vardon.

Moortown is classic moorland golf course with lovely peaty turf that provides the bouncy cushion-effect when walking – a course that is gentle on the feet. The fairways appear wide and inviting – many of the holes are flanked with silver birch, gorse and heather. But don't be fooled, it's no pushover. This golf course is tough and exacting.

It turned out to be a tough test for Walter Hagen, the 1929 Ryder Cup captain, and his American team. For it was here, at a cold Moortown, that Great Britain and Ireland, with George Duncan as captain, beat the USA 7-5. This was the first Ryder Cup to be held on home soil. The competition had been inaugurated two years earlier at the Worcester Country Club in the USA.

In addition to the Ryder Cup, Moortown has hosted numerous important professional competitions, Nick Faldo and Bernard Gallagher were amongst the Moortown winners. A host of important amateur events have also been contested over the moorland, and in the 1974 English Open Amateur strokeplay championship, Nigel Denham hit an over-zealous second shot into the billiard room of the in-bounds clubhouse. Undeterred, Denham marched inside and chipped through the open window to within five yards of the pin.

Moortown measures almost 6,500 yards from the regular tees, but accuracy will reap more rewards than length. Whilst the fairways appear to be wide, it's an optical illusion and the rough can be punishing. The course opens with two back-to-back par fives and these are both relatively short, so make the most of two great birdie opportunities. The 3rd is a testing par four, one of six par fours measuring in excess of 400 yards. The 10th is MacKenzie's signature hole, a cracking 158-yard par three called "Gibraltar". We are not entirely sure why it's called Gibraltar, clearly something to do with rocks or perhaps the dry stonewall behind the green. Does anybody know?

As Patric Dickinson stated in his book, *A Round of Golf Courses*: "The site of Moortown was chosen with courage and vision." There is absolutely no doubt that Moortown is an exciting place to play golf. The holes offer a great deal of variety, both in terms of look and feel and in shot-making requirements, and as always with MacKenzie's design, Moortown fits the land like a glove.

LINDRICK GOLF CLUB
Lindrick Common, Worksop, Notts, S81 8BH, England
Telephone: +44 (0) 1909 475282

Average Reviewers' Score:

Website: www.lindrickgolfclub.co.uk
Architect: Tom Dunn and Fred Hawtree
Visitors: Contact in advance – not Tue and weekends

Reviewers' Comments

Lindrick is an honest and friendly club that oozes tradition... A great course with excellent crisp turf - testing for the very best players... The course has a moorland cum heathland feel and I believe that it's sited on limestone. Either way, superb drainage... Categorising Lindrick is quite difficult... it's not really heathland, nor is it moorland, but whatever it is, it makes for great golf... Course is a picture in the spring when the gorse is in bloom... The start is a bit uninspiring but the course gets better and better... Some first rate holes; some poor ones... The best holes are across the busy road (mind how you go when you cross over)... Has some of the truest and fastest greens I've ever played on in England... Bring your best putting game... A good test but rather disappointing overall given its Ryder Cup pedigree... With so much history and tradition, Lindrick is a must-play course... It's a genuinely delightful place to play golf... Bring your jacket and tie along if you want to drink or eat in the main bar...Try it alongside Notts for a fantastic twosome.

Lindrick is remembered passionately because it was here in 1957 that Great Britain and Ireland beat the USA to win the Ryder Cup. Victory had been a long time coming; the last time GB&I had defeated the dominant Americans was way back in 1933 at Southport & Ainsdale. After the 1957 triumph, the Ryder Cup remained firmly in the grasp of the USA until 1985 when, at the Belfry, a combined team of GB&I and Europe managed to wrestle the cup from the Americans.

Clearly, the Ryder Cup put Lindrick firmly on the golfing map, but the Sheffield and District Golf Club, as it was originally called, was actually founded in the 19th century, 1891 to be precise, when Tom Dunn laid out the original nine holes on Lindrick Common. A second nine was added in 1894. Forty years later, the club changed its name to Lindrick Golf Club and Fred Hawtree made further revisions to the layout.

It's laid out on prime common land and the excellent turf has a mixed heathland and moorland feel. It's a wild but picturesque course with silver birch-lined fairways, heather and gorse. The fairways are generous and immaculately conditioned, the greens are subtly borrowed, lightning fast and well protected by bunkers. Accuracy, rather than length, is critical. We are stating the obvious here, but it is much more desirable to play from manicured fairways than dense rough.

There are a number of strong holes, especially on the back nine and the 4th, a short par five of 478 yards, is certainly fun and memorable, with a downhill drive and a blind approach to a hidden green, nestling in a hollow. According to the writing of Bernard Darwin in his original article for the Times, At Hollinwell and Lindrick, which was reprinted for his book, _Playing the Like_, the "secret and engaging dell" in the area of the 4th green, once bordered three counties - "York, Notts and Derby – and so it was once the ideal spot for prize-fighting." The 18th is a 210-yard par three. It's unusual to end with a one shotter and cruel to have such an exacting final tee shot, especially if the match is finely poised.

As with so many golf courses of this era, Lindrick, measuring a little over 6,600 yards, is simply not long enough to host today's professional men's tournaments. However, in 1966, it was the venue for the British Masters with Neil Coles emerging as the eventual winner and, in 1977, Vivien Saunders took the Women's British Open crown. Greg Norman somehow took 14 strokes at the 17th, a par four, during the final round of the 1982 Martini tournament, and then went on to win the British Masters by eight stokes at St Pierre a few weeks later.

The course still plays host to a number of important amateur events and Lindrick will certainly provide an excellent challenge for the visiting golfer, regardless of handicap.

LITTLE ASTON GOLF CLUB
Roman Road, Streetly, Sutton Coldfield, West Midlands
B74 3AN, England
Telephone: +44 (0) 121 353 2942

Average Reviewers' Score:

Website: www.littleastongolf.co.uk
Architect: Harry Vardon, Harry Colt
Visitors: Contact in advance – not on Saturdays

Reviewers' Comments

Little Aston is set in a salubrious area where the rich and famous Brummies live… It's quiet and peaceful despite being so close to Birmingham… It's immaculate, especially in the summer and this tree-lined course is an oasis…. Mature trees flank most of the holes and the bunkers are well positioned and well maintained…. Bunkering is quite superb… A good honest parkland course in immaculate condition… Holes are varied and offer up an excellent challenge… Little Aston has been hyped up as one of the best parkland courses in the land and it's up there, although I think Stoke Park is as good… I enjoyed it but somehow I expected a little bit more… Don't forget your jacket and tie or you'll be in the side bar - this is a traditional members' club. Well worth playing if you like parkland courses.

Little Aston   **91**st

Little Aston is set in 176 acres of tranquil, mature parkland in the former grounds of Little Aston Hall. The club is hidden away on the edge of exclusive suburbia, eight miles north of Birmingham city centre. "A pleasant park course of excellent turf," wrote Bernard Darwin in Golf Between Two Wars. "This is the kind of golf course which an eighteenth-century English gentleman would have approved." wrote Patric Dickinson in *A Round of Golf Courses*.

Harry Vardon reputedly laid out the course in 1908 for ten guineas. He had a charming and elegant piece of parkland to work with and succeeded in creating probably the best and toughest true parkland course in England. As it turned out, Vardon had created a course with long and challenging carries that ultimately proved too hard for the members, so Harry Colt was summoned to make the course friendlier. Mark Lewis (the club's professional for over 40 years during the first half of the 20th century) must also be credited for taking Little Aston through to maturity.

The course is always maintained immaculately. Even in the winter it plays well for a parkland layout and they are justifiably proud of the quality of their large greens. The undulating formal tree-lined fairways ensure that you get a private and picturesque walk in the park.

Above all, Little Aston is an honest golf course. There are no tricks, and everything is clearly laid out in front of you. The first two holes are fairly ordinary but at the third, things start to get better with a good downhill short par five that cajoles you into opening your shoulders. There are a number of good golf holes but it will take two or three rounds before you begin to really appreciate Little Aston.

Little Aston has hosted many important amateur and professional events, including the British Masters, held here on five separate occasions, most recently in 1969.

Birmingham isn't at the top of the list for golfing breaks, despite the fact that there are some excellent golf courses in this area, including Beau Desert, Whittington Heath and, of course, the Belfry. But if you do decide to visit this area, make sure you play Little Aston. It's one of the best courses in the Midlands.

FERNDOWN GOLF CLUB
119 Golf Links Road, Ferndown, Dorset, BH22 8BU
England
Telephone: +44 (0) 1202 874602

Average Reviewers' Score:

Website: www.ferndown-golf-club.co.uk
Architect: Harold Hilton
Visitors: Contact in advance - Not Thu and restricted at weekends

Reviewers' Comments

Ferndown is a lovely old course set in a beautiful part of the country and it compares well with some of the best of Surrey's heathland courses… The benefit of Ferndown is that Dorset is a great place to spend some time on a golfing break, unlike Surrey, which is in the middle of the commuter belt… Beautifully presented course wandering in and out of trees… Winds its way through the pines and its condition was outstanding in all respects… The course is always in great nick and the greens are slick too… Set up is excellent, as is the turf… A splendid experience… I was impressed with the warm and friendly welcome, they really make you feel at home… First class and a really friendly club too… Well worth a visit for all those who like classic heathland courses… A must-play course.

Ferndown (Old)

Ferndown is a pine and heathery heaven, set in pleasing manicured countryside and located a mile or two north of the popular seaside town of Bournemouth. This is where Peter Allis learnt his trade, for his father, Percy, was the professional here for more than a quarter of a century.

The club was founded in 1912 and Harold Hilton, one of the finest amateur golfers of all time, designed the course. It opened for play in 1914. Hilton won the British Open championship as an amateur twice, a feat only surpassed by Bobby Jones, who was British Open champion on three occasions, also as an amateur.

The Old course at Ferndown plays across a sandy outcrop of land where there is a proliferation of heather and pines. It's an inherently pretty golf course and sometimes it's bracketed alongside Augusta because of its immaculate tee to green grooming. The hazards are subtle – there are the obvious heather and trees to avoid, but the bunkers are especially well designed and positioned. The steep-lipped sand traps are invariably visible from the tees and the fairways and they certainly concentrate the mind. Many of the holes are doglegged in shape and tee shot position is critical, rather than sheer length. Ferndown is a course where scoring well depends entirely on whether or not the ball is kept in play.

By today's standards, the course is fairly short, measuring less than 6,500 yards from the medal tees, but the heathland layout will challenge the very best golfers and will enthral the average handicapper with its inherent beauty. Many important amateur and professional events have been contested over the Old course. In 1989, Ferndown hosted the Women's British Open. Jane Geddes carded a 67 on the first two days and dominated the tournament from thereon in.

There is no doubt that Ferndown is one of the prettiest and best-conditioned courses in the South and it's well worth a visit.

WOKING GOLF CLUB
Pond Road, Hook Heath, Woking, Surrey, GU22 0JZ
England
Telephone: +44 (0) 1483 760053

Average Reviewers' Score:

Website: www.wokinggolfclub.co.uk
Architect: Tom Dunn
Visitors: Contact 7 days in advance – no weekend visitors

Reviewers' Comments

Woking has bags of class despite being a traditional golf club in every respect... The course is short and during a hot summer it's almost links-like... It's good advice to leave the driver at home... There is enough to keep you interested all the way round... Greens with some significant undulations are kept in superb condition... Some heavy tree clearance underway, presumably to encourage the return of heather... This is one of the easier Top 100 courses I have played... Good course - but the lady members glare at one constantly, and seem to rule the roost here... Had a lovely day here... Well worth a visit and in the winter it's a bargain... A must-play course for the traditionalists... Thoroughly enjoyable... Would be a pleasure to be a member.

Woking

Woking is a charming Old England heathland course, laid out by Tom Dunn in 1893. The club was intended to provide relief for a few golf mad barristers who were sick and tired of playing on muddy clay. We must thank Woking wholeheartedly because nobody thought that heather and gorse-strewn land was viable ground for golf and this was the first experimental heathland layout.

At the turn of the 20th century, there were only a few heathland courses around London and Bernard Darwin described them as "the stars of sand and heather". He had a soft spot for Woking because it's the oldest and one of the best. He went on to say, "although my judgement may not be strictly an impartial one, I think it is still the pleasantest of all upon which to play, and the golf is undeniably interesting." Darwin was once a golf mad barrister himself and also a member here for more than sixty years.

There is absolutely no doubt that it's located in an idyllic spot and the unusual pavilion clubhouse only adds to the charisma. This is not a championship layout by any stretch of the imagination; the course only measures 6,340 yards from the medal tees. But Woking is a mature and strategic layout requiring well-positioned tee shots that must, at all costs, remain out of the heather and in play. We recommend that you leave your driver in the boot of the car to avoid any temptation.

Woking is not riddled with bunkers but those that are there are adroitly positioned. In 1900, a controversy raged when two bunkers were dug into the 4th fairway. The members were mortified that they might be penalised after hitting a good straight drive. Looking back at this, Woking was a pioneer in architectural terms, forcing the player to make a decision, lay up short or bravely aim on the right line.

In 1926, the club hosted a match involving captain Bobby Jones and the rest of the American Walker Cup team. The Americans were beaten 6-3 by the "Moles Golfing Society". Woking was also once home to the Alba Trophy, a celebrated amateur competition. These days, it's used to genteel peace and quiet in Surrey's suburbia. This is definitely a course for the connoisseur. Or as Darwin said in his 1910 book, *The Golf Courses of the British Isles*: "I can only end as I began by asserting that there is no more delightful course whereon to play golf."

WEST HILL GOLF CLUB
Bagshot Road, Brookwood, Surrey, GU24 0BH, England
Telephone: +44 (0) 1483 474365

Average Reviewers' Score:

Website: www.westhill-golfclub.co.uk
Architect: Cuthbert Butchart
Visitors: Contact secretary in advance

Reviewers' Comments

Lovely traditional course set next to Worplesdon and Woking... I've played Woking a good deal over the last ten years or so, but found West Hill to be superior in almost every aspect... Comparisons will be made with nearby Woking and, although similar looking, West Hill gets my nod as the 'toughest test' but Woking gets the vote for the 'better looking'... The course is absolutely superb with wonderfully designed holes that utilise the contours and surroundings very well indeed... It's a tough test with a par of 69, which includes five par fours over 400 yards... Possibly a bit on the short side but charming nonetheless... Straight driving is needed... Chances to get a score going on the two short par fives... Watch out on the 5th tee, there's heather right across the fairway over the hill... Very tricky greens to read - certainly beat me... You must have tea and a bacon sandwich at the snack hut by the 12th green, makes the memory of all those missed putts fade away... I would play this course again and again given the opportunity... I had a thoroughly enjoyable round.

West Hill

West Hill is the youngest of the trinity of "Ws" located in this most beautiful corner of Surrey (Woking and Worplesdon being the other two). Cuthbert Butchart, a Scottish professional from Carnoustie, laid out the course in 1910 on the instruction of the founder, Mrs Marguerite Lubbock, a keen golfer. At the time, ladies were not allowed to become members at other local Surrey clubs, so she decided to form one of her own. Butchart went on to become West Hill's first club professional and he also made a name for himself as a fine, forward-thinking clubmaker. His drivers were revolutionary, superbly balanced and fitted with innovative lead weights.

Butchart is not a household name in golf course architecture, but he created an excellent course, which has remained virtually untouched ever since (except for some recent bunker refurbishment). It's routed in an out and back fashion across undulating sandy ground. The fairways are lined with pine, birch and of course, tangly heather. Measuring slightly more than 6,350 yards, West Hill is not long by today's standards, but with only two par fives and a lowly par of 69, it represents an enjoyable and testing challenge. The key to scoring well at West Hill is the successful negotiation of the five short holes and the best of these is undoubtedly the 15th, which measures 212 yards from the back tees. British golf luminary Henry Cotton felt that the 15th was one of the best short holes in Britain and, for a while, Cotton shared the West Hill course record with a 67.

West Hill is home of the famous Father and Son Foursomes Tournament, which was first contested in 1931. The Times and The Telegraph report on this event as it progresses each year. The winning team become proud holders of the Geoffrey Lubbock Challenge Cup, which was donated by the husband of the founder Marguerite.

If it's charm that you are looking for, then you need look no further than West Hill. This is a truly delightful golf course.

PORTSTEWART GOLF CLUB
Strand Road, Portstewart, Co. Londonderry,
BT55 7PG, Northern Ireland
Telephone: +44 (0) 2870 832015

Average Reviewers' Score:

Website: www.portstewartgc.co.uk
Architect: Des Giffin
Visitors: Welcome weekdays and Sat/Sun pm

Reviewers' Comments

I'm sure the Top 100 connoisseurs out there already realise that there's some good golf to be had on the north Antrim coast, but I bet few people realise how good it really is... For me, the highlight of the trip was Portstewart... The Strand is a course for the dune junkies, the dunes are simply gigantic and the front nine is routed directly through them... This is the finest front nine I have ever played, bar none... The view from the first elevated tee is breathtaking... An inspiring start to the round... The front nine continues to wind its way through the sandhills, offering a striking landscape... The back nine by comparison is almost bland but that is more to do with the magnificence of the front nine... The challenges on the back nine are subtle with every hole offering something to make you think... The anti-climax is the last three holes... The back nine is good also... Looking back out over the course from the bar leaves the pleasant glow of another day's great golfing experience... I'd rather play the Strand front nine once than the whole of Royal Portrush twice. Simply stunning...Des Giffin thank you.

Portstewart (Strand)

The golf club at Portstewart was founded way back in 1894, but the origins of golf being played here date back even further to 1889. The Strand course is a bit of a hybrid, a mix of the old and the new. Major development took place in the late 1980s when the layout was updated and seven new holes were constructed in the virgin sand dune range called "Thistly Hollow". The new Strand course, designed by Des Giffin, opened for play in 1992.

And what an exhilarating golf course this is, set amidst imposing, gigantic sand dunes with panoramic views across the Atlantic mouth of Lough Foyle to the Inishowen peninsula beyond.

The Strand is an incredibly challenging and thoroughly enjoyable golf course, with one of the best opening nine holes in golf. The 1st hole is an absolute stunner, one of golf's most intimidating, a downhill 425-yard par four. There is a wealth of great holes here at Portstewart; especially memorable are two of the new par threes, the 3rd and the 6th. The 3rd is a challenging single shotter, measuring 207 yards, whilst the 6th, measuring a mere 140 yards with a plateau green, is also a tough cookie and will stay in the mind for a long time.

Credit must go to the designer because the new holes blend seamlessly with the old. Sometimes, when new land is taken in, there is punctuation between the old and the new. Not so at the Strand.

A golfing trip to Northern Ireland would not be complete without a round on the Strand course. The members here are very warm and welcoming and if you add this course to a round at both Royal Portrush and Royal County Down, you will have played three of the world's finest links courses.

LIPHOOK GOLF CLUB
Wheatsheaf Enclosure, Liphook, Hants, GU30 7EH
England
Telephone: +44 (0) 1428 723785

Average Reviewers' Score:

Website: www.liphookgolfclub.com
Architect: Arthur Croome
Visitors: Contact in advance – not Tue or competition days

Reviewers' Comments

Quaint and picturesque with the ability to suddenly jump up and bite when you least expect it... A pretty and exceptionally challenging heathland track... It isn't a long course but the shorter par fours make you position the tee shot instead of 'slashing' at it with the driver - strategy is the winner on these holes ... It requires a great deal of thought to score well... Downside is the par fives, which with a slight amount of work, could be made to be special without detracting from the overall feel of the course... The 13th is a belter... You'll need to keep out of that heather... Greens are excellent, some of the best and fastest I've ever putted on... Course was in great nick... Sneak onto the back tee of the par four 4th – the hole is fantastic and the view worth a look... In these days of the 7,400-yard championship course it is nice to re-visit Liphook and play golf in a lovely setting... An underrated course and it's up there with the best in this neck of the woods... Members are also very welcoming....A real gem and it should be ranked higher.

Liphook

96

Liphook is as pretty as a picture. A delightful, classic heathland course spanning Hampshire and Sussex's county boundaries. It's a course for the connoisseur, not for the dilettante. The club was founded in 1922. A teacher called Arthur Croome designed the course, his one and only. "He did it wonderfully well," wrote Bernard Darwin in *Golf Between Two Wars*, "all the better perhaps because he had not much money to do it with and must rely as far as possible on kindly Nature."

By today's standards, it's relatively short – measuring less than 6,200 yards – but with a lowly par of 69, playing to handicap is another matter. The heather, pine and birch place a premium on line rather than length. The sandy ground is wonderfully undulating with natural depressions and elevations and, in some ways, the land is reminiscent of that at nearby Hindhead, where there is another charming and understated golf course.

Liphook starts unusually with a par three. "For sheer beauty I think I like best the second hole," wrote Darwin, "a short one with its knowing little bunkers waiting by the fringe of the green and its clump of dark trees keeping watch and ward behind. The fifth, too, is picturesque with its big golden bunker and its stream." Bunkers are audacious, characterised not only at the 5th, but also at the 6th and 11th. The prettiest holes and probably the best sequence of holes is the trio from the 12th to the 14th. If we had to pick a favourite hole, we would plump for the 14th, a short par four doglegging to the right where a bold drive will leave a short pitch to the green, and a good birdie opportunity will be on offer following a well-positioned drive.

Liphook is a classy golf course which does everything well, but in an understated way. A charming course with friendly members – the perfect venue for golf.

DOWNFIELD GOLF CLUB
Turnberry Avenue, Dundee, DD2 3QP, Scotland
Telephone: +44 (0) 1382 825595

Average Reviewers' Score:

Website: www.downfieldgolf.co.uk
Architect: James Braid and C.K. Cotton
Visitors: Welcome - book in advance

Reviewers' Comments

Downfield in Dundee must surely rank as the best members' club inland course in the country... As a mark of respect, Downfield can be put in the same envelope as the leafy Surrey courses that we are well aware of - throw in a little bit of Woburn too... Better than Rosemount and Gleneagles for my money... This place is like Texas where everything is *big* – large tee boxes, wide fairways, tall trees on every hole and enormous greens... Even links lovers will like this delightful wooded test... It's easy to see why it is an Open Qualifying course... There's lots of variation and numerous long sweeping doglegs... If the course had a nickname it would be 'Rover' due to the amount of doglegs... 11th is one of the best inland holes I've played... From the 11th onwards – pure class... This venue does not receive the recognition that it deserves... The conditioning is quite superb and you can be assured of a genuinely warm welcome... It's not well known, but it should be... Don't pass this course by.

Downfield

On the outskirts of Dundee, lies Downfield, a stunning parkland course little known outside Scotland. Paul Lawrie came through Open Qualifying here in 1999 and went on to win the Open at Carnoustie. Downfield also hosted the inaugural 1972 Scottish Open, when England's Neil Coles won after a play-off with Wales's Brian Huggett. Undoubtedly, Downfield is a gem and one of the most beautiful inland courses in Scotland, with more than 100 species of trees lining the manicured fairways.

A modest nine-hole course was laid out at Downfield at the turn of the century but the land was returned to agriculture during the First World War. The club was reformed in 1932 and the great James Braid laid out a new course. Houses now occupy most of the 1930s layout – only five original holes are incorporated into the course we play today, which was laid out by a Downfield Golf Club member with advice and guidance from C.K.Cotton.

Downfield represents a differing challenge, depending on which tees are used. From the back tees, the course measures more than 6,800 yards against a par of 73, but from the regular men's tees, three par fives become testing, long par fours. There are six par fives for the ladies, against a par of 75. Water, in the shape of ditches and ponds, come into play on seven holes, adding to the obvious main hazard – the trees. The 11th through to the 13th are probably the best collection of holes. 11th and 13th are both tough par fours from the regular tees and the 12th is one of Gary Player's favourite par threes, called "Davy Jones's Locker".

Dundee isn't an obvious golfing destination, but include Downfield alongside Letham Grange and Edzell and you've got three of Scotland's very best and least known inland courses.

THE DE VERE BELFRY
Wishaw, North Warwickshire, B76 9PR, England
Telephone: +44 (0) 1675 470301

Average Reviewers' Score:

Website: www.thebelfry.com
Architect: Peter Alliss and Dave Thomas
Visitors: Welcome – Book in advance

Reviewers' Comments

Thoroughly enjoyed the challenge of playing such a famous and well-photographed course... Treading the turf of the Ryder Cup teams makes this a real treat... There's so much familiarity and history that you become totally absorbed... The experience is magical... This is one tough course... It's much tougher than it looks, water lurks everywhere and plenty of balls can be lost... To play this course well you need total faith in your driver... You have to be an exceptional golfer to hit some of these greens in regulation... 10th and 18th are special... there's more to the Brabazon than the 10th and 18th... The 3rd is a stunning risk/reward par five that will tempt the big hitters... Go for the 10th, you can dine out on hitting the green for years after... Excellent layout/design and as a test of golf... Design wise it's nothing special... Course suffers from wet conditions more than most... The course was in poor condition... The course was in excellent shape... Don't be put off playing this brilliant course because of past condition problems... Practice facilities are as good as any in England... We'll be back soon to try and play somewhere close to handicap.

206

Belfry (Brabazon)

The Brabazon course at The De Vere Belfry doesn't need introducing. After all, it's unique. This course has played host to more Ryder Cups than any other course on the planet - four in total. The Americans must dislike it, because team USA has only once triumphed here. Additionally, and for only the second time in Ryder Cup history, the 1989 biennial match was halved, but Europe retained the trophy because they were still the cup holders following their win in 1987 at Muirfield Village, Ohio.

The Belfry itself owes much to the vision and determination of one man, Colin Snape. In the mid 70s, Snape was the director of the financially struggling PGA. Over a pie and a pint, Peter Alliss told him that an old hotel on the outskirts of Birmingham was available as a potential new location for the PGA HQ. In 1977, The Brabazon - named after former PGA president, Lord Brabazon - opened for play with a challenge match, Seve Ballesteros and Johnny Miller against Tony Jacklin and Brian Barnes. The Belfry has never looked back and it's still the PGA's home.

Alliss and Thomas were given an unremarkable piece of farmland, which required significant sculpting to turn it into a remarkable golf course. For many visiting golfers, The Belfry, and The Brabazon course in particular, is Mecca. Everyone wants to play here; it's an exciting golfing venue, drawing thousands of visitors each year.

The excitement comes from playing memorable and familiar holes. And, following Dave Thomas's £2.7m makeover in the late 90s, there is more water on The Brabazon than just about any other inland course in the British Isles - take a few extra balls. The course has two outstanding holes, which have been popularised by television - the 10th and 18th. The former is a unique short par four, measuring about 300 yards, with water running along the right hand side of the fairway. It is drivable - you've seen Seve do it - so go on, you've got to go for it.

The 18th is another hole that is totally dominated by water and it's terrifying. This dramatic, par four closing hole, rewards the brave. Cut off as much of the water as you can from the tee, and you will be left with a shorter approach shot, which must carry a lake on its way to a long, narrow, triple-tiered green. This hole has seen more Ryder Cup emotion than any other hole in the world. For this reason alone, to follow in the footsteps of golf's greatest legends, The Brabazon is a must-play course.

ROYAL ASHDOWN FOREST GOLF CLUB
Chapel Lane, Forest Row, East Sussex, RH18 5LR
England
Telephone: +44 (0) 1342 822018

Average Reviewers' Score:

Website: www.royalashdown.co.uk
Architect: Archdeacon Scott
Visitors: Restrictions Tue and weekends – contact in advance

Reviewers' Comments

Special is the one word that comes to mind when I think about Royal Ashdown Forest... Wandering around here is a delight... Very natural and very old school but still top drawer... All so natural and unspoilt - babbling brooks around the greens... Totally natural and ever so tough to score well... Lots of sloping lies causing all types of shot-making difficulties... Play it in the summer when the heather is out and the fairways are hard and links-like... Having no bunkers does not make this easy - just try getting out of the gorse... You can certainly get lost in the forest here... 12th hole is my favourite, long par five downhill right to left... It's simply delightful in every respect... Very peaceful... Clubhouse felt a tad dated with the 'long sock rule' with shorts... The West course is also worth playing. It's very similar but much shorter, an ideal warm up course for a fantastic day's golf - 36 of nature's best... It's superb.

Winnie the Pooh and Christopher Robin had many adventures here in the dark and mysterious Ashdown Forest. Winnie invented "Poohsticks" on the edge of the Forest, a game we reckon is even more popular than golf! Oh, and by the way, watch out for bouncing Tigger.

The Ashdown Forest & Tunbridge Wells Golf Club (as it was originally called) was founded in 1888 and the course opened for play the following year. We are not entirely sure who designed it, but we know that the club's founder, Archdeacon Scott, was involved. Queen Victoria bestowed royal patronage in 1893 and in 1901, "Tunbridge Wells" was dropped from its name and the club became known simply as Royal Ashdown Forest.

It was originally a short course, measuring only 4,900 yards. Between 1910 and 1920, it was gradually lengthened to its present 6,400 plus yards. Little has changed since. The tremendous golfer, Abe Mitchell, was a member of the Cantelupe Club, Royal Ashdown Forest's Artisan section. Mitchell had the 1920 Open at Royal Cinque Ports in his grasp, but he lost to his greatest rival, George Duncan.

In his book, *Golf Courses of the British Isles*, Bernard Darwin wrote: "It is only at the end of a round that we realise with pleasurable shock that there is not a single hideous rampart or so much as a pot bunker". The only bunkers here are natural grassy pits. In fact, the whole course is natural. The challenge comes from the undulating land, streams, heather, bracken and, of course, the many trees.

The Ashdown Forest is protected by Acts of Parliament – no alterations are allowed to the terrain without the Conservators' approval. It is doubtful that the course would have remained so naturally beautiful without having these restrictions in place.

The 6th, the "Island Hole", is one of the best short holes anywhere. It's only 125 yards long from the medal tees, but it's fraught with danger, surrounded by a deep stream and a gully. If you hit the green, well done, but two-putting is not easy - there is a ridge running right across the middle of the green. The 17th is a fantastic downhill par four, measuring 480 yards from the back tees. A decent drive, with a bit of draw (for the right-hander), will leave a long second that needs to carry across gorse, bracken and a path!

The setting is really stunning, affording fantastic views from the high parts of the course across the forest and the rolling Sussex countryside. The resident professionals obviously like it here too. In Royal Ashdown Forest's long history there have been only three pros and Martyn Landsborough, the current pro, has served a mere 15 years at the club!

THE CARNEGIE CLUB AT SKIBO CASTLE
Skibo Castle, Dornoch, Sutherland, IV25 3RQ
Scotland
Telephone: +44 (0) 1620 842255

Average Reviewers' Score:

Website: www.carnegieclubs.com
Architect: John Sutherland, Donald Steel and Tom Mackenzie
Visitors: Contact for details

Reviewers' Comments

As an overall package and a completely indulgent treat, the Carnegie Club is hard to beat... A wonderful golfing experience but way too expensive for mere mortals... Best holes are set along the Dornoch Firth... Holes running alongside the Dornoch Firth are tight and very challenging... The course is understated and very natural with fine conditioning from tee to green... Give me the real Dornoch... The course is a must for links lovers... Take an intake of breath, dig deep and stay and play... Skibo is certainly worth playing as long as you don't mind putting a dent in your wallet... I got chatting to a member and managed to play their nine hole short parkland course (called Monk's Walk), which also doubles up as a par three layout. It's great fun, but reserved for members only... The hotel is stunning and the service is understated but perfect.

Skibo Castle

100th

Located on the edge of the beautiful Dornoch Firth with views of the Struie Hills, the 7,500-acre Skibo Castle estate is something special, very special. It's a place where fairytales meet reality. Schytherbolle, its Celtic name, roughly translated means fairyland. But it wasn't always like this – there was once much bloodshed when Sigurd the Mighty and Thorstein the Red, the early Nordic settlers, descended upon Dornoch. Things are much calmer these days and a trip to Skibo will make you feel like a millionaire.

In 1898, the original Laird of Skibo, Andrew Carnegie, commissioned Royal Dornoch's Secretary, John Sutherland to build a private nine-hole links course. But after Carnegie's death in 1919, Skibo Castle and the golf course soon became fallow. British entrepreneur Peter de Savary bought the Skibo estate in 1990 and he asked Donald Steel and Tom Mackenzie to resurrect the links. In 1992, a new Skibo Castle links was born.

"Love of traditional links lies at the core of our design principles", is the motto of Donald Steel's company. Steel and Mackenzie have created a links at Skibo that blends seamlessly into its natural surroundings. It's a cliché to say that any new course appears so natural that it seems as though it has been there forever, but if you didn't know better, you would think that the links at Skibo was much older than it actually is. Its age is given away only by the five sets of tees, which stretch the course from 5,500 yards to over 6,660 yards.

Very little is left of the original Sutherland design and the new Skibo contains many excellent holes at the start of the round, but then there is a slight lull in proceedings around the turn before the dramatic three closing holes kick in. The 17th is a risk-and-reward gem, a short par four measuring 267 yards with the green definitely in reach, but you'll need to flirt with the beach and the deep bunkers guarding the front of the green. The 18th, a sweeping par five, concludes a memorable and varied round. The hole doglegs left, hugging the salt marshes. Big hitters might reach it in two.

A visit to Skibo Castle is a breathtaking experience where you'll be treated as a member of the Carnegie Club for the duration of your stay. Expect pre-dinner drinks in the magnificent Edwardian reception room and then a piper will lead you to dinner. What a way to go!

YOUR TOP 100 COURSES

In the Editor's introduction on page 10, we explained how we derived our rankings. In summary, we blended and weighted the lists from publications (e.g. Golf World, Golf Digest etc.) to produce our own unique and comprehensive list of ranked courses. However, this book would not be complete without showing the Top 100 list according to our visitors' reviews posted on the website (www.top100golfcourses.co.uk).

The Top 100 list below is based on visitors' reviews up to April 2005 – from the Top 100 website. Biennially, we plan to publish a Top 100 based on visitors' reviews. We can't promise that it will be the most definitive list in existence but it will be based on the views of thousands of ordinary golfers who love playing our greatest courses. We'll then take this list and blend it into our overall ranking database.

We actively encourage people to post reviews onto the website and to rate the courses. There is also a facility for our visitors to nominate any course which they think should be included within the Top 100 website. We honestly believe that we have the most definitive list of our greatest courses. If you think we have missed any, let us know and if we agree, we'll add your favourite course to the "your gems" section of the Top 100 website.

1. Royal Dornoch (Championship)	51. West Hill
2. Royal County Down	52. Buckinghamshire
3. Lahinch (Old)	53. Chart Hills
4. Kingsbarns	54. Royal Troon (Old)
5. Royal Aberdeen	55. Brocket Hall (Melbourne)
6. Loch Lomond	56. Silloth-on-Solway
7. Turnberry (Ailsa)	57. Waterville
8. Ballybunion (Old)	58. Hillside
9. Carnoustie (Championship)	59. Portmarnock Hotel Links
10. Portmarnock (Old)	60. Perranporth
11. Woodhall Spa (Hotchkin)	61. Beau Desert
12. Royal Birkdale	62. Portstewart (Strand)
13. St George's Hill	63. Royal St David's
14. Western Gailes	64. Swinley Forest
15. Royal Portrush (Dunluce)	65. Sunningdale (New)
16. St Andrews (Old)	66. Hunstanton
17. Littlestone	67. St Enodoc (Church)
18. Ganton	68. Burnham & Berrow
19. Murcar	69. Alwoodley
20. Castlerock	70. Ballyliffin (Glashedy)
21. Pennard	71. Worplesdon
22. Carne	72. Malone
23. Sunningdale (Old)	73. St Andrews (New)
24. Nefyn (Old)	74. Woburn (Duke's)
25. Doonbeg	75. Downfield
26. Woburn (Duchess)	76. Gleneagles (King's)
27. Muirfield	77. Royal Porthcawl
28. Cruden Bay	78. West Lancashire
29. Old Head	79. St Andrews Bay (Devlin)
30. Wentworth (West)	80. Ballyliffin (Old)
31. Sandiway	81. Royal St George's
32. Brocket Hall (Palmerston)	82. Rye (Old)
33. Saunton (East)	83. Moor Park (High)
34. North Berwick (West)	84. Wentworth (East)
35. European Club	85. Leven Links
36. Notts	86. Royal Lytham & St Annes
37. West Sussex	87. Stoke Park
38. Prestwick	88. Machrie
39. Machrihanish	89. Formby
40. Druids Glen	90. Kilmarnock (Barassie)
41. Castletown	91. Ashridge
42. Rosapenna (Sandy Hills)	92. Royal Ashdown Forest (Old)
43. Delamere Forest	93. County Louth
44. Tralee	94. Aberdovey
45. Royal West Norfolk	95. Saunton (West)
46. Walton Heath (Old)	96. Pyle & Kenfig
47. Enniscrone	97. County Sligo (Championship)
48. Dooks	98. Hankley Common
49. Nairn	99. Donegal
50. Gleneagles (Queen's)	100. Ipswich (Main)

25 MORE GREAT COURSES

Here are 25 more great courses to whet your appetite. All of these are highly rated by the Top 100 team and visitors to the Top 100 website.

Ballyliffin Golf Club

Steve Smith

SEATON CAREW GOLF CLUB
Tees Road, Seaton Carew, Hartlepool, TS25 1DE
England
Telephone: +44 (0) 1429 296496

Average Reviewers' Score:

Website: www.sportnetwork.net/main/s235.php
Architect: Dr Alister MacKenzie, Frank Pennink
Visitors: Welcome after 10am

Reviewers' Comments

Seaton Carew, hidden within industrial Teesside, is proof that a classic course can be found in an apparently unpromising area... If you can overcome the stark views, you'll love Seaton Carew... A links course for the purist and a fair and honest test of golf... Though not long by modern standards, the wind, dunes, and whins make the course a severe test... The wind howls across this exposed strip of land... There are no unforeseen tricks and everything is laid out in front of you except for one semi-blind drive and the odd hidden bunker... You need the full repertoire of shots to play Seaton, this is certainly not target golf country and you need to run the ball in low or land the ball short of the green to get close to the pins... It's unpretentious and at the same time traditional... This is a course that gets better and better as you plot your way round... I made a special effort to play here and I wasn't disappointed... It's well worth making the detour to play... Playing the 17th "Snag" alone justifies a visit to Seaton Carew... Excellent value for money... A complete experience.

Seaton Carew

Dr Duncan McCuaig founded the Durham and Yorkshire Golf Club in 1874; this was the first golf club in the North East of England and originally it was laid out as a 14-hole course. Other golf clubs in this area were formed towards the end of the 19th century, so in 1887, the club changed its name to Seaton Carew. The course was extended to 18 holes in 1891.

Another doctor called MacKenzie came along in 1925 and modified the layout. Ten years later, Dr Alister MacKenzie went on to design Augusta National, home of the Masters. Continuing the doctor theme, the 3rd hole, called "Doctor", a short par three, remains as per its original design and serves as a tribute to Dr McCuaig, the club's founder.

There are now 22 holes following Frank Pennink's addition of four new holes. The members now have a number of playing options. The Old course, an out and back layout, is the original MacKenzie design. The Brabazon course incorporates 14 of the original holes; Pennink's four new holes come into play at the turn. The Brabazon, an uneven par 73 (35 out, 38 back), is now considered the championship course and is tougher and longer than the Old course. In 1985, Seaton Carew hosted the Brabazon Trophy (English Amateur Stroke Play Championship), producing a tie for first place between Peter Baker and Roger Roper.

Don't be put off by the industrial surroundings of chimneys and chemical works; this excellent golf course is one of the best on the East coast of England, a real MacKenzie treat. There are a few ridges of sand dunes and the fairways undulate gently, but otherwise this is a relatively flat links course, always at the mercy of the wind.

The 17th hole, called "Snag", is one of many great holes and the late Derek Hornby, a historian and author of the *History of Seaton Carew* poetically describes it: "The seventeenth's dangers are countless, beginning with whin, gorse and dune, the rough and gathering bunkers, and the green's undulating tune, to veer even slightly is fatal, the cost is distressingly high, many the card that's been torn up, just here with home oh so nigh".

DONEGAL GOLF CLUB
Murvagh, Co. Donegal, Ireland
Telephone: +353 (0) 73 34054

Average Reviewers' Score:

Website: www.donegalgolfclub.ie
Architect: Eddie Hackett
Visitors: Welcome - book online via Donegal website

Reviewers' Comments

"Murvagh", as the locals fondly know it, is an absolutely stunning course... One of Ireland's longest courses and you must drive well here... The views are simply breathtaking with the Atlantic crashing all around... Great setting with the mighty Blue Stack Mountains on show... Fairly new course - about 35 years old but has a distinctly older feel... It has recently been voted in the Top 10 Irish courses and I can't disagree... The best holes tumble through the dunes towards the sea... There are many excellent holes but special note is made of the par five 6th which offers a stunning view of the beach... I really can't fault this course... Highly thought-of course... With a traditional warm and friendly Irish welcome and, of course, a Guinness, you've got golfing paradise... Very memorable and great fun.

Donegal

The Murvagh peninsula, jutting out into Donegal Bay, is the home of Donegal Golf Club. It's an enchanting and isolated setting for a big links course. The panoramic view across the bay is sensational, with the Bluestack Mountains providing a dramatic backdrop.

The prolific architect, Eddie Hackett, laid out the course in 1973 and Murvagh is considered to be one of his finest creations. Hackett was given a naturally rugged and crumpled piece of links land to play with and he used it well to produce a monster championship-length layout. Donegal measures a mighty 7,200 yards from the back tees and we recommend that they be left well alone for the pros or for the very low single figure handicappers.

The layout is configured in two elongated loops of nine holes. The front nine runs anticlockwise and the back nine runs clockwise, sitting inside the outward nine. The first four holes are fairly ordinary, feeling inland in character, and then at the 185-yard par three 5th, we enter dune country. This one-shot hole, called "Valley of Tears", is a brute. A semi-blind tee shot to a narrow plateau green, means we must make sure that we select the right club to traverse the valley and the bunkers in front of and below the raised green.

The next three holes are stunning, where the fairways rollercoaster up and down, flanked by huge, shaggy sand dunes. At the turn, we are faced with a thrilling back nine, including the 12th, a monster par five, and the sadistic par three 16th, measuring nigh on 250 yards from the back tees.

There is no doubt that Donegal at Murvagh is a very challenging links course and it should be up at the top of the must-play list for any serious golfer.

LADYBANK GOLF CLUB
Annsmuir, Ladybank, Cupar, Fife, KY15 7RA, Scotland
Telephone: +44 (0) 1337 830814

Average Reviewers' Score:

Website: www.ladybankgolf.co.uk
Architect: Old Tom Morris
Visitors: Welcome weekdays - contact in advance

Reviewers' Comments

Ladybank is a very pleasant alternative to the links golf normally played when visiting the Kingdom of Fife… Had a great time – this is a really good test of golf but not impossible if you think your way around… It pays to keep to the straight and narrow because there is plenty of gorse just off the fairways to catch errant shots… The key to scoring well here is how well you play from the tee… The course is very flat and winds in and out of tree-lined fairways… The fairways were not as secluded as I imagined… Ladybank will once again be used for qualifying for the Open Championship… After the par three 12th hole, there is a very strong, demanding stretch of closing holes… The final three holes demand a high level of concentration to maintain your score… The clubhouse facilities were first class with separate visitors' changing area and an informal, well-appointed lounge… Visit Ladybank on the way to historic St Andrews – you'll have a fine time.

Ladybank

In the tranquil heart of the Kingdom of Fife lies an enchanting, sandy tract of land where the whin, heather and pine smell divine. The Howe of Fife provides Ladybank with a natural shelter in the valley of the River Eden between Strathmiglo in the west and Cupar to the east. It's one of those courses that really should be a Top 100 regular, because it is one of Scotland's very best inland courses. Clearly it's up against some serious competition in Fife, but mix in this peaceful heathland surprise, alongside the more famous links courses in and around the Home of Golf, and we guarantee you will not be disappointed. You'll certainly be less windswept!

In 1879, Old Tom Morris was charged with laying out a six-hole course. The layout was extended to nine holes in 1910, and in 1962, to 18 holes. Does anybody know who the architects were behind the new holes? Whoever it was, they did a fine job because it is hard to distinguish between the old holes and the new.

Regularly used as a Final Open Qualifier, Ladybank is a tough cookie, where accuracy and positioning are all important. The smallish greens are always in outstanding condition but your iron play will need to be on song to find the firm and fast putting surfaces. The crisp fairways are relatively flat and even – it is very rare to get an uneven stance. Measuring over 6,600 yards, it's a seriously challenging course – keeping the ball in play will pay dividends and save you from losing loads of shots and balls. The problem is that Ladybank teases and cajoles you into hitting a long ball – if you're accurate, you'll be rewarded handsomely. It's a tricky call.

We are sure that there is a sprinkling of Worplesdon, a dash of Woking and spot of West Hill at Ladybank. But wait a moment – perhaps it's the other way round, Ladybank was here first. Anyway, there is no doubt that it has got its own unique ambience and you will certainly receive an exceptionally warm welcome from the members. This is an absolute must-play course.

BALLYBUNION GOLF CLUB
Sandhill Road, Ballybunion, County Kerry, Ireland
Telephone: +353 (0) 68 27146

Average Reviewers' Score:

Website: www.ballybuniongolfclub.ie
Architect: Robert Trent Jones
Visitors: Contact in advance - not at weekends

Reviewers' Comments

Play this course before you play the Old course and make sure your legs are up for it... Super course - get a day ticket and play it alongside the Old... A wonderful, quirky ramble through the dunes of Ballybunion... Really enjoyable but a bit austere, especially if the weather is poor... Several blind shots reveal cheeky little greens with all the pace you need to test even the best putters... Alongside the Old it seems wanting, but when you compare it to a hundred other courses around these isles, you'll know you've played a little gem... Not to be missed when visiting Ballybunion.

Ballybunion (Cashen)

The Old course at Ballybunion is a tough act to follow and when new land was purchased in 1971, Robert Trent Jones had his work cut out to create a complementary second course. He was clearly thrilled to have been asked to fashion the new layout and he said: "When I first saw the piece of land chosen for the new course of Ballybunion, I was thrilled beyond words. I said that it was the finest piece of links land that I had ever seen, and perhaps the finest piece of links land in the world. With the ocean on one side and the river on the other, its tumbling, undulating, free-flowing rhythm of line is beauty beyond description."

In the early 1980s, the new Cashen course was ready for play and ever since, American visitors have besieged the place. Trent Jones has done an excellent job and it's just as well, because the links land is pure magic. The Cashen is set amongst even taller, more alarming, sand dunes than the Old course and its feel is slightly harder, despite being over 300 yards shorter in length, possibly because the fairways are tighter.

It is a cliché to say that the course looks natural and plays as though it has been laid out for a hundred years rather than a couple of decades, but it is a tribute to Trent Jones; he has resisted the temptation to do anything other than go with the flow of the land and use its natural form to full potential. The result is a dateless golf course.

Ballybunion is an unforgettable experience, with two thoroughly bewitching courses. Everyone comes here to play the Old course. That is understandable, but do not overlook the Cashen. It is an amazing second course and well worth playing in its own right.

WEST LANCASHIRE GOLF CLUB
Hall Road West, Blundellsands, Liverpool, L23 8SZ
England
Telephone: +44 (0) 151 924 1076

Average Reviewers' Score:

Website: www.westlancashiregolf.co.uk
Architect: Ken Cotton and Fred Hawtree
Visitors: Weekdays only, not before 9.30am

Reviewers' Comments

Very, very good - a nice variation of holes creating two loops of nine... The beauty of this course is its variety... The key to the course is to keep the ball on the fairway - if you stray into the rough, you will be lucky to find your ball... While the wind is always an influence, it is never overpowering as the layout of two loops of nine provides relief from what might otherwise be a constant battering... Hugely underrated, this is a cracking links course... It doesn't favour either hook or cut, just important to hit the fairway... Six par fours over 400 yards suggests a very long course but the four par threes are of average length, so a fine balance of length and difficulty is maintained... The clubhouse is rather unattractive, but who cares when the golf is as good and challenging as this... Despite a modern clubhouse, this course is a true "old links", very tough when the wind blows, and all-natural terrain... A great course... A belter!

West Lancashire

West Lancashire is the oldest surviving club in Lancashire, although, strictly speaking, Blundellsands is now part of the borough of Merseyside. In 1901, Harold Hilton, one of the finest amateur golfers of all time, was the Secretary of West Lancs Golf Club. That same year, he won the British Amateur Championship at St Andrews, beating J Low by one hole. Hilton was also the British Open champion in 1892 and 1897, a feat only surpassed by Bobby Jones, who won the British Open on three occasions, also as an amateur.

The club was founded in 1873. The course was originally designed by the hands of an unknown architect, but this is such a natural links that we suspect Nature did most of the work. We do know that Ken Cotton and Fred Hawtree made significant revisions to the layout in the early 1960s.

Its esteemed Royal neighbours keep West Lancs out of the limelight but it is a truly classical links course, located on a charming stretch of prime links land. On a clear day, to the north, Blackpool Tower can be seen in the distance. To the southwest, there are panoramic views across the Crosby Channel to the Birkenhead peninsula and Liverpool Bay beyond.

James Finnegan, in his book *All Courses Great and Small*, articulately sums up the characteristics of West Lancs: "On the 355-yard 13th, we fire away from an elevated tee, the fairway curving left along a dune-framed valley to a green on a cunning low plateau. The next hole, 412 yards, also begins on a high tee in the sandhills, but this time the downhill drive is blind, over a ridge, and the fairway bends sweepingly right, around a thick stand of pines, finally disclosing a raised green tucked in the lee of a wooded hillside."

The Guinness Book of Golf Facts and Feats tells the amazing story of Peter Richard Parkinson who, on 6th June, 1972, performed the British Isles' longest hole in one. It was on the 7th hole, and clearly it was a mistake because the 7th is called "Folly", a 393-yard par four. Either way, it was one hell of a biff!

SHISKINE GOLF & TENNIS CLUB
Shore Road, Blackwaterfoot, Isle of Arran, KA27 8HA
Scotland
Telephone: +44 (0) 1770 860226

Average Reviewers' Score:

Website: www.shiskinegolf.com
Architect: Willie Fernie and Willie Park
Visitors: Welcome - Contact in advance

Reviewers' Comments

A good little course that I appreciated much more on my second time round (having a better idea of what is required on the blind holes certainly helped!)... Shiskine is worth playing for the stunning views alone... The course itself is somewhat quirky but it's tremendous value and good fun too... When the weather is kind, the view from the 4th tee is awesome and views from elsewhere on the course do not disappoint either... It's good value and entertaining golf... If you visit the Isle of Arran, make sure you take your clubs and play this one at least once.

Shiskine

You will either love Shiskine or hate it. Either way, this is one of the most unusual courses featured in this book, a links that has attained true cult status.

Founded in 1896, originally as a nine-hole layout, it was designed by Willie Fernie. Shortly before the Great War, Willie Park was commissioned to extend the course to 18 holes and to revise Fernie's original nine holes. Six of the new holes fell into neglect during the Great War, leaving behind today's unusual 12-hole links.

Shiskine is located at Blackwaterfoot on the western side of the Isle of Arran, a small island often referred to as "Scotland in Miniature". This is a simply stunning location, affording majestic views across the Kilbrannan Sound to the Mull of Kintyre.

Notorious for its blind shots, Shiskine can only be described as idiosyncratic. Nevertheless, it's fun golf and immensely enjoyable. They employ sheep to keep the tight fairways trimmed, but somehow they manage to keep the greens in excellent condition. The 3rd and 4th holes, called "Crows Nest" and "The Shelf", offer real excitement, nestling underneath the Drumadoon Cliffs.

This is a links that needs to be played more than once. Only then will you begin to understand and appreciate its quirks.

ROSAPENNA GOLF LINKS
Downings, Co.Donegal, Ireland
Telephone: +353 (0) 74 91 55301

Average Reviewers' Score:

Website: www.rosapennagolflinks.ie
Architect: Pat Ruddy
Visitors: Welcome - Contact in advance

Reviewers' Comments

Had read very little about it but it's an absolute cracker... All 18 holes in among the dunes and no hole disturbing another... We heard about Sandy Hills from one of the locals and decided to play it. What a top decision... This is a golf course that makes you think your way around, rewarding sensible play and cruelly punishing wayward shots... The greens are still settling but already I would rank this course ahead of Glashedy, Donegal and the Old Rosapenna... After a spot of lunch we ventured into the dunes. Sandy Hills is a gobsmacking golfing orgasm, the proverbial big dipper... If you only play one course in Donegal, make it this one...A real gem and worth the trip alone.

Rosapenna (Sandy Hills)

The pretty fishing village of Downings lies on the edge of Sheep Haven Bay in the north of County Donegal. Donegal is rapidly becoming one of Ireland's best golfing destinations and the secluded Rosapenna is where the old meets the new.

Golf at Rosapenna dates back to 1891. A triumvirate of former British Open Champions – Old Tom Morris, James Braid and Harry Vardon – created the Old course and it still represents a fine challenge. But it was Pat Ruddy, the man behind the European Club, who put Rosapenna firmly on the map. His new course, Sandy Hills, will surely end up on every serious golfer's must-play list.

Sandy Hills quietly opened for play in June 2003 and slowly, but surely, the golfing world is beginning to recognise that this course is special. Old Tom chose to route the Old course alongside the dunes, but Pat Ruddy had different ideas – he decided to carve straight through them and this is presumably how the name Sandy Hills came into being. Right from the off, you are in a lunar landscape, amongst the gigantic dunes. Going over and through the dunes provides a platform to drink in the stunning views across the Old course to Sheep Haven Bay beyond. It's spectacular.

Measuring 7,155 yards from the back tees and with the par set at 71, it will test the very best. Each and every hole has precise definition with the hummocking fairways framed by the dunes, so the immense challenge is always clearly visible from the tees. Whatever you do, don't stray too far offline, otherwise you'll be lucky to find your ball in the dunes. And make sure that your approach shots are accurate too, because the greens are invariably cut into the dunes or sited on elevated plateaux.

Rosapenna was worthy of a visit just to play the Old course, but Pat Ruddy has improved on that, too, by remodelling the back nine. The new-look course is due to open in 2005. But it's his Sandy Hills course that everyone is talking about and there's only one way to find out how good it really is.

GLASGOW GAILES GOLF CLUB
Gailes, Irvin, Ayrshire KA11 5AE, Scotland
Telephone: +44 (0) 1770 860226

Average Reviewers' Score:

Website: www.glasgowgailes-golf.com
Architect: Willie Park Jnr.
Visitors: Contact in advance - not weekends am

Reviewers' Comments

Glasgow Gailes is a worthy Open Qualifier and straight driving is paramount in order to find these tight fairways otherwise thick, tangly heather and gorse await... There was a lot of major irrigation work going on around the course so the club were obviously not sitting back and resting on their Open qualifier status... The course has a feel very similar to nearby Barassie... There are no outstanding holes that live in the memory, just an overall impression of a good, above average links... The greens are some of the best around and they are like lightning in the summer... The greens were in great nick... This place has a solid reputation as being the best-conditioned course on the Ayrshire coast and it's true... It doesn't offer up quite as stern a test as Western Gailes but it's pretty tough nonetheless... The clubhouse atmosphere was a tad on the stuffier side... Their 'flip over' scorecard is easily the best I have come across yet - simple, concise and very practical... Make sure you play this one – you won't be disappointed.

Glasgow Gailes

"As one approaches Prestwick," wrote Bernard Darwin, in his 1910 book, *The Golf Courses of the British Isles*, "the train seems to be voyaging through one endless and continuous golf course – Gailes, Barassie, Bogside – I write them down pell-mell as they come into my head – Prestwick, St. Nicholas, St. Cuthbert, Troon, and several more beside." Add Turnberry, to Darwin's list, and you can see why this prodigious stretch of Ayrshire coastline is so special. Glasgow Gailes, and Western Gailes, its next-door neighbour, are the northernmost of these exceptional links.

Glasgow Gailes is home to the Glasgow Golf Club, founded in 1787 and the 9th oldest golf club in the world. In those days, golf was played some 30 miles away, in Glasgow City. It was surely an absolute joy for the members when the Gailes course opened for play in 1892 – at last, no more muddy, parkland golf. The opening of Gailes made Glasgow Golf Club unique, with two courses, 30 miles apart. We don't know who originally designed the course, but Willie Park Jnr. revised the layout in 1912. Thankfully, Gailes is open to visitors, unlike its older, parkland partner, which is only open to members' guests.

Glasgow Gailes is a classic links. "The turf is something softer – at least in my imagination – than that of the East Coast courses," wrote Darwin, "and the greens are wonderfully green and velvety." There is no doubt that the turf ensures tireless play, and it's just as well, because there are plenty of courses to play on the West Coast.

Notorious for its whin (gorse) and heather-lined fairways, Glasgow Gailes is a tough cookie. It's a final qualifying course when the Open is at either Turnberry, or Troon. Needless to say, it tests the very best professionals.

Many of the holes are fraught with danger, with out-of-bounds lurking beyond the railway line and the perimeter of the course. Straight and solid driving is required to card a good score. Beware of the wind – it can be a serious hazard.

Glasgow Gailes is kept out of the limelight by the many other superb links courses situated along this stretch of coastline. But you will be hard-pressed to find a better links. It really should be included on any must-play list – it's a genuine cracker.

HANKLEY COMMON GOLF CLUB
Tilford, Farnham, Surrey, GU10 2DD, England
Telephone: +44 (0) 1252 792493

Average Reviewers' Score:

Website: www.hankley.co.uk
Architect: James Braid and Harry Colt
Visitors: Weekdays and pm at weekends

Reviewers' Comments

It's located in a gorgeous spot, secluded and tranquil. It certainly compares favourably with the very best of the numerous heathland courses in this area (Sunningdale, Wentworth, Walton Heath, The Berkshire, etc)... As good as Walton Heath... A heathland delight, providing you can keep out of that heather... If you've got a natural draw, then this is the course for you - many of the holes are shaped from right to left... Course was in amazing condition... Hankley also represents great value for money in an area of England that is notorious for its high green fees... And for a pleasant change, the members and the staff are actually welcoming... It's no wonder this course is well regarded... Surely it should be ranked higher... Could play this course for the rest of my life.

Hankley Common

Hankley Common is situated on the North Downs, in a preservation area or to be precise, a 'Site of Special Scientific Interest', home to oak, rowan and the woodlark.

In many ways, it's reminiscent of Walton Heath, which is high praise indeed; the common at Tilford has the same ferocious heather and the same wide-open and windswept appearance as that of the heath at Walton on the Hill. If there was ever a place where seaside links golf meets inland heathery golf, it's here at Hankley Common.

Golf at Hankley commenced in 1897 with a modest nine-hole course but it remained an innocuous layout until James Braid added a further nine holes in 1922. Many people believe that it became a truly great course in 1936, after Harry Colt remodelled it.

There is an overwhelming feeling of spaciousness on this heathland course, so much so that it seems plausible that a second or third course could be intertwined between the existing 18 holes. To put everything into context, the course occupies 164 acres, but the club actually owns more than 850 acres of perfect heathland. Don't let this feeling of space lull you into a false sense of security – this is not the place to open your shoulders and let rip. Anything slightly off-line will be swallowed up by bunkers, or even worse, by the thick tangled heather.

Despite the fact that this is not a long course, measuring a little over 6,400 yards from the back tees, this is a really technically testing golf course. Regional Qualifying for the Open has been held here since 1984 and the club has hosted numerous other important amateur and professional events over the years.

The par threes, especially the 7th and the 11th, are extremely memorable and challenging, as are the opening and closing holes. Both are tough par fours, measuring well over 400 yards.

So, if you are looking for a memorable, testing and underrated golf course with outstanding greens, look no further than Hankley Common.

SOUTHERNDOWN GOLF CLUB
Ogmore-by-Sea, Bridgend, CF32 0QP, Wales
Telephone: +44 (0) 1656 880476

Average Reviewers' Score:

Website: www.southerndowngolfclub.com
Architect: Willie Fernie, Herbert Fowler, Willie Park and Donald Steel
Visitors: Welcome - contact in advance

Reviewers' Comments

Southerndown is a very enjoyable, hilly and exposed course, perhaps not in the same league as Royal Porthcawl in terms of the collection of holes or the condition, but the common land and the sheep account for that… Watch out for the sheep - they never respond to "fore"… Is it links, downland or heathland? Probably a bit of all three… You feel on top of the world, the course is really exposed to the elements… Hold on to your hat… Not an easy place to play to handicap and if the weather is against you, then this is really tough… An interesting layout with some fine views… The views from the 2nd are amongst the best… Good fun to play and a fair set of decent holes. 1st, 2nd and 18th my pick of the bunch… The opening and closing holes are superb, as is the par three 5th, known as "Carter's Folly"… Enjoyed my round at Southerndown… A warm clubhouse welcome and very friendly members - well worth listening to over a small libation… The views from the friendly and welcoming clubhouse are simply outstanding… Definitely worth playing.

Southerndown

"Not far from Porthcawl - as the aeroplane flies - is another excellent course, Southerndown," wrote Bernard Darwin, in *The Golf Courses of the British Isles.* "It is perched high aloft and looks down on Porthcawl, amid the many other glories of a beautiful view. You may look out far over the sea, or again over a wide stretch of English - or rather Welsh - landscape. The breezes blow cool and fresh here, and on a still and stifling August day, when the golfer is almost too limp to crawl round Porthcawl, he will be wise to refresh himself by a round on the heights of Southerndown."

Southerndown's elevated site, high above the Ogmore River Valley, provides arresting views across the Bristol Channel. Over time, sand has blown up from the seashore, coming to rest on the rolling slopes and giving the turf a rather links-like character. In fact, you would be hard pressed to categorise the course - it's quite unique, but one thing is for sure, it's absolutely natural. There are no trees or artificial water hazards, just bracken, gorse and bunkers waiting to trap the wayward drive. Oh yes, we'd almost forgotten, there are a couple of other things – the ever-present wind and the sheep, serious hazards in their own right.

Willie Fernie originally laid down the course in 1905. But this wasn't the same Willie Fernie who won the British Open Championship in 1883 - it was his namesake - a fact we learnt from Southerndown's knowledgeable Secretary. The hands of a number of great architects have touched Southerndown over the years - Herbert Fowler, Willie Park and, more recently, Donald Steel - but its lineage remains intact.

"Bracken to the left of you, bracken to the right - and a fairway rising up to the sky," was how the great Henry Cotton saw Southerndown's opening hole. It's certainly a most challenging two-shot hole and it's followed by two more, which are equally tough. The four par threes are noteworthy, especially the 4th hole, known as "Carter's Folly" - it's expertly bunkered and calls for an accurate iron shot.

James Braid and Harry Vardon predicted that Southerndown would become a great course, and they were right. It's hosted a number of important events including the Piccadilly Masters and the Martini International. The most notable current event is the Welsh amateur competition, called the Duncan Putter, an annual 72-hole competition, which has seen Peter McEvoy and Gary Wolstenholme emerging as winners.

No trip to South Wales would be complete without a game at Southerndown - it's an exciting experience with a warm and inviting clubhouse, which completes the perfect day.

DE VERE SLALEY HALL
Hexham, Northumberland, NE47 0BY, England
Telephone: +44 (0) 1434 673350

Average Reviewers' Score:

Website: www.deveregolf.co.uk
Architect: Dave Thomas
Visitors: Welcome - contact in advance

Reviewers' Comments

Slaley Hall has much to commend it... Could be one of the best, if not the best course in the North East but it needs a facelift... Backdrop is spectacular but Dave Thomas's original design is tired... Ground is perfect for golf with some excellent elevation changes and huge stands of mature pines... Modern course built on a great piece of land... Some of the holes, particularly the 9th are stunning... Some truly magnificent holes and the closing six or seven are amongst the best I have ever seen but there are a few bland holes which could easily be spiced up... You really do feel like you are playing at Augusta... After a poor start to the back nine, the course comes to life at the 13th... A big last hole – plenty of drama to end your matchplay games here ... "As tough as nails" championship test and don't expect to play to handicap... The course as a whole lacks consistency... They do allow you to play from whichever tee you like, which is nice, but it obviously gets harder the further back you go... It's certainly worth playing and the hotel and facilities are really good.

Slaley Hall (Hunting)

Critics have described Slaley Hall as the 'Gleneagles of the North East', the 'Woburn of the North' the 'Augusta of the North' and the 'Gleneagles of the South' but it was Golf World which described Slaley Hall as the "Manchester of the North East – every time a tournament goes there, such is the deluge." Regardless of the weather, the Hunting course is a great layout, located in a county devoid of many decent golf courses except for Berwick-upon-Tweed and Bamburgh Castle.

The Hunting course opened for play in 1989 and was designed by Dave Thomas. The resort at Slaley Hall is now part of the De Vere Group, formerly Greenalls. It's a big golf course, carved through a dense pine forest. Rhododendrons and cherry trees provide welcome seasonal colour, but it's the pines that will punish the wayward shot, for they are predominant throughout the round.

Dave Thomas is renowned for designing unique and interesting holes and he's done himself proud at Slaley Hall. His bunkering design is masterful. No doubt there was some land to be moved, but he has skilfully used nature's features effectively, especially the streams on the front nine.

As we have already said, it's a big course, measuring over 7,000 yards from the back tees. The layout plays across varied ground, and whilst the majority of holes are park-like in nature, there are some holes that have distinct moorland characteristics with springy crisp turf. Either way, the Hunting has been immortalised by the European Grand Prix, formerly called the Slaley Hall Northumberland Challenge, and it's seen some famous champions, including Retief Goosen and Colin Montgomerie.

There's an American feel to the course and the resort in general. With plenty of tees to choose from, make sure you select wisely, because the Hunting plays its length. The layout is invariably in excellent condition and there is absolutely no doubt that the Hunting is one of the best young courses in England.

HANBURY MANOR GOLF &·COUNTRY CLUB
Ware, Hertfordshire, SG12 OSD, England
Telephone: +44 (0) 1920 885000

Average Reviewers' Score:

Website: www.hanbury-manor.com
Architect: Harry Vardon and Jack Nicklaus II
Visitors: Contact in advance

Reviewers' Comments

The hotel and leisure facilities along with the golf course make Hanbury Manor a special place to visit… A great setting and an overall interesting course… An interesting course invariably in good nick… Generally not very challenging as it is set up for Corporate, so you can hit it almost anywhere off the tee… The layout is well designed and has excellent true greens and uses the contours to provide a variation of shots… The front nine is a bit open but the back nine more than makes up for it… Off the daily tees this course is too open and short to be a true 'championship' test… Very good condition and worth playing… A surprisingly straightforward yet nonetheless charming course in a lovely setting… A track that will suit all handicap levels, yet be challenging enough for the low handicapper… The facilities are great, the hotel, in particular, being superb.

Hanbury Manor

The Jacobean-style manor house was built in 1890 for the Hanbury family and in 1923, it was converted into a girls' boarding school. It remained a school until 1986, when it was ambitiously transformed into a luxury hotel and country club.

Harry Vardon originally laid out a nine-hole course in the majestic parkland grounds in the early 1900s, but it was Jack Nicklaus's eldest son who brought the golf course back to life. Behind the manor house was an undulating piece of farmland and this was used for the addition of nine new holes and the original Vardon parkland layout was completely revised. The official opening took place in 1991, with an exhibition match between Tony Jacklin and Dave Stockton. Jack Nicklaus II was there too.

Nicklaus II has done a great job. He has used many of his father's tricks of the trade and created an exciting golf course with double fairways and plenty of threatening water. The golf course is PGA championship standard and it plays its length, measuring over 6,660 yards from the medal tees. The two nines are distinctly contrasting, each having a completely different look and feel. The newer front nine is much more exposed, laid out on undulating land in a modern American style. The back nine feels traditionally park-like with fairways flanked by stately trees.

Hanbury Manor's tournament potential was quickly recognised and, in 1996, Trish Johnson won the Women's European Open by five clear shots. The following year, the Men's PGA European Tour arrived in the shape of the English Open and the tournament remained at Hanbury until 1999.

Scoring well on this demanding course is easier said than done. The 8th hole is the toughest on the course, measuring 425 yards with out-of-bounds all the way along the right hand side. The approach shot to the green is tricky, even from the middle of the fairway. The green is elevated and protected by a lake on the left and a grassy hollow to the right. The ground and the green slope cruelly towards the lake. The back nine features some memorable holes, playing through majestic oaks and across numerous lakes.

Hanbury Manor stands on its own in an area without any great golf courses. There's a lovely ambience here, an English rural version of an American Country Club.

DOOKS GOLF CLUB
Glenbeigh, Co. Kerry, Ireland
Telephone: +353 (0) 66 9768205

Average Reviewers' Score:

Website: www.dooks.com
Architect: Eddie Hackett, Donald Steel and Martin Hawtree
Visitors: Contact in advance

Reviewers' Comments

Ah Dooks - a little beauty if ever there was one... A lovely variety of holes, which aren't too long but they're interesting... This is fun golf with a capital F... The holes are so varied, exciting and unusual... Where else can you be 5ft away from a skylark, hear the sound of a cuckoo, see beautiful orchids and hear the Atlantic at the same time - only at Dooks... The views are to die for... An amazing course on the edge of Dingle Bay - every hole is different and the 13th a dream of a rollercoaster green... They are undergoing some significant changes, but I hope and pray that they don't lose the charm of this delightful links course... Course is being modified and if the current four new holes are anything to go by, Dooks will go on from strength to strength... Course is great for the avid golfer and the higher handicapper alike... The members are the most engaging and friendly that I have ever come across... Views are unsurpassed... Whatever you do - don't miss Dooks, it's an absolute delight... Play it and rejoice.

Dooks

Environmentally, Dooks has to be one of the most natural golf courses in the world. Everything is in harmony with its surroundings – it's a beautiful place for golf. The course is enchantingly located on a promontory on the southern side of Dingle Bay. The MacGillycuddy's Reeks Mountains stand guard to the southeast and stretched out in the foreground to the north and west are the sandy peninsulas of Rossbehy and Inch Point. The vista is simply breathtaking.

Officers from the Royal Horse Artillery laid out a short nine-hole course in 1889 and they introduced the local gentry to the game of golf. This establishes Dooks as Kerry's oldest golf course. Around 1900, the course was extended to 18 holes, but due to escalating costs, the club soon reverted back to nine holes.

In 1963, a shockwave arrived through the Dooks letterbox. The letter was from the land agent, serving notice to hand back possession of the golf course and club. The course was laid out on leased land, but unfortunately the original lease wasn't signed. Immediately, a "Save Dooks" campaign was launched and for the next two years the golf club was front-page news. £7,000 was eventually raised and in 1965, the members became the proud owners of Dooks Golf Club.

After all the publicity, Dooks grew in popularity and soon became overwhelmed with golfers wanting to play the now famous links. Clearly, the course needed extending to 18 holes, but funds were tight. Lateral thinking was needed. After much debate, nine members volunteered to form and lead teams to construct nine new holes. In September 1970, against all odds, and inside a meagre £3,000 budget, a newly extended 18-hole course opened for play – designed and built by the members. The outcome is fantastic, the new holes blend perfectly with the old.

It's a tranquil, engaging and fun golf course. It also provides a true and traditional links experience. It's not of championship length, measuring just over 6,000 yards, but don't let this put you off. It's a thoroughly enjoyable challenge. Beware of the toads though – the warm, sandy linksland at Dooks is home to the Natterjack, and is one of the amphibians' last remaining habitats. The club has adopted the Natterjack toad as their emblem. Don't worry if you're squeamish, these little creatures are nocturnal, emerging only when the golfers have gone home.

There are numerous memorable holes, but the 13th will remain etched in the mind for a very long time. Many of the greens are undulating, but the green of the par three 13th is the big dipper in rollercoaster terms. Dooks is certainly an inspirational golf course, a very special place. It is also one of the most sociable and friendly golf clubs on the planet and visitors can certainly be assured of a warm and friendly Irish welcome.

ST ANDREWS BAY GOLF RESORT & SPA
St Andrews Bay, St Andrews, Fife, KY16 8PN, Scotland
Telephone: +44 (0) 1334 837000

Average Reviewers' Score:

Website: www.standrewsbay.com
Architect: Bruce Devlin
Visitors: Contact in advance

Reviewers' Comments

The Devlin is a great new course... I had low expectations of the Devlin but I thoroughly enjoyed it... It's an excellent, understated layout which entertains and makes you think... I was very taken with its 'Kingsbarns-like' risk/reward design on many holes... In a similar vein to Kingsbarns, the location and the dramatic coastal views are going to set this place up as a course that will become known across the world... Cracking design, excellent condition and great views back towards the town... The condition was stunning and the whole experience was rather good. In fact, it was very good. I like the choice of tee position... I think the Torrance is a better course... The greens are as links-like lightning fast and as firm as you will find along the road at the other St Andrews courses... I'd thoroughly recommend the Devlin to anyone... Oh, and the views from the clubhouse overlooking St Andrews and beyond, up the East coast into Angus are just breathtaking... Make sure you add this to the list if you're in the area... Come for the day and play both courses.

St Andrews Bay (Devlin)

Travelling to St Andrews is much more than a visit - it's a reverent pilgrimage. It's a joy to see an entire town given up to golf, but there is inevitably an air of expectation when a new course is built so close to the "home of golf". All eyes were on Bruce Devlin the designer, former Australian Open champion and himself an Aussie. Assisting Devlin with the design on a consultancy basis was "the Squire", the legendary late Gene Sarazen. In the summer of 2002, the Devlin course at St Andrews Bay opened for play to a rapturous standing ovation.

You'll find the five star St Andrews Bay resort a couple of miles outside the "auld grey toon", en route to Kingsbarns. It's an amazing location with the resort's flagship Devlin course sited on elevated ground next to the cliff-tops. The views across the River Tay estuary with the famous medieval town in the background are simply breathtaking. The design is dramatic too, with the natural features of the land being used to great effect, most notably a deep ravine called Kittock's Den, which cuts frivolously through the course. Undoubtedly, the most striking holes are those that border the rugged North Sea shoreline, a number of which will remain etched permanently in the mind.

Bruce Devlin's design goal was "to build great golf courses within the contours of the natural surroundings which challenge the best golfers and yet can be equally enjoyed by the novice". We think he's definitely achieved his target with four distinctly different teeing areas. You'll need to be either an exceptionally good player or a masochist to play this par 72 from the back tees (7,049 yards) but with four areas to choose from, there's a tee for all abilities (5,195 yards from the forward tees).

The Devlin has been constructed in an American-style with two man-made lakes, but the layout honours the tradition of golf at St Andrews with two double greens, numerous deep pot bunkers and, of course, the most important ingredient, the feeling.

After a fairly gentle start, the Devlin goes wild when the par five 7th stretches along the edge of Kittock's Den. The vista opens up and the land begins to pitch and roll. From here on in, there's no looking back... from the par four 9th, which is squeezed up against the rugged coastline with its green perched on a promontory to the awe-inspiring signature hole, the long par four 17th, which doglegs towards the hanging cliff-edge green. The round concludes with an excellent par three, where the cliff-edge eagerly waits to catch anything struck offline to the right.

The Devlin is a valuable addition to the St Andrews experience. It's a course to be savoured and should be included on any serious golfer's must-play list.

THE WESTIN TURNBERRY RESORT
Turnberry, Ayrshire, KA26 9LT, Scotland
Telephone: +44 (0) 1655 334032

Average Reviewers' Score:

Website: www.turnberry.co.uk
Architect: Philip Mackenzie Ross and Donald Steel
Visitors: Contact Golf Reservations Office

Reviewers' Comments

Maturing nicely is the Kintyre... Greens were as well presented in January as most inland courses in the summer – honestly... Early holes are fairly tight and gorse-lined... The dogleg 7th is rather out of place, then the signature 8th divides golfers - love it or loathe it you'll never forget it ... Interesting elevation around the turn at Bains Hill... The back nine bears a resemblance to the back nine on the Ailsa... Hard to concentrate over the last six holes without casting occasional envious glances towards the closing holes on the Ailsa... But at least the 18th on the Kintyre is a *far* better closing hole than that on the Ailsa... The last is a particular challenge... Not as memorable as the Ailsa (naturally) but an interesting and demanding course... What a double day out it would be to play both; golfing nirvana... Turnberry is without doubt one of the very top golfing destinations in Scotland.

Turnberry (Kintyre)

"Mull of Kintyre – oh, mist rolling in from the Sea...my desire is always to be here – oh, Mull of Kintyre!" Whether you like the McCartney song or not, it conjures up certain ravishing images and these images are many at Turnberry. Gazing across the Firth of Clyde, above and beyond the nearby Ailsa Craig, lie the majestic peaks of Arran's mountains and further still, beyond Arran, the curvy Mull of Kintyre. On a crystal clear day you can see right across the Irish Sea to Northern Ireland. It's quite a spectacle.

As most people already know, the Kintyre course is Donald Steel's re-creation of the old Arran course, which was originally laid out in 1909. Just like the Ailsa, the Arran was re-built by Philip Mackenzie Ross after the ravages of the Second World War and for many years it provided an excellent accompaniment to the Ailsa.

The Kintyre opened for play in 2001 and it's much more than an Arran redesign. Steel took some new land into the equation – Bain's Hill – and reutilised much of the old Arran topography. The result is a championship standard links, which stretches out to 6,853 yards, and, in 2004, it was used to host Open Championship Final Qualifying.

It must be a tough job to try and create a new course, which must sit alongside and complement an existing masterpiece. Donald Steel should take a bow. The Kintyre is an exhilarating course, which pitches and rolls quite delightfully along the Ayrshire coastline.

Towards the turn, the Kintyre reaches Bain's Hill and things really come alive. First of all, the view at the 8th, a short par four, measuring a mere 298 yards, is awe-inspiring – then there's the blind approach shot to a green, nestling in a rocky cove. The tee shot at the short par five 9th, along the edge of the sea, is nerve-wracking and the approach shot is also challenging, especially for those brave enough to go for the green in two. Then there's the climb up to the 10th, a challenging and robust par four, which is the highest point on the course. It's a magnificent stretch of holes. Having said that, the rest of the course is also good, albeit a more traditional test of links golf.

With the addition of the new Kintyre course, Turnberry can now boast two excellent links courses. Whilst it's doubtful that the Kintyre will push the Ailsa off its pedestal, it is a great layout in its own right and it's a welcome addition to the rich collection of links golf courses along this famous stretch of Ayrshire coastline.

MURCAR GOLF CLUB
Bridge of Don, Aberdeen, AB23 8BD, Scotland
Telephone: +44 (0) 1224 704354

Average Reviewers' Score:

Website: www.murcar.co.uk
Architect: Archie Simpson and James Braid
Visitors: Contact in advance

Reviewers' Comments

One of *the* most underrated links courses in Scotland… "Hidden gem" is too often applied to golf courses but this one deserves the moniker…It suffers because of the reputation and quality of its next door neighbour, Royal Aberdeen, but believe me, for much of this course, the holes are as good… Don't go expecting to play a classic… Murcar dispels the misconception that a so-called short course is any less of a challenge… Murcar was the "find" of this year's 17 courses we played… Miss this one out at your peril… Fairways pitch and roll in an alarming fashion, keeping your ball in play requires pinpoint accuracy… Stray too far on many holes and you are heavily penalised… Nice gentle start on holes 1 and 2 but from then on, it's tough and some of the opening holes would not look out of place anywhere… Hole after hole we were not only blown away by the course but by the stunning scenery too… Views across the steely North Sea are dramatic and the elevated tees are breathtaking… Can't speak highly enough of the place… Friendliness of the club was unique… This is a Top 50 course, not to be missed.

Murcar

Murcar golf club was founded in 1909. Archie Simpson, the professional from Royal Aberdeen, designed the course. Simpson didn't have too far to travel because Royal Aberdeen golf club is literally next door, and, apparently, he popped over to Murcar in his lunch break to get to grips with the design. As with so many courses of this era, Murcar was later revised by James Braid.

Located on a classic stretch of links land with huge sand dunes, crumpled fairways, whins, burns and heather. There are some magnificent views from the elevated tees across the North Sea and to Aberdeen City in the south. It's a beautifully rugged course with lots of natural of appeal.

Murcar is not a championship monster, but it's a seriously challenging course which belies its meagre yardage. From the back tees, the course measures 6,300 yards with par of 71. But the par fives disappear from the card when the regular tee boxes are used and par drops to a lowly 69. Murcar asks some serious questions. The hummocking fairways are sometimes cruelly tight and the ball has a habit of bouncing off the knolls and into vicious rough. Add this to the odd blind shot and you can find yourself leaving quite a few balls behind for the members.

Having said this, the experience is stunning and the elevated tees provide that wonderful on-top-of-the-world feeling. The greens are most exquisitely sited on raised tables and amongst the dunes. There is little need for bunker protection around the greens, but to make life even more difficult there are pot bunkers sited there too.

There is a bundle of excellent and memorable holes, especially those in the dunes. The 7th is considered to be the signature hole and it's called "Serpentine". Here, we must scramble up to the high tee and soak up that panoramic view of the North Sea, and then we realise why this hole is called "Serpentine". This par four, measuring 423 yards, requires a drive over a looping, snaking burn, avoiding the ravine on the right and the vicious rough on the left. Somewhere out there, there's a narrow fairway wedged between towering dunes. Now, let's think about this one for a moment and take a deep breath. Perhaps it's time to find that old dog-eared ball that's hiding at the bottom of the golf bag.

When the wind blows, Murcar can be an absolute brute. Whatever the weather, this is an absolute must-play golf course. It's tremendous entertainment all the way round.

STOKE PARK CLUB
Park Road, Stoke Poges, Buckinghamshire, SL2 4PG
England
Telephone: +44 (0) 1753 717171

Average Reviewers' Score:

Website: www.stokeparkclub.com
Architect: Harry Colt
Visitors: Contact in advance

Reviewers' Comments

A classical parkland course, always maintained in sublime condition... An exceptionally memorable experience... It's better than Little Aston, which is widely considered to be the best parkland course in Britain... For a course of its age this is a great test of golf, even for those with their monster drivers in the bag... Off the back tees, the bunkers sit carefully waiting for those big hits... Bring your best driving game with you - this is a tough course... The greens require precision and, above all, it all sits on some beautifully manicured grounds... The front eighteen are the ones to play. The remaining nine need some time and refinement to match the former... It's a bit pricey but worth every penny... They certainly know how to look after you... Clubhouse is simply delightful... Well worth playing.

Stoke Park

In Bernard Darwin's 1910 book, *The Golf Courses of the British Isles*, he wrote: "Stoke Park is a beautiful spot, and there is very good golf to be played there; the club is an interesting one, moreover, as being one of the first and the most ambitious attempts in England at what is called in America a Country Club."

Capability Brown originally landscaped the historic parkland in the late 18th century. Harry Colt then came along and designed the golf course, which opened for play in 1908. The signature hole, the 7th, the inspiration for Augusta National's 12th, is considered to be one of Colt's finest holes. The 7th has been recently remodelled and now features a lake and a waterfall.

Stoke Park is surely one of the finest parkland golf courses in the South of England. There is no heather here at all (which is unusual for the location); the main line of defence is the abundance of huge stately trees and Colt's clever design. The fairways appear wide and generous from the tees. However, it is important to get the line and distance right, otherwise you will face challenging second shots.

More famous than the majestic parkland golf course is the 18th century mansion designed by James Wyatt (architect to George III), housing the clubhouse, hotel and restaurant. "The clubhouse is a gorgeous palace," wrote Darwin, "a dazzling vision of white stone, of steps and terraces and cupolas, with a lake in front and imposing trees in every direction."

Stoke Poges was also used as the setting for the golf scenes in the 1964 James Bond movie Goldfinger, in which 007 had his famous match with Goldfinger. The film featured the scene whereby Harold Sakata, as Oddjob, spun his steel-rimmed bowler hat at Sean Connery. It missed 007 but beheaded a statue! The clubhouse was also featured in the later Bond movie, Tomorrow Never Dies.

Recently, the course has been extended to 27 holes. Each of the three loops of nine is named: Colt, Alison and Jackson. The original course is made up of the Colt and Alison nines.

BALLYLIFFIN GOLF CLUB
Ballyliffin, Inishowen, Co. Donegal, Ireland
Telephone: +353 (0) 7493 76119

Average Reviewers' Score:

Website: www.ballyliffingolfclub.com
Architect: Eddie Hackett, Charles Lawrie, Frank Pennink and Nick Faldo
Visitors: Welcome - contact in advance

Reviewers' Comments

It's far more traditional and to an extent, far more engaging than the Glashedy... A course for the purist... Standing on the first tee it appears as if a hundred elephants have been buried in the fairway – humps and hillocks as far as you can see... This piece of land was made for golf - fairways and greens just blend into the landscape as if they were always there - it's a wonderful place to play... I've never seen fairways like this...they make the fairways at St Andrews Old and Rye look tame... The Faldo work was taking place when I played and there's no doubt that this will be a much-improved course once it's completed... Playing the course your stance will be awkward and varied, just like the wind, especially on the run of holes from 13 to 17 next to the Atlantic... The terrain is up and down, left and right in every direction possible... Heaven help golfers when the wind from the Artic blows over hundreds of miles to the North Shore of Donegal... Look out Glashedy – in time to come, the Old might well upstage you... What a venue for links golf.

Ballyliffin (Old)

Ballyliffin is Ireland's most northerly golf club, located off Tullagh Point on the Atlantic edge of the Inishowen Peninsula. The location is divine; the course hugs the shoreline overlooking the golden beach of Pollan Strand and Glashedy Rock (Ballyliffin's equivalent of Turnberry's Ailsa Craig).

It's difficult to pin a date on the earliest origins of the game of golf at Ballyliffin, though it is clear that the Ballyliffin Golf Club was founded in 1947. The Old course originally started out in life as a very ordinary nine-hole course and the club progressed very slowly, often struggling financially. In the late 1960s, Martin Hopkins, a local agricultural advisor, identified a prime stretch of links land nearby, ideal for golf. Eddie Hackett, Charles Lawrie and Frank Pennink were engaged in shaping the new links course and in 1973, the brand new "Old" course opened for play.

The Old is a classic links, with fairways that pitch and roll through wild dunes. This is links golf at its most traditional, where the perfect drive will often find an awkward lie. If you are afflicted with a lack of balance, you will struggle, because you'll rarely get a flat stance.

For about 20 years, the Old course remained well and truly outside of the limelight. Only those in the know, and the lucky members, knew the secret. Then, in June 1993, a helicopter dropped out of the blue sky and landed next to the clubhouse with the world number one on board. After a quick thrash around the Old course, Nick Faldo was spellbound, falling under its trance. "One of the most natural courses I have ever played," he commented. And from that point onwards, Ballyliffin came of age. The Faldo design team is currently engaged in the renovation of the Old course. With new rivetted bunkers, new 'Faldo' tees and two enlarged greens, the Old course is set to rise much higher in the Top 100 rankings. Renovation work should be finished before Easter 2006.

There are many memorable holes, but the 190-yard par three 5th, called "The Tank", will stick in the mind for a very long time. It's an intimidating tee shot to an elevated plateau, almost stage-like green that is surrounded by dunes.

Ballyliffin's new Glashedy course has recently upstaged the Old, but don't make a trip to County Donegal without playing it. Both courses contrast and complement each other supremely well. But for the true links purist, the Old course is the one.

EAST DEVON GOLF CLUB
North View Road, Budleigh Salterton, Devon,
EX9 6DQ, England
Telephone: +44 (0) 1395 443370

Average Reviewers' Score:

Website: www.edgc.co.uk
Architect: Robert Tosswill, Herbert Fowler and Harry Colt
Visitors: Contact in advance - not before 9am

Reviewers' Comments

There is no doubt - East Devon is enchanting, a course which has a bit of everything... This is a total gem if ever there was one... Not as well known as it should be but possibly all the better and certainly quieter as a consequence... For me, this is one of the most enjoyable courses I have played and for my money it should be a Top 100 regular... It's a great test of golf but at the same time completely enjoyable for both the low man and for the higher handicapper... The 10th is truly magnificent and the 16th hole is even better – the drive is a real test of courage... If you like golf by the sea, fantastic views, the softness of heathland and lots of undulations you're at the right place... Make a special trip - you will *not* be disappointed... I would return again in a heartbeat.

East Devon

East Devon is absolutely enchanting. The golf course is laid out on high ground, 400ft above the sea, close to the clifftops, where one can drink in the most spectacular views in golf. The sweeping panorama of Lyme Bay is in view, and on a clear day, you can spot the Isle of Portland, jutting out into the English Channel.

The fairways have been cut through a profusion of gorse and heather. It's as pretty as a picture, an undulating seaside heathland course with an overwhelming feeling of spaciousness because wide tracts of gorse and heather divide each fairway. Robert Tosswill, a retired army officer laid down the original course, working with the natural lie of the land, and it opened for play in March 1902. Herbert Fowler changed the layout in 1913 and after the First World War, Harry Colt remodelled the course. This is the layout largely played today.

Measuring a little over 6,200 yards, East Devon is not championship material, but with a lowly par of 70 and some tight drives, this is a challenging and attractive test of golf. Right from the off, the course wends its way slowly but surely to the clifftops. The climb is gradual and certainly not hard work. Many of the holes are memorable and certainly the 9th, a downhill par four, was a record breaker for T. Aydon. In 1934 he entered the *Guinness Book of Records* for hitting the longest recorded drive. It was measured at 450 yards and he reached the edge of the green. It is no longer featured in the current records, but bear in mind that this drive was struck 70 years ago without the aid of modern technology.

East Devon's one-shotters are charming, and the pick of the bunch is the 10th, a stunning par three played from an elevated tee across a valley clad in gorse and heather to a well protected, three-tiered green. "The best view in golf", according to Peter Alliss, can be taken in on the 16th tee, a 406-yard par four. This is the start of the downhill stretch back to the clubhouse. Don't go too far right here – there are cliffs and out-of-bounds waiting to catch the slice. Anything too far left will be caught by heather or blocked out by trees. The 17th is a delightful long par four with another lovely view and loads of heather and gorse. A par here will feel like a birdie.

East Devon is an elegant course on charming heathland. It's relatively unknown, but it's certainly discerning and immensely enjoyable – well worth a visit.

CROWBOROUGH BEACON GOLF CLUB
Beacon Road, Crowborough, East Sussex, TN6 1UJ
England
Telephone: +44 (0) 1892 661511

Website: www.cbgc.co.uk
Architect: Unknown
Visitors: Contact in advance - weekends after 2pm

Average Reviewers' Score:

Reviewers' Comments

A lovely hidden gem with links-like fairways in the summer and beautiful springy turf in the winter… Lovely springy turf makes the walk a real joy… The views are worthy of the green fee alone and the club itself is warm and friendly… Bouncy fairways, very long rough and the greens were rock hard and fast… Really enjoyable golf and good fun too… Tough but enjoyable… Well worth a visit.

Crowborough Beacon

Crowborough Beacon is an undulating heathland delight. The course is laid out on the southern slopes of the East Sussex High Weald, 800ft above sea level, affording panoramic views of the South Downs.

Golf at Crowborough began modestly in 1895, with nine holes laid out simply on the Alchorne estate. In 1905, the course was extended to 18 holes. Can anyone answer the elementary question as to who designed the course? Or perhaps we should assign Sherlock Holmes to the case? The author of the famous novels, Sir Arthur Conan Doyle, was the Club Captain of Crowborough Beacon in 1910, and he lived close to his beloved course.

There are similarities between Crowborough and its delightful near neighbour, Royal Ashdown Forest, with spectacular views across the treetops and springy heathland/moorland turf. There are, however, bunkers at Crowborough that punctuate an otherwise natural landscape.

Accuracy, rather than length, is all-important. The course measures a little over 6,200 yards but finding the right position on the fairways is easier said than done, and hitting the small greens is also a challenge. There are many fine holes, but the signature hole is a par three called "The Speaker". Measuring 190 yards from the back tees, the tee-shot must be struck across a gully, whilst avoiding a large, threatening pit that lurks to the left of the green.

It's an enchanting, pretty golf course and also a genuine members' golf club. But you can be assured of a warm welcome. They will make your visit enjoyable and memorable because they have a long history of entertaining. We're sure that you'll be captivated by the charm of Crowborough Beacon.

DUNBAR GOLF CLUB
East Links, Dunbar, East Lothian, EH42 1LL, Scotland
Telephone: +44 (0) 1368 862317

Average Reviewers' Score:

Website: www.dunbar-golfclub.co.uk
Architect: Old Tom Morris & Young Tom Morris
Visitors: Not before 9.30am - contact in advance

Reviewers' Comments

Dunbar should be on your must-play list, just as Muirfield and North Berwick will be for any serious golfing trip to East Lothian… After an average start, this course proved how it is possible to fit holes into a narrow strip of land… The first two holes and the last are certainly the weakest, but the rest are simply superb… The greens, and indeed, the green sites are quite stunning – firm, fast seriously contoured and tough to read. End up in the wrong place on the green at your peril… Out of bounds wall to the right of the 4th and the 18th on the home stretch was a little strange… Dunbar is reminiscent of Kingsbarns and North Berwick, the main difference is that you feel more shoehorned between the huge stone wall and the coastline. This makes each hole look tight but well defined… Some wonderful holes, tricky greens, and teeing off at times almost on the seashore… A beautiful setting where the sea seems to dominate every view and inevitably where the wind's influence was constant… It is a complete gem and naturally there is so much history attached to this outstanding club.

Dunbar

The North Sea coastal town of Dunbar is steeped in history, its ancient ruined castle stands guard over the town's twin harbours. Golf has been played in and around Dunbar since the early part of the 17th century, but the Dunbar Golf Club wasn't formed until 1856. Old Tom Morris originally designed the course circa 1850, originally as fifteen holes and then, in 1880, it was extended to eighteen holes. In 1893, Young Tom Morris was called in to alter six holes and to further extend the course. Extra land, part of the ancient deer park of Broxmouth estate was acquired at the turn of the 20th century and four new holes were built.

The course is laid out on a narrow strip of land with the best holes hugging the rocky coastline affording resplendent views across the North Sea to Bass Rock, a huge volcanic lump rising up out of the water.

The first two holes at Dunbar play up and down the old deer park and they are flat, ordinary and park-like. The 2nd green was once a shelter where the deer were fed. The 3rd has an interesting story to tell, a par three called "Jackson's Pennies". Mr Jackson was a retired local businessman and in the 1920s he used to sit behind the green and award a penny, a king's ransom in those days, to those who played the hole well. At the 4th, a lovely par four called "Shore", Dunbar begins to play like a classic links course, the views open up and the wind becomes a more prominent factor. The next thirteen holes are wedged between the coastline and a fine-looking old stone wall where out-of-bounds threatens beyond. The finishing hole, aptly called "Hame", plays back to the clubhouse across the old deer park.

Dunbar East Links is a relatively short course, measuring 6,404 yards from the medal tees, but the wind generally makes the round thoroughly challenging and immensely entertaining. There is so much history to be absorbed in East Lothian and a visit to Dunbar will help to complete the lesson.

MOOR PARK GOLF CLUB
Rickmansworth, Hertfordshire, WD3 1QN, England
Telephone: +44 (0) 1923 773146

Average Reviewers' Score:

Website: www.moorparkgc.co.uk
Architect: Harry Colt
Visitors: Contact in advance - not at weekends

Reviewers' Comments

The first thing that strikes you about Moor Park is the amazing clubhouse. A mammoth building that smacks of history and elegance... Lovely well-maintained parkland course - you'd never believe you were so close to London... Enjoy a summer's day golf here if you can... The course is pretty and fair, with a variety of holes... Course opens up with a welcoming first... The 2nd is where it really begins... Par fours make this course... Dogleg right 8th is my pick; a drive just right of centre is what's required... My only single complaint about this thoroughly enjoyable track is that for the longer hitter the par fives are simply too short... Lovely greens that are fair and true... Was mightily impressed with the condition... An honest collection of golf holes... Probably one of the Top 5 courses inside the M25... Food is terrific and very well organized for big societies... A real treat... Always look forward to visiting Moor Park, great welcome and a very interesting golf course, in top condition.

Moor Park (High)

Located conveniently near to London, but sufficiently protected by mature trees to shield us from suburbia, the elegant High course layout will provide a challenging test of golf in pleasant park surroundings.

The clubhouse at Moor Park is an elegant 17th century mansion, the most photographed clubhouse in golf, perhaps, with the exception of the R&A clubhouse at St Andrews. It has been used for many purposes throughout its illustrious history: home to the gentry, religious hierarchy and requisitioned as the HQ for the Parachute Regiment during the Second World War. It was here that the doomed battle of Arnhem was planned. The club also made it into the *Guinness Book of Golf Facts and Feats* as the club with the highest membership in England (1600).

Harry Colt designed the High course and it opened for play in 1923. Two years later it hosted the PGA Matchplay Championship. The Bob Hope Classic was held here during the 1980s, along with numerous other professional tournaments. A number of blue-ribbon junior events have been held on the High course, including the Boys' Amateur Championship and the English Boys' Stroke Play Championship, formerly the Carris Trophy.

There are some good holes on the 6,700-yard layout, opening with a friendly par four. The 2nd is a good driving hole, requiring a solid tee shot across a valley to a fairway that doglegs to the right. The 4th is a long downhill par four, two mighty shots are required to reach this green in two. The 8th, 440 yards, is one of our favourites, sweeping downhill and then back uphill to a sloping green protected by a lurking pond with the half-way house sitting welcomingly behind the green.

The homeward nine is really more of the same, some strong and long par fours with a couple of short and reachable par fives. If anything, the back nine is more memorable and certainly a much tougher proposition than the outward nine. Two troublesome holes are the par three 12th, requiring a bold tee shot over a valley and the 14th, a fantastic long par four where the approach shot must carry a hidden gully dissecting the fairway.

Moor Park oozes quality. It's a classy golf course and a warm welcome awaits in the clubhouse mansion.

BEAU DESERT GOLF CLUB
Rugeley Road, Hazel Slade, Cannock, Staffordshire
WS12 5PJ, England
Telephone: +44 (0) 1543 422626

Average Reviewers' Score:

Website: www.bdgc.co.uk
Architect: Herbert Fowler
Visitors: Contact in advance

Reviewers' Comments

The drive into the club gives you a feeling for the grandeur... Lovely golf course, full of quality... Course takes you into Cannock Chase with views that are truly the best for many miles... Best views from any course in the Midlands... Every hole is tree-lined, with gorse, heather, fern and bracken that surround the fairways - this is special in a Walton Heath sort of way... Every hole is worthy of a mention and difficult to pick the best (maybe the 12th)... Key to scoring well, more so than nearly any other course that I have visited, is do not leave the fairway... Most of the holes are played out in their own little chapter, with almost every hole bordered by immense trees... 2nd hole is where this course comes to life and it doesn't sit down until you hole your final putt... 18th is rightly the signature hole – a shortish par five that requires pinpoint accuracy off the tee... Beau Desert can stand proud under the 'gem' umbrella... Given the choice to play here or at the Belfry, Beau Desert would get my vote every time... A true hidden gem and a course I would thoroughly recommend.

Beau Desert

The Midlands is not necessarily considered a hotspot for golf courses, but Beau Desert is one of the few exceptions.

This is the Marquess of Anglesey's golf course. He commissioned Herbert Fowler to design it and in 1913, Fowler completed the job. The golf club was formed seven years later, affording the poor Marquess some tax benefits and some income from the lease.

Beau Desert, or "Beautiful Wilderness", is an unusual name for a golf course, especially for a course located in such a picturesque landscape. The land once formed part of the Marquess's Beaudesert Estate. Once upon a time, the area may well have been wild, but it isn't any more. This is a stunning heathland course with heather and gorse-lined fairways, framed by acres of firs and spruces.

It's certainly not a long course, measuring 6,300 yards from the medal tees, but it's narrow. You need accuracy from the tee. The greens are quite large, especially the 18th, and they are full of wicked borrows, so expect a few three putts. Beau Desert is no pushover; on numerous occasions it has hosted Open Championship qualifying rounds. Invariably, the course is maintained in excellent condition.

One of the many treats is that you play most holes in splendid isolation; you can lose yourself in the trees here. Additionally, the holes are varied and memorable. If you take Beau Desert alongside Whittington Heath and Little Aston, you will be hard-pressed to find three better inland courses in the British Isles, except in Surrey and Berkshire.

CASTLEROCK GOLF CLUB
65 Circular Road, Castlerock, Co Londonderry
BT51 4TJ, Northern Ireland
Telephone: +44 (0) 28 7084 8314

Website: www.castlerockgc.co.uk
Architect: Ben Sayers and Harry Colt
Visitors: Contact in advance - limited at weekends

Average Reviewers' Score:

Reviewers' Comments

Castlerock has the potential to be an absolute crackerjack golf course... Links golf of great standard... Mussenden is certainly a must-play when visiting the North and the course stands up well against Royal Portrush... No better links course in Britain... Great opening, dogleg right uphill... After a strong start, you reach the 3rd, which is closest to the railway line, and it's these holes (3rd and 5th) that inspire the least... If only the 5th (and some of the par threes) on the excellent nine-hole Bann course could be incorporated into the Mussenden... It's a feast for the eyes as it contains some of the most scenic holes in golf... The greens are lightning fast which means bad putters will soon be found out... Links golf of the very highest order... Castlerock has *great* potential, but it's well worth a visit and it certainly won't disappoint... Had a fantastic time here and I recommend it highly... I would advise you to play this course as soon as possible, before word gets out... A warm welcome is assured from the fantastic Irish people... No idea as to why Castlerock is not rated more highly.

Castlerock (Mussenden)

Castlerock is a seaside village, located on the Causeway Coast. The course lies at the mouth of the River Bann, where it meets the mighty Atlantic Ocean. On a clear day, the Isle of Islay is visible to the north, and to the west, the rolling hills of Donegal.

It was founded in 1901, originally as a nine-hole layout. The famous Scottish club maker, Ben Sayers, extended the course to 18 holes in 1908. In 1925, Harry Colt made further modifications.

Living in the shadow of its famous neighbours, Portstewart and Royal Portrush, Castlerock is every bit as good, and will not disappoint. This is one of the toughest links courses around, with some fantastic holes. Play close to your handicap and you are doing exceptionally well.

The wind is a huge factor and when it blows, hold on to your hat. This will no doubt affect scoring. So much so, that in 2001, during the Ireland PGA International, Paul McGinley registered the course record of 64 on a calm day. The previous day, when the wind was up, the eventual winner Des Smyth, was the only player to score better than par. As with most links courses, you need to keep your ball in play. Your short game must be of the highest standard because these greens are very quick, even during the winter. Maintaining concentration is important all the way round, because there are no easy holes.

The 4th, a 200-yard par three, is a fantastic hole, known as "Leg O' Mutton". The tee-shot is played to a raised green, with the railway line running the full length of the hole on the right and a meandering burn running diagonally from right to left. Do not try to bump and run your approach shot to the short par four 6th – the hidden burn runs across the front of the green. The 15th is a great par five, called "Homewards". A blind tee shot needs to be struck slightly right of centre, providing a great chance to score well. The 18th is a lovely finishing hole – a tough dogleg to the right and the highest, double-tiered, green on the course.

We recommend a visit to Castlerock as part of a triple deal (with Portstewart and Royal Portrush). If you cannot obtain this package, Castlerock is definitely worth playing anyway. During 2003, the actor Michael Douglas was a visitor and he loved the place too – a fatal attraction, you might say!

As a closing note, Castlerock also has a 9-hole course called the Bann. The layout is similar to the main Mussenden course, and the par five 5th is considered to be "one of the most scenic holes in Irish golf" – we can't disagree.

PERRANPORTH GOLF CLUB
Budnic Hill, Perranporth, Cornwall, TR6 0AB
England
Telephone: +44 (0) 1872 573701

Average Reviewers' Score:

Website: www.perranporthgolfclub.com
Architect: James Braid
Visitors: Welcome - contact in advance

Reviewers' Comments

11 blind tee shots - yep 11... Played this course six times now and have just managed to work out how to play it... Lots of blind tee shots become easy if you hit the ball in the right place. If you don't, it's a double bogey/lost ball... Fantastic links but one which you need to get to know - so many blind shots can leave you in deep trouble... An excellent links course with great views and some interesting and exciting holes... Extremely natural and those views are amazing... The views on this cliff-top course are great on nearly every hole... Be prepared for aching legs, unless by some miracle you can keep on the fairways you'll be traversing dunes all day in search of your ball... This course is not for beginners or the very unfit as it is very hilly... Like it or loathe it, this course is unadulterated links at its best... I bet James Braid must have rubbed his hands together as he surveyed this bumpy piece of land... Probably the most natural course I've ever played... Outstanding value for money... Would never get tired of this course.

Perranporth

Located in Poldark country, on North Cornwall's dramatic Atlantic coastline, this natural links course is sited on high ground, ensuring enchanting views across Perran Bay, where the sandy beach glistens and the aquamarine ocean sparkles.

In 1927, the great James Braid designed the links and his layout has remained virtually unchanged ever since. J. Hamilton-Stutt (golf course consultant and architect) was impressed with Braid's Perranporth and he said that the course "is not only a rare and priceless heritage, but the inspiration on which all other golf courses ever built throughout the world are based".

If you don't like blind shots, steer clear of Perranporth. There are plenty of blind drives and numerous blind/semi-blind approach shots, causing a few challenges, especially when playing the links for the first time and when the ground is hard and fast. The Perranporth landscape is lunar, with a capital L. The holes wend their way relentlessly up and down the dunes. It's a tiring, fun and totally engaging experience.

The course measures a modest 6,252 yards from the back tees, with a par of 72. It is by no means long, but rest assured, Perranporth will challenge the very best golfers because every shot in the book will be required. If you suffer from a lack of balance, take your stabilisers; you will be presented with many varied sloping lies. A quick word about the greens - they are excellent, hard, undulating and fast. Many are sited on raised plateaux, calling for skilful approach shots.

Perranporth is a natural and honest golf course that you need to get to know to love. Play it more than once. It is probably the most underrated links course in the South West of England and should be taken alongside St Enodoc, Trevose and West Cornwall. The stunning views are worthy of the excellent value green fee alone. The welcome is warm and friendly too. What more can any serious golfer wish for?

Index

Bold page numbers indicate course main entry.